■ SCHOLASTIC

Grades 6–8
....
Readability
3.0–7.0

Hi-Lo
Nonfiction Passages
for *Struggling Readers*

80 High-Interest/Low-Readability Passages With Comprehension Questions and Mini-Lessons for Teaching Key Reading Strategies

New York ○ Toronto ○ London ○ Auckland ○ Sydney
New Delhi ○ Mexico City ○ Hong Kong ○ Buenos Aires

p. 3l and tr: © Photo Spin, br: © PictureQuest; p. 4bl: © Bettman/Corbis, tl: © Photos.com/IndexOpen, br and tr: © Photo Spin; p. 5t: © Photo Spin, b: 338: © Royalty-Free/Corbis; p. 10l: © AbleStock/IndexOpen, r: Artville/ SODA; p. 11: © Corbis; p. 13: © Photo Spin; pp. 16-7: © PictureQuest; p. 20: Stanley Bach/ SODA; p. 21t: © PictureQuest, b: Tom Raymond/SODA; pp. 24-5: © PictureQuest; p. 28: © Photos.com; p. 29: © Matt Hage/AlaskaStock.com; p. 32tl and tr: © Photodisc/SODA; p. 33t: © Mike Blake/Reuters, b: © Photodisc/SODA; p. 36: © AbleStock/IndexOpen; p. 37: © photos.com; p. 40: © U.S. Department of the Interior, National Park Service, Edison National Historic Site; p. 41t: © Nancy Carter/North Wind Picture Archives, b: © Photo Spin; p. 44: © FogStock LLC/IndexOpen; pp. 46-7: © Photo Researchers; pp. 50-1: The Granger Collection, New York; pp. 54-5: © NASA; pp. 58-9: © PictureQuest; p. 62: © Artville/SODA; pp. 62-3: © Michael S. Yamashita/Corbis; p. 66: ©Paul J. Richards/AFP/Getty Images; p. 67t: © Photos.com/IndexOpen, b: Richard C. Williams; p. 70: © H. Lorren Au Jr./MCT/Newscom; p. 71: © Scott Camazine/Photo Researchers; p. 74: The Armand Hammer Collection; p. 75: © FogStock LLC/IndexOpen; p. 78: © Mitchell Gerber/Corbis; p. 79: © Ron J. Berard/Corbis; p. 82: © Lisette Le Bon/SuperStock; p. 83: © PictureQuest; p.86: © Dave G. Houser/Corbis;, background: © Photos.com/IndexOpen; pp. 90-1: © Paulo De Oliveira/Oxford Scientific/jupiter Images; p. 94: © PictureQuest; p. 95: Jaime Lucero; p. 96: © Hot Ideas/Index Open; p. 100: Courtesy Early Television Museum; p. 101: © Devin Jeffrey/Istockphoto; p. 104t and b: © Photodisc/SODA; p.105t: © PictureQuest, b: © Christopher Pattberg/Istockphoto; p. 108 background: © Photos.com, inset: Library of Congress; p. 109: Naval Battle with the Spanish Fleet (oil on canvas) by Pierre Puget (1620-94) © Private Collection/Johnny Van Haeften Ltd., London/The Bridgeman Art Library; p. 112: © Photos.com; p. 116: © John McColgan/National Interagency Fire Center; p. 117t: © Photos.com, b: © Photo Spin; p. 120: © Marie Dorigny/REA/Redux; p. 124: Russell Lee / Library of Congress; p. 125 © Flavia Bottazzini/Istockphoto; p. 129: © Bettmann/Corbis; p. 132: © Amos Nachoum/Corbis; p. 133: © Arthur Morris/Corbis; p. 134: © Chris Lisle/Corbis; p. 135: © Gunter Marx Photography/Corbis; p. 138: © DesignPics Inc./IndexOpen; p. 139t: © FogStock LLC/IndexOpen, b: © Ben Greer/Istockphoto; p. 142t: John Snelgrove/Istockphoto, pp.142-3b: © PictureQuest; p. 146: © AbleStock/IndexOpen; p. 147: © Photos.com; p. 150: © AP Images/San Diego Wild Animal Park; p. 151: © Luis C. Tejo/MorgueFile; pp. 154-5: NASA; p. 158: © VStock LLC/IndexOpen; p. 159: © FogStock LLC/IndexOpen; p. 160: © Greg Nicholas/IStockphoto; p.161: © Darroch Putnam/IStockphoto; p. 164: © Photos.com/IndexOpen; p. 165: © Fogstock LLC/IndexOpen; p. 168: © FogStock LLC/IndexOpen; p. 169: © Bettman/Corbis; p. 172: © Mark Jones/OSF/Animals Animals; p. 176: © AbleStock/IndexOpen; pp. 180-1: Terry Sirrell; p. 185: © Photos.com/IndexOpen; p. 187: © PictureQuest; pp. 190-1: courtesy Rob Armstrong; p. 194: Rose Zgodzinki; p. 198: © The Granger Collection; p. 199: © Photo Researchers; p. 202: © AP Images/Daily Press, Adrin Snider; p. 206: © Bettman/Corbis; p. 207: © Gillian Darley/Corbis; p. 210: © Mitchell Gerber/Corbis; p. 214: Joann Fraiser-Dasent c/o Ashley Bryan; p. 220: © Photo Spin; pp. 224-5: Dan Brawner; p. 228: © Artville; p. 233: © Nik Wheeler/Corbis; p. 236: © Kim Kulish/Corbis; p. 240: © Photolibrary.com/IndexOpen; p. 241: © PictureQuest; p. 245: © Photos.com/IndexOpen; p. 246: © Hyungwon Kang/Reuters/Corbis; pp. 250-1: © PictureQuest; p. 254: Frank Spooner/Gamma; p. 255: © AP Images/Ed Andrieski; p. 258: © G.Baden/Zefa/Corbis; p. 262: © Robert Caputo/Aurora Photos; p. 266: © Maximilian Weinzierl/Alamy; p. 267: © Michael Freeman/Corbis; p. 270 Portrait of Mary Queen of Scots: © Archivo Iconografico, S.A./Corbis; Pu-Yi, Emperor of China: © Hulton Archive/Getty Images; p. 274: Ruth J. Flanigan; p. 278: © Getty Images; pp. 282-3: Dan Brawner; p.286: © Bettman/Corbis; p. 287: © Photos.com; p. 288t: © Artville, b: © Corbis; p. 292: © Photo Spin; p. 296: © Karl Crutchfield/Ai Wire/Newscom; p. 297: © Photo Spin; p. 300: © Marc Sulszny/Gamma Press; p. 304: © DesignPics Inc./Index Open; p. 308: © PictureQuest; p. 308-9b: © DesignPics Inc./Index Open; p. 312: © Keith Levit Photography/IndexOpen; p. 316: © Photo Spin; p. 317: © PictureQuest; pp. 320-1: © The Granger Collection, New York; p. 324: Rose Zgodzinski; p. 328: © James Denk/IndexOpen; pp. 330-1: © PictureQuest; p. 334: © PictureQuest; p. 338: © Royalty-Free/Corbis; p. 342: © Bettman/Corbis

Cover design by Jason Robinson

Interior design by Grafica, Inc.

ISBN-10: 0-439-69498-1

ISBN-13: 978-0-439-69498-8

Copyright © 2006 by Scholastic Inc. All rights reserved.

Printed in the U.S.A.

11 12 13 14 15 16   40   15 16 17 18 19/0

Table of Contents

Introduction **6**

Making Inferences **10**

Rocket Man! (3.0–3.5) 12

Quiet Creatures:
Two Poems (3.0–3.5) 16

Kids Help Pass
Safety Laws (3.5–5.0) 20

The Talking Otter (3.5–5.0) 24

She Climbed to the Top (4.0–4.5) 28

Who Says Ball Games Are
for the Birds? (4.0–4.5) 32

Written by Anonymous (4.0–4.5) 36

Lights! Camera! Invention! (5.0–5.5) . . . 40

Identifying Main Idea & Details . . . **44**

Giants of the Earth (3.0–3.5) 46

Long Ago in Timbuktu (3.0–3.5) 50

Astronauts Walk on
the Moon (3.5–5.0) 54

Rain-Forest Medicines (3.5–5.0) 58

Baseball Is a Hit in Japan (4.0–4.5) . . . 62

May You Have a Long Life (4.5–6.0) . . . 66

The Truth About AIDS (4.5–6.0) 70

Hail to the Chief! (5.0–5.5) 74

Not Just Black or White (5.0–5.5) 78

The Real Dracula (5.0–5.5) 82

Old Bones Dug Up (5.0–5.5) 86

Creatures of the Deep (6.0–6.5) 90

Recognizing Cause & Effect **94**

One Cool-Looking
Cowhand (3.0–3.5) 96

Americans Discover TV (3.0–3.5) 100

Collectors Strike It Rich! (4.5–6.0) 104

Victory at Sea (4.5–6.0) 108

The Earth Heats Up (4.5–6.0) 112

Fire in Their Eyes (5.0–5.5) 116

Children at Work (5.0–5.5) 120

The California Gold Rush (5.0–5.5) . . .124

Deborah Samson,
Secret Soldier (6.0–6.5) 128

Table of Contents

Identifying Problem & Solution . . **132**

Stories That Reach Toward
the Sky (3.5–5.0) 134

A Bridge to a New World (3.5–5.0). . . 138

Saving the Sphinx (4.0–4.5) 142

Scum Energy (5.0–5.5) 146

Condor Comeback (6.0–6.5) 150

Exploring Jupiter (6.0–6.5) 154

Categorizing **158**

The King's Things (3.0–3.5) 160

What's It Like to Live
in China? (3.0–3.5) 164

Unsolved Mysteries (4.0–4.5) 168

The Galápagos—
Can They Survive? (4.5–6.0) 172

What's the Word? (5.0–5.5) 176

Who Dropped the Ball? (6.0–6.5) 180

Sequencing **184**

Triathlon: The Sport That
Does It All (3.0–3.5) 186

Life in the Comics (3.0–3.5) 190

Driving Through Time (3.0–3.5) 194

Marie Curie: A Woman Ahead
of Her Time (4.0–4.5) 198

Lost and Found:
The First Fort (4.0–4.5) 202

The Case of the
Missing Globe (5.0–5.5) 206

Jim Carrey: Class Clown
Makes Good (5.0–5.5) 210

Making Stories
Come Alive (6.0–6.5) 214

Comparing & Contrasting **218**

Yo-Yos Are Forever (3.0–3.5) 220

Giving TV the Boot! (3.0–3.5) 224

Sports: For Fun or Money? (4.5–6.0) . .228

The Water Festival (4.5–6.0) 232

Cartoons Come to Life (4.5–6.0) 236

Foods With a Difference (4.5–6.0). . . .240

Table of Contents

Summarizing **244**

Presidential Pets and Kids (3.0–3.5) . . .246

History of Marbles (3.0–3.5) 250

Flying Friends of the
Air Force (4.0–4.5) 254

Flying Machine (4.5–6.0) 258

Fighting for Their Lives (4.5–6.0) 262

Crunchy Critters (5.0–5.5) 266

Children Who Ruled (5.0–5.5) 270

Friendly Rooms (6.0–6.5). 274

Pedal Power (6.0–6.5) 278

The Story That Stretched (6.0–6.5) 282

Drawing Conclusions **286**

Mary McLeod Bethune (3.0–3.5) 288

Does Music Make
You Smarter? (3.0–3.5) 292

Grant Hill: Straight
Shooter (3.5–5.0) 296

Surf's Up—Way Up! (4.0–4.5) 300

Coral Crisis (4.5–6.0) 304

A Trash Collector's Work
Is Never Done (5.0–5.5) 308

The Animals of the
Arctic Tundra (5.0–5.5) 312

Wildlife for Sale (6.0–6.5) 316

So, How About
Those Vikings? (6.0–6.5) 320

High-Tech Highways (6.0–6.5) 324

Distinguishing Fact & Opinion . . . **328**

A Panda for a Pet? (3.5–5.0) 330

Faithfully Ours (3.5–5.0) 334

Cleopatra's City—
Lost & Found (4.0–4.5) 338

Searching for the
"Real" King Arthur (5.0–5.5) 342

Rock Around the Clock (6.0–6.5) 346

Answer Key **350**

Introduction

Welcome to *Hi-Lo Nonfiction Passages for Struggling Readers*, your one-stop resource for leveled, high-interest articles complete with comprehension and vocabulary questions. This collection of nonfiction passages, leveled from 3.0 to 7.0, covers a wide range of topics in science, history, and geography, as well as sports, art, entertainment, and more—a perfect motivator for even your most reluctant readers.

Why Use Nonfiction?

As students move up in grade level they encounter more nonfiction when they tackle content-area textbooks, reference materials, newspapers, and Internet articles. What's more, about half of the passages students will find on standardized tests are nonfiction. Reading nonfiction, however, presents a different set of challenges from fiction. Whereas fiction tells a story, nonfiction conveys facts and information—and students need to learn how to comprehend that information in order to succeed in school and in the real world.

The vocabulary contained in nonfiction texts can be tricky for struggling readers. Not only does each content area have its own special set of words, but some of these are familiar words that have specialized or alternate meanings, which can be confusing for students. In addition, identifying main ideas and details, recognizing cause and effect, distinguishing fact from opinion, and synthesizing information can all pose difficulties for students as they read nonfiction texts. *Hi-Lo Nonfiction Passages for Struggling Readers* can help your students navigate these challenging texts.

What's Inside

This book is divided into ten sections, with each section focusing on a specific reading strategy: making inferences, identifying main ideas and details, recognizing cause and effect, identifying problem and solution, categorizing, sequencing, comparing and contrasting, summarizing, drawing conclusions, and distinguishing fact and opinion.

Each section opens with an introduction to a key reading strategy, and offers simple, bulleted suggestions to help students read effectively. A sample passage models the strategy in a meaningful way, and a graphic organizer helps students visualize the strategy and record important points from the passage. Students can then practice this key strategy as they read a second nonfiction passage.

Following each reading strategy are several reproducible nonfiction passages with test-formatted questions so that students can apply their understanding. The high-interest passages are written below grade level to help motivate struggling readers and build their confidence. You'll find the readability range for each passage in the table of contents.

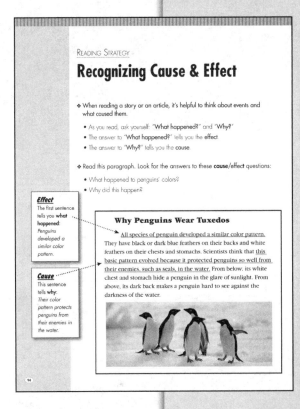

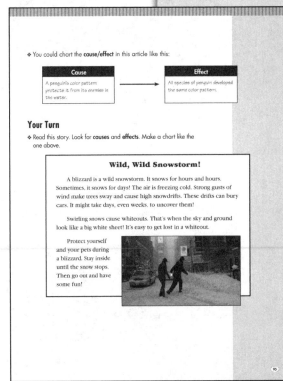

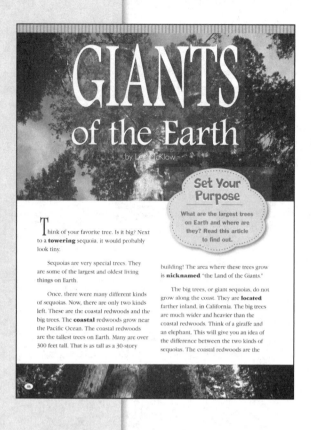

The book includes 80 reading passages in all. Each starts with a "Set Your Purpose" question that helps focus students before they begin reading. A critical-thinking question at the end of the passage helps readers reflect on what they've read. In addition, after each passage, you'll find mini-quizzes that assess students' comprehension, vocabulary, and word-attack skills in a bubble-format test. The comprehension questions reinforce the particular reading strategy, while context clues help students develop their vocabulary. In "Word Work," students review or develop word-attack skills, including phonics and structural analysis. Finally, a "Write Now" section invites students to write an open-ended summary or response to the passage. Graphic organizers help them organize their thoughts about the selection they read. The writing activities—ranging in format from business letters to posters, journal entries, articles, and more—provide excellent practice for the short-answer essays students will encounter on standardized tests and writing assessments. An answer key is at the back of the book.

How to Use This Book

Hi-Lo Nonfiction Passages for Struggling Readers is a great supplement to your current reading/language arts program or curriculum. It includes direct instruction and demonstrations of key reading strategies to help students better decode and comprehend nonfiction text. You can use this book in a number of ways:

- Introduce a reading strategy to the whole class. Copy the reading strategy pages onto transparencies and display them on an overhead projector. You may also want to distribute photocopies of the strategy pages to students. Work with students to help them understand how to use the particular strategy—for example, summarizing or making inferences. Together review the model passage before letting students practice on the additional passage provided.

- Work with a small group (preferably at the same reading level). Give each student a copy of a passage, making sure it is appropriate to the group's level. Guide students through the process and strategies for reading the passage. Model how to refer back to the article to find the answers to the mini-quizzes.

- For homework, assign individual students passages based on their interest, reading level, or the skills they need to work on. You may also want to provide a copy of the relevant reading strategy pages for students who need extra help or reinforcement.

- Select reading passages that focus on science or social studies topics, to teach students strategies for reading in the content areas.

However you decide to use this book, you'll find great satisfaction in watching your students become more confident readers as their literacy soars. Enjoy!

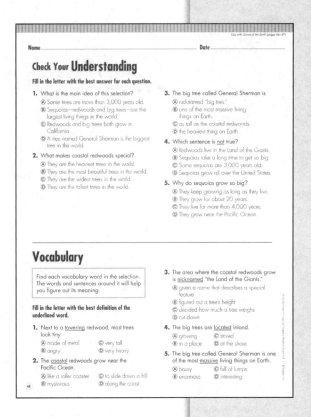

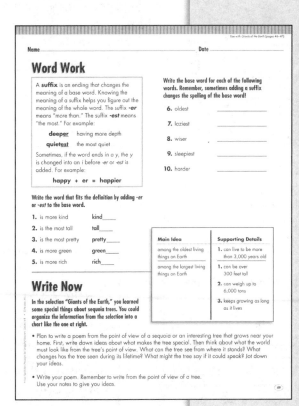

Making Inferences

❖ When you read, you can use clues, along with what you already know, to help you figure out what the author doesn't tell you.

- As you read, ask yourself: "What is the author leaving out that is important to understanding the article?"
- Look for clues in the text.
- Ask yourself: "What do I already know about something like this?"
- Use clues and your own experience to figure out what the author means or does not tell you.

❖ Read this story. Use story clues and what you already know to **make inferences** that will answer these questions:

- What can you figure out about Mark McGwire's batting ability?
- What can you figure out about Sammy Sosa's ability as a ballplayer?

Clue
These sentences give clues to how amazing Mark McGwire's accomplishment was.

Clue
Sosa's 66 home runs are a clue to his hitting ability.

Race for the Record

On September 8, 1998, Cardinals slugger Mark McGwire hit his 62nd home run of the season. In doing so, <u>he broke Roger Maris's record, which had stood for 37 years. McGwire went on to hit a total of 70 home runs.</u> <u>The 66 homers pounded in by the Cub's Sammy Sosa that same year would have been a record-breaking event in any other season!</u>

❖ You could chart the clues that helped you **make inferences** in the paragraph like this:

Clues
Roger Maris's home-run record stood for 37 years.
Mark McGwire broke Maris's record and hit 70 home runs in one season.
Sammy Sosa hit 66 home runs in the same season.

What I Know
If a record is not broken for a long time, it must have been a hard thing to do.
Someone who breaks a record and then sets an even bigger record has done something amazing.
Sosa also broke Roger Maris's record.

What I Can Figure Out
Mark McGwire is a great batter.
Sammy Sosa is also a great batter.

Your Turn

❖ Read this story. What **inferences** can you make about the stone blocks? Make a chart like the one above.

The Mystery of the Great Stones

In many places around the world there are large blocks of stone. Some of these stand alone. Others form rings or lines. Still others look like huge tables. They are some of the earliest buildings.

Most of these stones are on flat land. No other stones are around them. We think people from long ago used ropes and logs to move the stones. This took many years.

What did the stones mean? It's still a mystery. Some rings may have been calendars. Maybe they were meeting places. What do you think?

Rocket Man!

adapted by Lee McKlow

Set Your Purpose

What's it like to be in outer space? Read this interview for some inside information.

Do the words "blast off" thrill you?

Would you like people to say that you have "the right stuff"? That is the best **compliment** an astronaut can give someone. NASA astronaut Tom Jones has the right stuff. He has blasted into space three times. Here he tells an interviewer what it is like:

Interviewer: When did you decide to become an astronaut?

Tom Jones: When I was 10. It was 1965, and U.S. astronauts were practicing for the first trips to the moon.

Interviewer: What does it feel like when you blast off in the space shuttle?

Tom Jones: First, there's a **rumble** as the engines fire up. Then there's a huge **jolt**, followed by steady shaking. In the eight minutes it takes to get to orbit, the pressure (heavy feeling) against your chest builds. It feels like a 700-pound gorilla is sitting on top of you. Once in orbit, the pressure is gone and you are weightless.

Interviewer: What does it feel like to be weightless?

Tom Jones: It's very peaceful, like you're floating underwater. With a touch of your finger, you can push off and **glide** wherever you want.

Interviewer: What's cool about being in space?

Tom Jones: The view of Earth. At any point, you can "swim" over to the window and catch a **glimpse** of oceans, snow-covered forests, and deserts. The colors are amazing.

Interviewer: What advice would you give kids who want to be astronauts?

Tom Jones: Work hard in school. You need a college degree. You also need three years of work experience before you can apply to NASA to become an astronaut.

If you don't get picked the first time, keep trying. And don't give up!

Backpack

Inside is Tom's life-support system: electricity, oxygen, water, and a radio.

Helmet

Three layers protect Tom from the sun's ultraviolet rays.

Chest Pack

Tom can control the temperature inside his suit by pressing buttons on his chest pack.

Safety Straps

These are attached to a thin steel cable from the spaceship so Tom can walk in space without floating away!

Think About It

Would you like to travel to outer space? Why or why not?

Name _____   Date _____

Check Your Understanding

Fill in the letter with the best answer for each question.

1. From Tom Jones's description, you can infer that when astronauts blast off, they

Ⓐ feel no pain or unpleasant pressure.
Ⓑ "swim" around feeling peaceful.
Ⓒ must put up with unpleasant pressure.
Ⓓ take a nap.

2. People who want to become astronauts

Ⓐ do not have to work hard in school.
Ⓑ must work hard in school.
Ⓒ should watch TV instead of studying.
Ⓓ do not need any work experience.

3. According to Tom Jones, what causes you to feel like you're "floating underwater"?

Ⓐ blasting into space
Ⓑ looking at oceans
Ⓒ becoming an astronaut
Ⓓ being weightless

4. Which words best describe people who have "the right stuff"?

Ⓐ silly and lazy
Ⓑ foolish and weightless
Ⓒ brave and hardworking
Ⓓ sleepy and likely to give up

5. According to Tom Jones, the cool thing about being in space is

Ⓐ having a gorilla sit on your chest.
Ⓑ feeling a jolt as the ship blasts off.
Ⓒ listening to the rumble of the engines.
Ⓓ seeing amazing views of the Earth.

Vocabulary

Find each vocabulary word in the selection. The words and sentences around it will help you figure out its meaning.

Fill in the letter with the best definition of the underlined word.

1. "The right stuff" is the best <u>compliment</u> an astronaut can give someone.

Ⓐ space suit   Ⓒ words of praise
Ⓑ forests and oceans   Ⓓ engine

2. First, there's a <u>rumble</u> as the engines fire up.

Ⓐ kind of bee   Ⓒ peaceful feeling
Ⓑ deep, long   Ⓓ explosion
   rolling noise

3. Then there's a huge <u>jolt</u>, followed by steady shaking.

Ⓐ good time   Ⓒ sudden jerk
Ⓑ heavy gorilla   Ⓓ gentle touch

4. With a touch of your finger, you can push off and <u>glide</u> wherever you want.

Ⓐ hold down
Ⓑ turn upside down
Ⓒ have trouble moving
Ⓓ move smoothly and easily

5. Through the window, you can catch a <u>glimpse</u> of oceans, forests, and deserts.

Ⓐ quick look   Ⓒ movie
Ⓑ type of airplane   Ⓓ far-off sound

Name _____ Date _____

Word Work

> **Antonyms** are words that have opposite meanings. For example, *weightless* and *heavy* are antonyms.

Write the word that means the opposite of the words in dark type.

compliment   noise

glide   peaceful   amazing

1. The astronaut heard the **silence** of the engines as the space shuttle blasted off. _____

2. The astronaut felt very **troubled**. _____

3. He could **stumble** easily from one end of the spaceship to the other. _____

4. From the window, the astronaut had a glimpse of Earth's **ordinary** colors. _____

5. It was a big **insult** for him to say that she had the "right stuff." _____

> The letter combinations **sh**, **th**, and **ch** each stand for a special sound that is different than the sounds of the two letters pronounced separately.
>
> **fi<u>sh</u>   <u>th</u>irteen   <u>ch</u>icken**

Read the definitions. Complete the word by adding the letters *sh*, *th*, or *ch*. Write the word.

6. a rocket ship that can fly into space and land again on earth   ____uttle

7. to tremble or shiver   ____ake

8. to select or pick   ____oose

9. to stretch toward something   **rea**____

10. an exciting moment   ____rill

Write Now

Tom Jones gave a description of his journey into space. This word web highlights what he saw and felt.

• Plan to write a journal entry about traveling in space. First, imagine that you went with Tom Jones on an expedition in space. Create your own word web with the words "My trip with Tom Jones" in the center circle. Add words that describe what you might see and feel.

• Write your journal entry. Remember to use your word web. Add descriptive details to make your journal interesting to read.

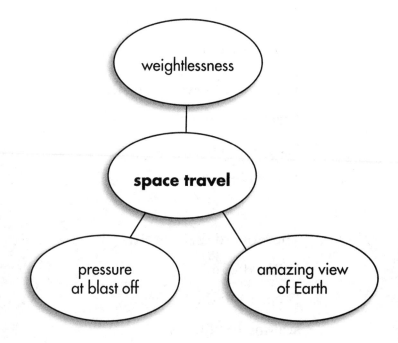

weightlessness

space travel

pressure at blast off

amazing view of Earth

Hi-Lo Nonfiction Passages for Struggling Readers: Grades 6–8 • Scholastic Inc.

15

Quiet Creatures: Two Poems

It's nighttime in the jungle, and all seems peaceful. Don't be fooled! Under cover of darkness, a deadly game of hide and seek is being played out. The hiders are animals that feed on plants. The seekers are predators. Predators hunt and kill prey for food. One of the most feared predators is the leopard.

The leopard is a big cat. Adult leopards are about six feet long. They weigh between 100 and 150 pounds. The leopard's coat is sandy-colored with black spots. These markings are good **camouflage**. They make the leopard hard to see as it lurks in the shadows. Few animals are a match for the fast, fierce, powerful leopard.

Set Your Purpose

As you read these two poems, try to picture the animals and the scene.

The Leopard

The leopard **creeps** quietly
Creeps in the night
Creeps when the stars
And the moon are bright.

The leopard creeps softly
Up on the hill
Peeps from the bushes
Waiting to kill.

– Anonymous

You rarely see or hear the mysterious snake. Snakes tend to avoid other creatures. They slither away in a quick, quiet motion.

The Silent Snake

The birds go fluttering in the air,
The rabbits run and skip,
Brown squirrels race along the **bough**,
The May-flies rise and dip;
But while these creatures play and leap,
The silent snake goes creepy-creep!

The birdies sing and whistle loud,
The busy insects hum,
The squirrels **chat**, the frogs say "Croak!"
But the snake is always **dumb**.
With not a sound through grasses deep
The silent snake goes creepy-creep!

– Anonymous

Think About It

Why do animals fear the leopard? How is the snake different from most other animals?

Name _____ Date _____

Check Your **Understanding**

Fill in the letter with the best answer for each question.

1. The poem implies that leopards
  (A) are the prey of other animals.
  (B) are big cats.
  (C) eat other animals.
  (D) have a sandy-colored coat.

2. We know that we won't hear a leopard come toward us because
  (A) it weighs about 100 pounds.
  (B) it is tawny and black.
  (C) it creeps when the stars and moon are bright.
  (D) it creeps quietly and softly in the night.

3. We rarely see snakes because they
  (A) fly away too quickly.
  (B) look like leopards.
  (C) tend to hide from other creatures.
  (D) live in trees.

4. Unlike snakes, all the other creatures in the poem "The Silent Snake"
  (A) make noise.
  (B) crawl through the grass.
  (C) never make a sound.
  (D) flutter in the air.

5. According to the poems, leopards and snakes both
  (A) are big cats.
  (B) creep about quietly.
  (C) move about only at night.
  (D) eat plants.

Vocabulary

Find each vocabulary word in the selection. The words and sentences around it will help you figure out its meaning.

Fill in the letter with the best definition of the underlined word.

1. Brown squirrels race along the <u>bough</u>.
  (A) bend forward   (C) ribbon
  (B) spider web   (D) tree branch

2. When squirrels <u>chat</u> with each other, what do they say?
  (A) talk happily   (C) hunt prey
  (B) fall down   (D) fly away

3. The leopard's markings are good <u>camouflage</u>.
  (A) ideas
  (B) coloring that makes an animal look like its surroundings
  (C) resembling a camel
  (D) shape that makes an animal move swiftly

4. The leopard <u>creeps</u> quietly through the night.
  (A) large, green plants
  (B) leaps
  (C) moves slowly and quietly
  (D) moves quickly and joyfully

5. Other animals make noises, but the snake is always <u>dumb</u>.
  (A) singing   (C) talkative
  (B) humming   (D) silent

Hi-Lo Nonfiction Passages for Struggling Readers: Grades 6–8 • Scholastic Inc.

Name _____ Date _____

Word Work

> **Synonyms** are words that have similar meanings. For example, *little* and *small* are synonyms.

Read the sentences and the words below. Write the word that means almost the same as the word in dark type.

markings   powerful   creeps   skip   dumb

1. The leopard **crawls** softly so it will not be heard. _____

2. Unlike most animals, the snake is **silent**. _____

3. The leopard has black **spots** on its light brown coat. _____

4. Most animals fear the leopard because it is a **strong** predator. _____

5. The child watched the rabbit **hop** away. _____

> Some words have more than one meaning. You can often figure out the meaning of a word by looking at how the word is used in a sentence.
>
> **1. row** (*noun*) – a line
> We sat in the *row* behind our parents.
>
> **2. row** (*verb*) – to paddle a boat
> Let's *row* the boat to the island.

Decide if each underlined word has meaning A or B. Fill in the letter with the correct answer.

6. Animals try to <u>hide</u> from predators.
   Ⓐ stay out of sight   Ⓑ an animal skin

7. A leopard is <u>hard</u> to see through the grass.
   Ⓐ not soft   Ⓑ difficult

8. What <u>kind</u> of animal is spotted?
   Ⓐ type   Ⓑ friendly

9. Don't get too <u>close</u> to a leopard.
   Ⓐ near   Ⓑ shut

10. Sometimes I see squirrels in my <u>yard</u>.
   Ⓐ a measurement   Ⓑ a grassy area around a house

Write Now

Think about an animal that you have watched. Draw a picture of that animal. Then look at the chart below.

- Plan to write a poem describing your animal. First, make a chart like the one shown. Write words that describe your animal's color, body parts, movements, and sounds.

- Write a descriptive poem about your animal. Your poem can rhyme, but it doesn't have to. Use words from your chart. Choose words and sounds that help make the picture of the animal come alive.

Ways to Describe	Examples
color	red, black, white, green
body parts	wings, paws, tail, hair
movement	fly, run, hop, swim
sound	sing, bark, moo, roar

Hi-Lo Nonfiction Passages for Struggling Readers: Grades 6–8 • Scholastic Inc.

19

Kids Help Pass Safety Laws

adapted by Sharon Dederian

When Sean Aiken bought a bike helmet, he never thought it would help him so soon. Only a week later, it saved his life. He was hit by a car while riding home from school in Tucson, Arizona. His bike didn't survive the crash. But Sean did. His helmet protected him from **serious** head injuries. "I used to think helmets were **unnecessary**. I thought I would never get hurt," Sean said. "But it can and will happen to you if you're not careful." Sean later spoke before the Tucson City Council about the need for bike-helmet laws. This led to a new Arizona law that **requires** people under the age of 18 to wear a bike helmet while cycling.

Fifteen-year-old Mike Jones of Sioux Falls, South Dakota, knows about safety. Two years ago, he was seriously hurt in a car accident. Mike had a skull fracture and brain damage when he was thrown from

Set Your Purpose

How can kids and adults save lives? Read this newspaper article to find out.

Kids know that safety is important.

a van. "I don't know why I didn't wear a safety belt that day. Now I always buckle up," Mike said. Today, he is still reminded of that experience. "I used to love sports, but I can't do them anymore. I can't risk getting another serious injury," he said.

Like Mike, many people around the U.S. are becoming more safety-wise. "Parents can't watch kids every minute. Kids must know how to be safe. It's in their control and power," says Susan Gallagher, director of the Safety Network.

New technology is also helping to **prevent** injuries. More people than ever before use products such as smoke detectors in their homes and seat belts in their cars. Most cyclists know that they should use bike helmets. New laws, such as the bike-helmet law Sean Aiken helped pass, are also making more people use these products. The number of **fatal** injuries caused by car crashes and fires has gone down over the years.

Kids are taking action to help prevent injuries. Like Sean Aiken and Mike Jones, they know that safety works.

Think About It

What can people do to make life safer?

Name_____   Date_____

Check Your Understanding

Fill in the letter with the best answer for each question.

1. If Sean Aiken weren't wearing a helmet when he and his bike were hit by a car, he probably would have been
   - Ⓐ a survivor.
   - Ⓑ a hero.
   - Ⓒ walking away from the accident.
   - Ⓓ seriously hurt or killed.

2. People in the U.S. are becoming safety-wise because
   - Ⓐ awards are being given to them.
   - Ⓑ they love sports.
   - Ⓒ too many people are getting hurt.
   - Ⓓ they wear bike helmets.

3. To help save lives, kids can
   - Ⓐ take control of cars.
   - Ⓑ put out fires.
   - Ⓒ not play sports.
   - Ⓓ ask for new safety laws.

4. Why has the number of fatal injuries caused by car crashes and fires decreased?
   - Ⓐ New technology keeps a more accurate count.
   - Ⓑ More people use safety-related products than ever before.
   - Ⓒ Fewer people ride cars.
   - Ⓓ Fires are no longer dangerous.

5. Why is it important to wear a bike helmet while riding?
   - Ⓐ to protect the rider against head injuries
   - Ⓑ to keep the rider from falling off his bike
   - Ⓒ to keep the rider from seeing well
   - Ⓓ to be different from all other riders

Vocabulary

> Find each vocabulary word in the selection. The words and sentences around it will help you figure out its meaning.

Fill in the letter with the best definition of the underlined word.

1. His helmet protected him from <u>serious</u> head injuries.
   - Ⓐ dangerous
   - Ⓑ tiny
   - Ⓒ beautiful
   - Ⓓ easy

2. I used to think helmets were <u>unnecessary</u>; I thought I would never get hurt.
   - Ⓐ required
   - Ⓑ important
   - Ⓒ not needed
   - Ⓓ unhappy

3. A new law <u>requires</u> people to wear a bike helmet while cycling.
   - Ⓐ rides
   - Ⓑ quizzes
   - Ⓒ returns
   - Ⓓ orders

4. New technology is also helping to <u>prevent</u> injuries.
   - Ⓐ cure
   - Ⓑ make worse
   - Ⓒ keep from happening
   - Ⓓ let happen

5. Safety laws have brought down the number of <u>fatal</u> injuries.
   - Ⓐ minor
   - Ⓑ deadly
   - Ⓒ healed
   - Ⓓ faked

Hi-Lo Nonfiction Passages for Struggling Readers Grades 6–8 • Scholastic Inc.

Name _____ Date _____

Word Work

> The letter **y** can stand for several different sounds. Look at the examples.
>
> **long-e sound:** necessary
>
> **long-i sound:** my
>
> **short-i sound:** gym

> The letter combinations **sh**, **th**, and **ch** each stand for a special sound that is different than the sounds of the two letters pronounced separately.
>
> **shoe   tooth   cheese**

Read each word in dark type. Fill in the letter of the word that has the same vowel sound.

1. bicycle
Ⓐ necessary   Ⓑ my   Ⓒ gym

2. seriously
Ⓐ necessary   Ⓑ my   Ⓒ gym

3. safety
Ⓐ necessary   Ⓑ my   Ⓒ gym

4. try
Ⓐ necessary   Ⓑ my   Ⓒ gym

5. injury
Ⓐ necessary   Ⓑ my   Ⓒ gym

Read the definitions. Complete the word by adding the letters *sh*, *th*, or *ch*.

6. a sandy shore   bea____

7. to move quickly back and forth   ____ake

8. a playground game   hopscot____

9. a storm noise   ____under

10. a pumpkin   squa____

Write Now

In this selection, you learned about safety laws that help prevent injuries in daily life. Look at the chart. It shows some safety rules for bicycling. Can you think of rules for other sports?

- Plan a safety poster showing safety rules for a sport you like. First, think of a sport to write about. Then make a chart like the one shown. List two or three rules of safety for that sport.

Sport	Bicycling
Rules	1. Always wear a helmet. 2. Watch out for cars. 3. Obey traffic rules.

- Are you ready to design your own safety poster? Choose one or more rules to illustrate in a single picture. Write the rules at the top of the poster and draw your picture underneath.

Hi-Lo Nonfiction Passages for Struggling Readers: Grades 6–8 • Scholastic Inc.

23

The Talking Otter

adapted by Ian Alexander

Martin and Chris Kratt are the stars of a TV show called *Kratts' Creatures*. Their co-stars are the wild animals they introduce to their audience. To find these creatures, Martin and Chris sometimes travel to remote parts of the world. When the Kratts are on a mission to find a creature, things can get pretty tough. They once had to travel 200 miles in an oxcart. What a bumpy ride!

These tough missions are **worthwhile** when they find interesting creatures. Of all the animals they know, the giant otter of South America is one of the Kratts' favorites. Why? Many animals **communicate**, but giant otters have a language all their own.

Set Your Purpose

Some people say that their pets "talk" to them. Read this article to find out how the giant otter uses different sounds to send messages.

Whistles, whines, squeals, and snorts are all part of the otters' vocabulary. As with other animals, each sound means a different thing. One sound may mean "Come quickly!" Another might mean "Here is food!" Some sounds are warnings. For example, one otter will warn others if a human hunter gets too close. They do this by snorting, "Pffttt." Understanding this warning can save an otter's life. Hunters kill them for their thick fur. There are now only 4,000 giant otters left.

Giant otters are as much fun to watch as they are to listen to. They travel in **packs**, hunting and playing together in the South American jungle. The otters communicate with others in the group as they **prowl**. They use teamwork to hunt for fish. The otters make different sounds to help each other find or catch their food.

The otters must also work together to protect themselves from other animals. Crocodiles and jaguars like to eat baby otters. But giant otters can be very fierce. A giant otter can grow as long as six feet. Even a jaguar will get out of the way of a pack of angry giant otters. Giant otters really know how to take care of one another. And "talking" helps them do just that!

Think About It

What kinds of messages can a giant otter send? Do the otters communicate only when there is danger?

Name_____ Date_____

Check Your Understanding

Fill in the letter with the best answer for each question.

1. The Kratts became stars of a TV show because
- Ⓐ they can talk like otters.
- Ⓑ traveling in an oxcart for 200 miles is interesting.
- Ⓒ they sometimes travel to remote parts of the world.
- Ⓓ people like to see wild animals they haven't seen before.

2. The author says that giant otters have a language because
- Ⓐ they speak English.
- Ⓑ they use different sounds to communicate with each other.
- Ⓒ they speak, write, and read otter languages.
- Ⓓ the otters told the Kratts that they communicate.

3. We know that giant otters can be fierce because
- Ⓐ they communicate with each other.
- Ⓑ they use teamwork.
- Ⓒ even a jaguar will get out of their way.
- Ⓓ they attacked the Kratts.

4. The greatest threats to the giant otters are
- Ⓐ human hunters.
- Ⓑ television stars.
- Ⓒ oxcarts.
- Ⓓ fish.

5. The giant otter probably got its name because
- Ⓐ its fur is very thick.
- Ⓑ it has a large vocabulary.
- Ⓒ it is a large, powerful cat.
- Ⓓ it can grow to six feet long.

Vocabulary

Find each vocabulary word in the selection. The words and sentences around it will help you figure out its meaning.

Fill in the letter with the best definition of the underlined word.

1. Martin and Chris sometimes travel to remote parts of the world.
- Ⓐ close by
- Ⓑ in the neighborhood
- Ⓒ faraway
- Ⓓ on television

2. Tough missions are worthwhile when the Kratts find interesting creatures.
- Ⓐ useless
- Ⓑ rewarding
- Ⓒ worldly
- Ⓓ alarming

3. Many animals communicate, but giant otters have a language all their own.
- Ⓐ remain silent
- Ⓑ look away
- Ⓒ share information
- Ⓓ get together

4. They travel in packs, hunting and playing together in the South American jungle.
- Ⓐ suitcases
- Ⓑ groups
- Ⓒ book bags
- Ⓓ cartons

5. The otters communicate with others in the group as they prowl.
- Ⓐ search quietly
- Ⓑ growl like a dog
- Ⓒ stay in one place
- Ⓓ fall asleep

Hi-Lo Nonfiction Passages for Struggling Readers: Grades 6–8 • Scholastic Inc.

Name _____ **Date** _____

Word Work

A **compound word** is made of two shorter words. Combining the meanings of the two shorter words often explains the compound word. For example, *worthwhile* is made up of the words *worth* and *while*.

Make compound words by combining each word on the left with a word on the right. Write the compound words.

1. some   away   _____

2. ox   tellers   _____

3. team   times   _____

4. far   cart   _____

5. story   work   _____

Look at the compound words below. Write the word that best completes each sentence. Then draw a line between the two shorter words that make up the compound word.

sometimes   oxcart   teamwork

faraway   storytellers

6. I would like to visit _____ countries and see interesting creatures.

7. Riding in an _____ would be a different way to travel.

8. The Kratts _____ go to the jungle, but they also go to the desert.

9. The Kratts use _____ to get everything ready for their TV show.

10. I like to listen to the Kratts talk about animals because they are good _____.

Write Now

In the article, you learned that each sound that a giant otter makes sends a different message to other members of its pack. Look at the chart. It lists some of the sounds that giant otters make. It also gives the purpose of one of the sounds and how that sound might be written in English.

- Plan to write a message in otter language. First, imagine what some of the other sounds listed might mean in English.

- Use your chart to write a message in otter language. *Hint:* Think about what otters might have to communicate—danger, hunger, happiness.

Sound	English Meaning
Snort	A human hunter is nearby!
Whistle	
Whine	
Squeal	

She Climbed to the Top

adapted by Pam Halloran

Set Your Purpose

Read this article to find out about the youngest person to climb Denali, the highest mountain in North America.

The wind was **howling**. Twelve-year-old Merrick Johnston, her mom, and a guide had to take cover, but where? They were more than 14,000 feet up on Denali, America's highest mountain. There was nowhere to go but down into the snow. The group dug a deep snow cave to protect themselves. They waited inside for five days until the storm blew over. Then they continued their record-breaking climb.

That was just one adventure Merrick had on Denali. On June 26, 1995, she became the youngest person ever to reach the top of the 20,320-foot-high **peak** in Alaska.

Merrick's trip took 26 days. Each person in the group carried a backpack full of food and other supplies. Temperatures sometimes **dipped** to 30 degrees below zero. The team had to cross more than one dangerous ice **canyon** and climb icy slopes. Falling into a canyon could have been deadly, but they never gave up. After more than three weeks of climbing, Merrick's group reached the top.

"We were in the clouds most of the time. But right when we got to the top, we were above the clouds," Merrick said. "All of the clouds were pink because of the sun. It was really neat."

Why did Merrick attempt such a tough climb? "It seemed interesting," she told reporters, "and my mom said it was OK."

Now that Merrick has tackled North America's tallest mountain, she's looking for a new **challenge**. What are her plans? She hopes to climb Vinson Massif, the highest peak in Antarctica.

Think About It

What experiences did Merrick Johnston have on her climb up Denali?

Name _____   Date _____

Check Your Understanding

Fill in the letter with the best answer for each question.

1. Why did Merrick's team dig a cave in the snow?

   Ⓐ They were tired and needed a place to rest.

   Ⓑ They needed a place to put their supplies.

   Ⓒ They needed to find shelter from the strong winds.

   Ⓓ They were looking for food.

2. Which of these supplies do you think the climbers did <u>not</u> have in their backpacks?

   Ⓐ warm clothing

   Ⓑ games and newspapers

   Ⓒ tents and sleeping bags

   Ⓓ food and water

3. What kind of a person do you think Merrick Johnston is?

   Ⓐ determined and adventurous

   Ⓑ shy and quiet

   Ⓒ conceited and loud

   Ⓓ sad and lonely

4. Why did Merrick Johnston stand out when she climbed Denali?

   Ⓐ She climbed alone.

   Ⓑ Other climbers could not keep up with her.

   Ⓒ She was the best in the group.

   Ⓓ She was the youngest in the group.

5. How did Merrick react to the view when her group reached the mountaintop?

   Ⓐ She was tired and bored.

   Ⓑ She thought it was really neat.

   Ⓒ She could hardly breathe.

   Ⓓ She felt it was cool to be on top.

Vocabulary

Find each vocabulary word in the selection. The words and sentences around it will help you figure out its meaning.

Fill in the letter with the best definition of the underlined word.

1. The wind was <u>howling</u>.

   Ⓐ making a sound like a loud, wailing cry

   Ⓑ making a giggling sound

   Ⓒ kind of monkey

   Ⓓ joking

2. Denali is a 20,320-foot-high <u>peak</u> in Alaska.

   Ⓐ snow cave   Ⓒ clouds above a mountain

   Ⓑ become sickly   Ⓓ highest point of a mountain

3. Temperatures sometimes <u>dipped</u> to 30 degrees below zero.

   Ⓐ dug a cave   Ⓒ dropped down

   Ⓑ soaked to the skin   Ⓓ broke a record

4. The team had to cross more than one dangerous ice <u>canyon</u>.

   Ⓐ long, narrow valleys   Ⓒ narrow, light boats

   Ⓑ big guns or weapons   Ⓓ lakes or rivers

5. She's looking for a new <u>challenge</u>.

   Ⓐ business deal   Ⓒ public announcement

   Ⓑ someone's opinion   Ⓓ exciting and difficult opportunity

Name_____ Date_____

Word Work

> **Synonyms** are words that have similar meanings. For example, *little* and *small* are synonyms.

Read the sentences and the words below. Write the word that means almost the same as the word in dark type.

hazardous   top   adventure

leader   dropped

1. The climbers reached the **peak** of the mountain just before nightfall. _____

2. The **guide** showed the group how to handle the icy slopes. _____

3. Conditions on the mountain were **dangerous** at times. _____

4. At night, temperatures **dipped** below zero degrees. _____

5. The climbers described their trip as a challenging **experience**. _____

Fill in the letter with the word or group of words that means the same or about the same as the underlined word.

6. Another word for <u>howling</u> is
- Ⓐ walking.
- Ⓑ digging.
- Ⓒ wailing.
- Ⓓ climbing.

7. To <u>climb</u> is to
- Ⓐ run.
- Ⓑ go up.
- Ⓒ work.
- Ⓓ go down.

8. Something that is <u>interesting</u> is
- Ⓐ exciting.
- Ⓑ boring.
- Ⓒ frightening.
- Ⓓ easy.

9. To <u>reach</u> is to
- Ⓐ fall.
- Ⓑ leave.
- Ⓒ arrive at.
- Ⓓ tell.

10. To <u>tackle</u> is to
- Ⓐ fasten.
- Ⓑ handle.
- Ⓒ lift.
- Ⓓ fall down.

Write Now

In the selection "She Climbed to the Top," you learned how Merrick Johnston and her fellow climbers survived a bad storm on the slopes of Denali.

The Storm on Denali

See	Hear	Feel and Think	Say and Do

- Plan to write your own descriptive paragraph of the storm on Denali. First, imagine you were there. What do you think it was like? What could you see? What could you hear? What did you feel and think? What did you and your companions say and do? Write your ideas on a chart.

- Write your description. Use words that help your reader imagine what it looked, sounded, and felt like on the mountain. Then explain how you and your companions escaped the storm.

Who Says Ball Games Are for the Birds?

by Joshua Wink

Set Your Purpose

What do ball games and birds have in common? More than you think! Read this article to find out.

The Trinity College Bantams were proud of their name. Bantams are a type of small fighting rooster, and the name suited the **spunky** spirit of this basketball team. One day in 1954, the Trinity Bantams were set to battle the Yale University team.

The Trinity fans wanted to support their players. They hatched a "fowl" plan. On the day of the game, they were prepared. When the Bantams scored their first basket, the fans cheered. Then they gently released dozens of live chickens onto the court! The chickens raced wildly around the floor. The

game had to be **suspended** until all the birds were collected. Unfortunately, all that team spirit was not enough. The game was won by Yale. You might say the Bantams "fowled" out of that game!

Casey Stengel was an old-time baseball player. He played with the Brooklyn Dodgers until 1918. Then he was traded to the Pittsburgh Pirates. Casey loved playing jokes. The fans loved his **antics**. When Casey returned to his old home stadium for the first time as a Pirate, he planned a special prank for his old fans. When the stadium announcer called out Casey's name in the lineup, Casey jogged onto the field to tip his cap to the crowd. When he did that, a canary that he had hidden in his cap

flew out. The crowd was delighted. They welcomed Casey back with loud applause.

Ballparks are great places for birds to hang out. Pigeons, seagulls, and other small birds can often be seen feasting on spilled popcorn. However, sometimes fans are lucky enough to catch sight of a larger-than-life bird, the Famous San Diego Chicken. The Chicken travels the nation, attending sports events. He **entertains** the crowds at baseball, basketball, hockey, and football games. The human inside the chicken costume is Ted Giannoulas. He's been a "chicken" since 1974. At that time, he was a student working at a college radio station, hoping to break into the world of professional radio. When a San Diego radio station put out a call for a volunteer to wear a chicken suit for a **promotional** stunt, Ted jumped at the chance. He was short enough; the chicken suit fit. The Famous San Diego Chicken was hatched that day, and it's never returned to its shell.

Think About It

Which "birds at the ball park" piece do you think was the most amusing? Why?

Name _____ Date _____

Check Your Understanding

Fill in the letter with the best answer for each question.

1. Why did the Trinity fans release chickens at the ball game and not some other animal?

   Ⓐ Chickens are funnier than other animals.

   Ⓑ The Trinity team name is the Bantams. Bantams are a type of chicken.

   Ⓒ Chickens were easy to sneak into the stadium.

   Ⓓ Chickens can fly, so they wouldn't get hurt.

2. Why was his return to the Brooklyn stadium a special occasion for Casey Stengel?

   Ⓐ He had never been to Brooklyn.

   Ⓑ He used to play on the Brooklyn team, and the fans used to cheer for him.

   Ⓒ It was the best stadium in the world.

   Ⓓ He loved to watch the birds that gathered at the stadium.

3. From this article, you can infer that sports fans

   Ⓐ dislike animals.

   Ⓑ love chickens.

   Ⓒ like jokes.

   Ⓓ wish athletes were more serious.

4. Ted Giannoulas agreed to wear a chicken suit because he

   Ⓐ was short.

   Ⓑ wanted people to appreciate chickens.

   Ⓒ wanted to work in professional radio.

   Ⓓ needed the money.

5. What would be another good title for this article?

   Ⓐ The Famous Chicken

   Ⓑ When Birds and Sports Mix

   Ⓒ Professional Sports

   Ⓓ How Casey Made the Day

Vocabulary

Find each vocabulary word in the selection. The words and sentences around it will help you figure out its meaning.

Fill in the letter with the best definition of the underlined word.

1. The name Bantam suited the <u>spunky</u> spirit of this basketball team.

   Ⓐ short   Ⓒ lively and energetic

   Ⓑ sleepy   Ⓓ underground

2. The fans loved Casey's <u>antics</u>.

   Ⓐ jokes and pranks   Ⓒ funny clothes

   Ⓑ athletic skills   Ⓓ relatives

3. The game had to be <u>suspended</u> until all the birds were caught.

   Ⓐ stopped for some time

   Ⓑ speeded up

   Ⓒ recorded on tape

   Ⓓ sent home from school

4. The Famous Chicken <u>entertains</u> the crowds at ball games.

   Ⓐ annoys   Ⓒ goes in with

   Ⓑ amuses   Ⓓ introduces

5. Ted first wore the chicken suit for <u>promotional</u> reasons.

   Ⓐ formal dance   Ⓒ athletic

   Ⓑ health   Ⓓ advertising

Name_____ **Date**_____

Word Work

Some words have more than one meaning. You can often figure out the meaning of a word by looking at how the word is used in a sentence.

1. rule (*verb*) – to decide
   Umpires can *rule* the runner safe.

2. rule (*noun*) – an official instruction
   You will be fined if you break a *rule*.

A **contraction** is formed by putting two words together and replacing one or more letters with an apostrophe (').

did + not = didn't

Decide if each underlined word has meaning A or B. Fill in the letter with the correct answer.

1. The runner made a <u>dash</u> for home plate.
   Ⓐ sprinkle   Ⓑ quick run

2. The catcher managed to <u>tag</u> the runner out.
   Ⓐ to touch a player with the ball
   Ⓑ a label, such as a price tag or name tag

3. My friend hopes to <u>pitch</u> in the next game.
   Ⓐ throw a baseball to a batter
   Ⓑ the highness or lowness of a musical note

4. The <u>season</u> ended, so the players went home.
   Ⓐ to add spices
   Ⓑ a part of the year

5. There are chickens on the basketball <u>court</u>!
   Ⓐ a place where legal cases are heard
   Ⓑ an area where games are played

Fill in the letter of the contraction that can be formed by the underlined words.

6. <u>He is</u> trying to put some fun into the game.
   Ⓐ He's   Ⓑ He'd   Ⓒ He'll   Ⓓ Haven't

7. The umpire <u>had not</u> decided which call was best.
   Ⓐ haven't Ⓑ hasn't   Ⓒ hadn't   Ⓓ didn't

8. The manager argued that his player <u>was not</u> out.
   Ⓐ wasn't   Ⓒ wouldn't
   Ⓑ weren't   Ⓓ won't

9. It was the zaniest thing <u>we have</u> ever seen.
   Ⓐ we'll   Ⓑ we've   Ⓒ we'd   Ⓓ we're

10. Do you think <u>you will</u> ever see that again?
   Ⓐ you're   Ⓑ you'd   Ⓒ you've   Ⓓ you'll

Write Now

In the article "Who Says Ball Games Are for the Birds?" you read several sports pieces that involve birds.

• Plan to write a short news article about one of the three events described in the selection. Create a flowchart and describe what happened first, second, and third.

• Write your article. Be sure to use your own words to describe what happened. Your flowchart will help you. Finally, write a headline for your article. Your headline should be short, clear, and clever. It should catch the reader's attention and capture the main idea of the article.

Written
by Anonymous

Many famous poems and songs were signed "Anonymous." Who is this mysterious writer?

Well, the truth is that "anonymous" means unknown. Poems are signed anonymous when the true author is unknown.

In the first poem, Anonymous is in an **upbeat** mood, juggling sound-alike words. And Anonymous manages to say something **meaningful**, too.

Set Your Purpose

The poems that follow might make you think and laugh. Read and enjoy them.

The Weather

Whether the weather be fine
Or whether the weather be not,
Whether the weather be cold
Or whether the weather be hot,
We'll weather the weather
Whatever the weather,
Whether we like it or not.

— *Anonymous*

In the next poem, Anonymous makes fun of a friend's joke in a **mocking** tone.

The Joke

The joke you just told isn't funny one bit.
It's pointless and dull, wholly lacking in wit.
It's so old and stale, it's beginning to smell!
Besides, it's the one I was going to tell.

— *Anonymous*

In the next poem, a frog's question gets a centipede so confused she loses her **capacity** to walk.

The Puzzled Centipede

A centipede was happy quite
Until a frog in fun
Said, "Pray, which leg comes after which?"
This raised her mind to such a pitch,
She lay distracted in the ditch
Considering how to run.

– *Anonymous*

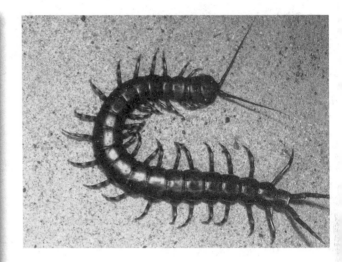

Now Anonymous wonders why the ptarmigan spells his name in such an odd way! Then Anonymous shows us what would happen if everyone **adopted** this strange spelling.

The Ptarmigan

The ptarmigan is strange,
As strange as he can be;
Never sits on ptelephone poles
Or roosts upon a ptree.
And the way he ptakes pto spelling
Is the strangest thing pto me.

– *Anonymous*

The last poem is the story of a flea and a fly who are trapped in a flue—a pipe inside a chimney.

Think About It

Which poem did you like best? Why?

A Fly and a Flea in a Flue

A fly and a flea in a flue
Were imprisoned, so what could they do?

Said the fly, "Let us flee!"
"Let us fly!" said the flea,
And they flew through a flaw in the flue.

– *Anonymous*

Name _____   Date _____

Check Your Understanding

Fill in the letter with the best answer for each question.

1. In "Weather," you can infer that the poet believes that people should

  Ⓐ dress properly for bad weather.

  Ⓑ try to get away from bad weather.

  Ⓒ learn to accept all sorts of weather.

  Ⓓ pay attention to predictions about bad weather.

2. In "The Joke," you can infer that the poet felt

  Ⓐ pleased.   Ⓒ upset.

  Ⓑ happy.   Ⓓ kind.

3. In "The Puzzled Centipede," you can infer that the reason why the centipede can't walk is

  Ⓐ she has broken all her legs.

  Ⓑ she feels the frog has insulted her.

  Ⓒ she is ashamed of her many legs.

  Ⓓ she is too confused to move.

4. Compared to the frog, the centipede has

  Ⓐ lots of spots.   Ⓒ a huge head.

  Ⓑ many legs.   Ⓓ tiny eyes.

5. The fly and the flea managed to escape because

  Ⓐ a larger insect carried them off.

  Ⓑ rain washed them down the water spout.

  Ⓒ they found a hole in the chimney pipe.

  Ⓓ a human being opened the flue.

Vocabulary

Find each vocabulary word in the selection. The words and sentences around it will help you figure out its meaning.

Fill in the letter with the best definition of the underlined word.

1. The poet is in an <u>upbeat</u> mood, joyfully juggling sound-alike words.

  Ⓐ cheerful   Ⓒ serious

  Ⓑ sad   Ⓓ peaceful

2. Anonymous makes a <u>meaningful</u> point even if the poem doesn't seem to make sense.

  Ⓐ nonsense   Ⓒ sensible

  Ⓑ short   Ⓓ weak

3. The poet makes fun of a friend's joke in a <u>mocking</u> tone.

  Ⓐ friendly   Ⓒ quiet

  Ⓑ crying   Ⓓ teasing

4. The centipede is so confused, she loses her <u>capacity</u> to walk at all.

  Ⓐ ability   Ⓒ company

  Ⓑ interest   Ⓓ movement

5. The bird <u>adopted</u> a strange spelling for his name.

  Ⓐ wanted   Ⓒ changed

  Ⓑ chose   Ⓓ rejected

Hi-Lo Nonfiction Passages for Struggling Readers: Grades 6–8 • Scholastic Inc.

Name _____ **Date** _____

Word Work

Synonyms are words that have similar meanings. For example, *little* and *small* are synonyms.	Antonyms are words that have opposite meanings. For example, *weak* and *strong* are antonyms.

Read the sentences and the below. Write the word that means almost the same as the word in dark type.

puzzled   wondering

crack   boring   nest

1. Your joke is pointless and **dull**. _____

2. The centipede was **confused** by the frog's question. _____

3. She was **considering** how to run. _____

4. The ptarmigan won't **roost** in a tree. _____

5. They flew through a **flaw** in a flue. _____

Read the sentences and the words below. Write the word that means the opposite of the word in dark type.

fresh   sad   hot   freed   strange

6. The weather may be **cold**. _____

7. This bread is very **stale**. _____

8. The centipede was quite **happy**. _____

9. The ptarmigan is an **ordinary** bird. _____

10. The fly and the flea were **imprisoned**. _____

Write Now

The chart shows two of the funny things you read about in the poems by Anonymous.

a centipede	couldn't remember how to run
a fly and a flea	couldn't fly out of a flue

- Plan to write a paragraph telling a funny animal story. Build the story around something that you've seen or observed. You can also make it up.

- Write your story. Describe the situation. Add details to make your story come alive.

Lights! Camera! INVENTION!

by John James

Set Your Purpose

How did Thomas Edison change the world? Read this article to find out.

Young Thomas Edison was bored. It was Saturday afternoon, and he was stuck at home. He was supposed to be **attending** a concert in the park with his friends. But Mother Nature had made other plans. Heavy rains had forced the band to **postpone** the concert until Sunday. Now what was he supposed to do?

Disappointed as he was, Tom wasn't one to mope for long. He **rummaged** through his bookcase until he found a story he liked. Soon, he was lost in a tale about pirate treasure. It was too bad the flickering light from the oil lamp made it so hard to see.

Tom closed the book and let his imagination drift. What if people could hear band music whenever they wanted? What if they could flip a switch and have

bright, steady light for reading? What if they could see pictures of pirate ships on the ocean—pictures in which the people, the boats, and the waves moved the way they did in real life?

Years passed, but Tom never forgot his dreams. In the 1870s, he invented a phonograph, or talking machine. He had found a way to record, or copy, sounds onto a thin, flat, round disk. People could sit at home and listen to band music whenever they wanted.

Tom wasn't finished. A few years later, he invented the first electric lightbulb people could use in their homes. His lightbulb had two **advantages** over those being used in street lamps at the time. First, it was **inexpensive** because it used very little electricity. Many people could afford to use it in their homes. Second, the lamp gave off a steady light, softer than the harsh brightness of the streetlight bulbs.

For some people, these would have been enough bright ideas for one lifetime. But they weren't enough for Tom. He still had plenty up his sleeve. In 1888, he invented the motion-picture camera. Audiences could watch pirates, clowns—almost anyone or anything they wanted—on film. But that wasn't all.

Several years later, Tom Edison built the world's first film studio so he could make movies for others to enjoy, rain or shine!

Most of us dream about how we'd like to change the world. Tom Edison did more than dream. He made his dreams come true.

Think About It

How do you think the world would be different without electric lights, recorded music, and movie cameras?

Name _____   Date _____

Check Your **Understanding**

Fill in the letter with the best answer for each question.

1. Tom Edison was someone who
- Ⓐ never had any dreams.
- Ⓑ thought dreams were important.
- Ⓒ did not like to read.
- Ⓓ liked being bored.

2. Which of the following sentences best describes Tom Edison?
- Ⓐ He liked the world just the way it was.
- Ⓑ He thought trying to change the world was impossible.
- Ⓒ He thought it was too much trouble to try changing the world.
- Ⓓ He thought people could change the world if they tried.

3. People admire Tom Edison because he
- Ⓐ found pirate treasure.
- Ⓑ found a way to hold concerts in the rain.
- Ⓒ worked to make his dreams come true.
- Ⓓ invented expensive electric street lamps.

4. Voices and music could be heard clearly on the
- Ⓐ park concert.
- Ⓒ electric lightbulb.
- Ⓑ film studio.
- Ⓓ phonograph.

5. Edison's bulb brought light inexpensively into people's
- Ⓐ streets.
- Ⓒ cars.
- Ⓑ homes.
- Ⓓ parks.

Vocabulary

Find each vocabulary word in the selection. The words and sentences around it will help you figure out its meaning.

Fill in the letter with the best definition of the underlined word.

1. Tom was supposed to be <u>attending</u> a concert in the park, but it was raining.
- Ⓐ writing
- Ⓒ being present at
- Ⓑ reading
- Ⓓ inventing

2. Heavy rains had forced the band to <u>postpone</u> the concert until Sunday.
- Ⓐ show
- Ⓒ begin
- Ⓑ stop
- Ⓓ delay

3. He <u>rummaged</u> through his bookcase until he found a story he liked.
- Ⓐ destroyed
- Ⓒ looked through
- Ⓑ played
- Ⓓ put on film

4. Tom's lightbulb had <u>advantages</u> over those being used in street lamps.
- Ⓐ movements
- Ⓒ failures
- Ⓑ benefits
- Ⓓ flower seeds

5. The lightbulb was <u>inexpensive</u> because it used very little electricity.
- Ⓐ low in cost
- Ⓒ quiet
- Ⓑ loud
- Ⓓ painful

Name _____ **Date** _____

Word Work

> **Antonyms** are words that have opposite meanings. For example, *dark* and *light* are antonyms.

Read the sentences and the words below. Write the word that means the opposite of the word in dark type.

delay   indoors   succeed

advantages   harsh

1. pleasant The first recorded music sometimes had a _____ sound.

2. hurry We had to _____ the baseball game because of the weather.

3. outdoors The heavy rains forced Tom to stay _____.

4. fail When Edison's inventions didn't _____, he tried again.

5. drawbacks Edison's lightbulb had two _____ over those of earlier inventors.

> A **suffix** is a word part that comes at the end of a base word. The suffixes **-er**, **-or**, and **-ion** can be added to base words to form new words. For example:
>
> photograph + er = photographer
>
> sail + or = sailor
>
> select + ion = selection

Each word on the left contains a base word and a suffix. Complete the definition by writing the correct form of the base word.

6. inventor a person who can _____

7. dreamer someone who can _____

8. direction something that can _____

9. invention something that one can _____

10. actor a person who can _____

Write Now

The article "Lights! Camera! Invention!" mentions quite a few inventions by Thomas Edison. If you could invent something, what would it be?

- Plan to write a paragraph about an invention that you think will improve your world. First, think about what current problem you would like to solve. What kind of invention will solve the problem? Make a chart like the one shown.

- Write a paragraph about your invention. Use as many details as possible to help your reader visualize the finished product.

Problem	Invention
It's too difficult to clean the bathtub.	a self-cleaning bathtub

Identifying Main Idea & Details

❖ Identifying the main idea a writer is trying to get across will help you understand and remember the writer's most important points.

- The **main idea** is the most important idea about a topic.

- **Details** are used to support the main idea.

- To find the **main idea**, list supporting details and think about how they are related.

- If there is no sentence that states the main idea, make up one using the supporting details.

❖ Read this paragraph. Look for the **main idea** and **details** that support the main idea.

Main Idea

This sentence tells what the whole paragraph is about. It states the **main idea** of the paragraph.

Details

These sentences give **details**. They give more information about the main idea.

A Long Friendship

Dogs and people may have been companions for far longer than was previously thought. Recent research indicates that dogs and humans joined company more than 140,000 years ago. DNA evidence shows that dogs evolved from wolves in Europe at about the same time that early humans left Africa. One scientist believes this shows that dogs and people formed a hunting partnership soon after humans arrived in Europe.

❖ You could chart the **main idea** and **details** in the paragraph like this:

Main Idea
Dogs and humans have been companions for far longer than was previously thought.

Supporting Details
Research shows that dogs and humans joined company more than 140,000 years ago.
DNA evidence shows that dogs evolved from wolves in Europe at about the same time that early humans left Africa.
Dogs and humans formed a hunting partnership soon after humans arrived in Europe.

Your Turn

❖ Read this selection. Look for the **main idea** and **details**. Make a chart like the one above.

Here Comes the . . . Maildog?

For three years, from 1883 to 1886, the town of Calico, California, had a very unusual mail carrier—a dog named Dorsey.

Dorsey was the pet of the town's postmaster, Jim Stacy. He went along on Stacy's rounds with him. When Stacy fell ill and was unable to deliver the mail, he counted on Dorsey to take over. Stacy made a

 special harness for Dorsey and attached a pair of saddlebags to it. Then he sent Dorsey off with a note tied to his collar. The note requested that people place any return mail in the saddlebags. Dorsey completed his rounds successfully.

When Stacey recovered, Dorsey didn't retire. Instead, he was rewarded with his own official mail route.

GIANTS
of the Earth

by Lee McKlow

Set Your Purpose

What are the largest trees on Earth and where are they? Read this article to find out.

Think of your favorite tree. Is it big? Next to a **towering** sequoia, it would probably look tiny.

Sequoias are very special trees. They are some of the largest and oldest living things on Earth.

Once, there were many different kinds of sequoias. Now, there are only two kinds left. These are the coastal redwoods and the big trees. The **coastal** redwoods grow near the Pacific Ocean. The coastal redwoods are the tallest trees on Earth. Many are over 300 feet tall. That is as tall as a 30-story building! The area where these trees grow is **nicknamed** "the Land of the Giants."

The big trees, or giant sequoias, do not grow along the coast. They are **located** farther inland, in California. The big trees are much wider and heavier than the coastal redwoods. Think of a giraffe and an elephant. This will give you an idea of the difference between the two kinds of sequoias. The coastal redwoods are the "giraffes." The big trees are the "elephants."

The biggest sequoia of all is a big tree called General Sherman. It is one of the most **massive** living things on Earth. This tree is 275 feet tall. It is not as tall as some of the redwoods, but its trunk is the widest. It is more than 100 feet around. Scientists think it weighs more than 6,000 tons!

Sequoias take a long time to get so big. Humans grow for about 20 years, then they stay the same height. Sequoias keep growing as long as they live, and that can be a long time! Scientists say that General Sherman is between 3,000 and 4,000 years old. Think of everything that tree has seen in its lifetime!

Did You Know?

- The sequoia trees were named after a great Cherokee leader.

- General Sherman was a famous American soldier.

Think About It

What did you find out about the largest trees on Earth?

Name_____ Date_____

Check Your Understanding

Fill in the letter with the best answer for each question.

1. What is the main idea of this selection?

Ⓐ Some trees are more than 3,000 years old.

Ⓑ Sequoias—redwoods and big trees—are the largest living things in the world.

Ⓒ Redwoods and big trees both grow in California.

Ⓓ A tree named General Sherman is the biggest tree in the world.

2. What makes coastal redwoods special?

Ⓐ They are the heaviest trees in the world.

Ⓑ They are the most beautiful trees in the world.

Ⓒ They are the widest trees in the world.

Ⓓ They are the tallest trees in the world.

3. The big tree called General Sherman is

Ⓐ nicknamed "big tree."

Ⓑ one of the most massive living things on Earth.

Ⓒ as tall as the coastal redwoods.

Ⓓ the heaviest thing on Earth.

4. Which sentence is not true?

Ⓐ Redwoods live in the Land of the Giants.

Ⓑ Sequoias take a long time to get so big.

Ⓒ Some sequoias are 3,000 years old.

Ⓓ Sequoias grow all over the United States.

5. Why do sequoias grow so big?

Ⓐ They keep growing as long as they live.

Ⓑ They grow for about 20 years.

Ⓒ They live for more than 4,000 years.

Ⓓ They grow near the Pacific Ocean.

Vocabulary

Find each vocabulary word in the selection. The words and sentences around it will help you figure out its meaning.

Fill in the letter with the best definition of the underlined word.

1. Next to a towering redwood, most trees look tiny.

Ⓐ made of metal

Ⓑ angry

Ⓒ very tall

Ⓓ very heavy

2. The coastal redwoods grow near the Pacific Ocean.

Ⓐ like a roller coaster

Ⓑ mysterious

Ⓒ to slide down a hill

Ⓓ along the coast

3. The area where the coastal redwoods grow is nicknamed "the Land of the Giants."

Ⓐ given a name that describes a special feature

Ⓑ figured out a tree's height

Ⓒ decided how much a tree weighs

Ⓓ cut down

4. The big trees are located inland.

Ⓐ growing

Ⓑ in a place

Ⓒ stored

Ⓓ at the shore

5. The big tree called General Sherman is one of the most massive living things on Earth.

Ⓐ bossy

Ⓑ enormous

Ⓒ full of lumps

Ⓓ interesting

Name _____ Date _____

Word Work

A **suffix** is an ending that changes the meaning of a base word. Knowing the meaning of a suffix helps you figure out the meaning of the whole word. The suffix **-er** means "more than." The suffix **-est** means "the most." For example:

deep<u>er</u>   having more depth

quiet<u>est</u>   the most quiet

Sometimes, if the word ends in a *y*, the *y* is changed into an *i* before *-er* or *-est* is added. For example:

happy + er = happier

Write the base word for each of the following words. Remember, sometimes adding a suffix changes the spelling of the base word!

6. oldest _____

7. laziest _____

8. wiser _____

9. sleepiest _____

10. harder _____

Write the word that fits the definition by adding *-er* or *-est* to the base word.

1. is more kind   kind_____

2. is the most tall   tall_____

3. is the most pretty   pretty_____

4. is more green   green_____

5. is more rich   rich_____

Main Idea	Supporting Details
among the oldest living things on Earth	**1.** can live to be more than 3,000 years old
among the largest living things on Earth	**1.** can be over 300 feet tall
	2. can weigh up to 6,000 tons
	3. keeps growing as long as it lives

Write Now

In the selection "Giants of the Earth," you learned some special things about sequoia trees. You could organize the information from the selection into a chart like the one at right.

- Plan to write a poem from the point of view of a sequoia or an interesting tree that grows near your home. First, write down ideas about what makes the tree special. Then think about what the world must look like from the tree's point of view. What can the tree see from where it stands? What changes has the tree seen during its lifetime? What might the tree say if it could speak? Jot down your ideas.

- Write your poem. Remember to write from the point of view of a tree. Use your notes to give you ideas.

Long Ago In
TIMBUKTU

Mansa Musa, King of Mali, is shown seated on his throne.

by Jay Dinsmore

Set Your Purpose

What ancient cultures have you learned about in history? Read this article to find out about a great African kingdom from the past.

Imagine living in Africa 600 years ago. What would it have been like? You might have lived in a small village. Or you might have lived in the wealthy city of Timbuktu! Timbuktu was the most important city in Mali, a great kingdom in the western part of Africa.

The most powerful king of Mali was a man named Mansa Musa. He lived in the 14th century. Mansa Musa controlled several secret gold mines. He used these riches to build Timbuktu into a magnificent city filled with **splendor**.

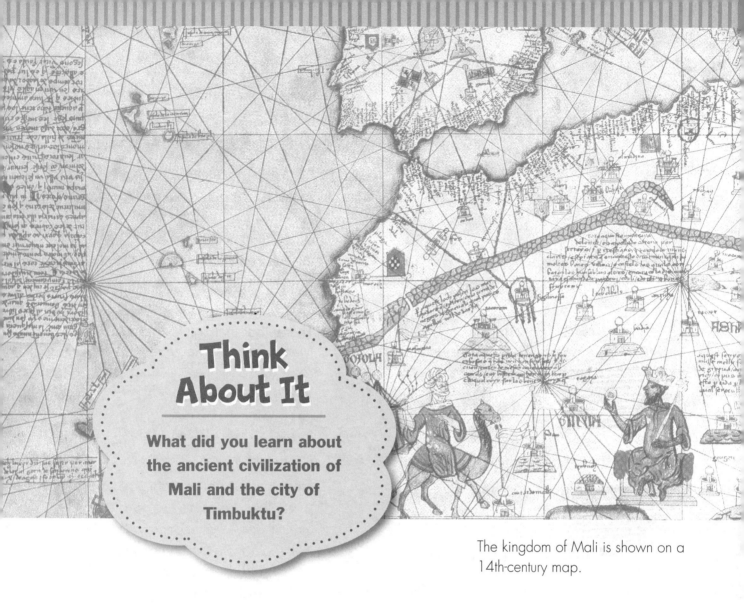

Think About It

What did you learn about the ancient civilization of Mali and the city of Timbuktu?

The kingdom of Mali is shown on a 14th-century map.

Have you ever heard someone complain, "I had to go all the way to Timbuktu"? That means the person had to travel to some remote, faraway place. Going all the way to Timbuktu was worth the trip 600 years ago! Mali was a very advanced **civilization**. The city of Timbuktu had huge libraries and marvelous schools. Poets, scholars, and artists gathered there. Traders from all over the world came to **seek** their fortunes.

Mansa Musa was a Muslim. He practiced the religion of Islam. Once in their lives, all Muslims are supposed to make a trip to the city of Mecca. Although Mecca was hundreds of miles away, Mansa Musa made the trip in style. His **caravan** included hundreds of camels and servants. He carried more gold in his caravan than most kings could hold in their royal **vaults**.

After the death of Mansa Musa, the great civilization of Mali began to crumble. Eventually, the kingdom fell apart. But the fame of Timbuktu and the stories of Mansa Musa's fabulous wealth live on.

Name _____ Date _____

Check Your Understanding

Fill in the letter with the best answer for each question.

1. During the reign of King Mansa Musa, Timbuktu was

Ⓒ a wealthy city in the kingdom of Mali.

Ⓓ an imaginary city.

Ⓔ a city to which Mansa Musa traveled in a caravan.

Ⓕ a small village in Africa.

2. Which detail supports the idea that Timbuktu was worth visiting?

Ⓒ Mansa Musa lived in the 14th century.

Ⓓ The king of Mali made a trip to Mecca.

Ⓔ Timbuktu had huge libraries and marvelous schools.

Ⓕ Timbuktu was a remote, faraway place.

3. How was King Mansa Musa able to build Timbuktu into a magnificent city?

Ⓒ He used riches from secret gold mines.

Ⓓ He borrowed money from other kingdoms.

Ⓔ He made a trip to Mecca.

Ⓕ He taxed traders from all over the world.

4. The author mentions Mansa Musa's trip to Mecca because he wants to

Ⓒ compare Islam to other religions.

Ⓓ describe the route.

Ⓔ describe the camels.

Ⓕ compare Mansa Musa's wealth to that of other kings.

5. From the last paragraph, you can guess that

Ⓒ Timbuktu is no longer a wealthy city.

Ⓓ the great civilization of Mali continues.

Ⓔ the gold mines never existed.

Ⓕ Timbuktu is not so far away after all.

Vocabulary

Find each vocabulary word in the selection. The words and sentences around it will help you figure out its meaning.

Fill in the letter with the best definition of the underlined word.

1. Timbuktu was a magnificent city filled with <u>splendor</u>.

Ⓒ weapons   Ⓔ warmth

Ⓓ glory   Ⓕ people

2. Mali was a very advanced <u>civilization</u>.

Ⓒ station   Ⓔ society and culture

Ⓓ high school   Ⓕ college life

3. Traders from all over the world came to <u>seek</u> their fortunes.

Ⓒ look for   Ⓔ sink

Ⓓ run away from   Ⓕ bury

4. Mansu traveled to Mecca with an enormous <u>caravan</u>.

Ⓒ city   Ⓔ parade of travelers

Ⓓ robe   Ⓕ food common in Africa

5. The kings stored their gold in their royal <u>vaults</u>.

Ⓒ palaces

Ⓓ locked rooms or compartments

Ⓔ libraries

Ⓕ towers or prisons

Name _____ **Date** _____

Word Work

> **Synonyms** are words that have similar meanings. For example, *small* and *tiny* are synonyms.

Read the sentences and the words. Write the word that means almost the same as the underlined word.

faraway   strong   enormous

old   traders   ruined   journeyed

1. Timbuktu was a <u>distant</u> city.   _____

2. Mansa Musa was its <u>powerful</u> ruler.   _____

3. Many artists <u>traveled</u> to Timbuktu.   _____

4. Wealthy <u>merchants</u> traveled there, too.   _____

5. Scholars visited the <u>huge</u> libraries.   _____

6. Years later, the kingdom was <u>destroyed</u>.   _____

7. The <u>ancient</u> buildings crumbled.   _____

> **Connotation** is the emotional meaning of a word. It affects the tone or mood of the sentence. For example, the word *stomped* below conveys an angry mood. The word *skipped* conveys a happy mood.
>
> **Jesse *stomped* down the hall.**
>
> **Jesse *skipped* down the hall.**

8. Fill in the letter of the word that suggests that Mansa Musa was kind.

Mansa Musa was a _____ king.

   Ⓐ powerful   Ⓒ generous
   Ⓑ wealthy   Ⓓ stern

9. Fill in the letter of the word that suggests that there were lots of finely prepared food at the banquet.

The king invited them to an _____ banquet.

   Ⓐ interesting   Ⓒ elaborate
   Ⓑ awful   Ⓓ unusual

10. Fill in the letter of the word that suggests that the goods in the store were unusual and from all over the world.

The shop was filled with _____ goods.

   Ⓐ antique   Ⓒ useful
   Ⓑ expensive   Ⓓ exotic

Write Now

Did "Long Ago in Timbuktu" give you some new insights into what life was like in ancient Africa? If asked to describe ancient Africa, many people would write words such as *jungles, elephants, lions,* and *zebras.* But, as you now know, there was much, much more.

- Plan to write a short description of a place you know well. First, choose a place. Then list the things you know about that place.

- Write your description. Use your list to help you.

Astronauts Walk on the Moon

by Carol Domblewski

The United States won the space race today. The *Eagle* landed on the moon, and the first human being walked on its surface.

Apollo 11 astronaut Neil Armstrong took those first steps. "That's one small step for man, one giant leap for mankind," said Armstrong.

Millions of people around the world were watching the event. It was carried live on television. Some watched both the landing on the moon last night and the walk on the moon early this morning. The landing stirred strong feelings of pride and joy on planet Earth. Millions of people cheered, and some people cried. All were amazed. Armstrong did what no one has ever done before.

The landing also **fulfilled** a promise made by President John F. Kennedy. During his term in office, Kennedy said that the United States

Set Your Purpose

What was it like when the first astronauts walked on the moon? Read this newspaper article to find out what one reporter wrote.

Neil Armstrong steps onto the moon.

would land a man on the moon by the end of the **decade**. Today his dream came true. So did the dreams of millions.

Armstrong and fellow astronaut Edwin "Buzz" Aldrin spent more than two hours walking on the moon. In their space suits, they found walking—and even running—easy. This is due to the moon's **gravity**, which is one-sixth of Earth's. The astronauts planted a U.S. flag on the moon. They set up three experiments. They collected rock samples from the moon's surface. They also made satellite contact with the White House. This led to another **historic** moment. Richard M. Nixon became the first President to chat with someone on the moon.

While Armstrong and Aldrin walked, the third *Apollo 11* astronaut, Michael Collins, stayed on board. He was still in orbit, circling the moon. After their walk, Armstrong and Aldrin used the *Eagle* to get them back to *Apollo 11.*

The flight was launched five days ago, on July 16. It has been attracting worldwide attention ever since.

Astronaut Neil Armstrong—the first man to walk on the moon

Think About It

What did the astronauts do when they landed on the moon? Why was this an important event?

Name _____ Date _____

Check Your **Understanding**

Fill in the letter with the best answer for each question.

1. The main idea of this selection is that
  Ⓐ Neil Armstrong took a small step.
  Ⓑ walking on the moon is easy.
  Ⓒ astronauts landed and walked on the moon.
  Ⓓ the astronauts talked to the President.

2. What did the astronauts do when they were on the moon?
  Ⓐ They set up a space station.
  Ⓑ They drove a moon buggy.
  Ⓒ They were fishing.
  Ⓓ They collected rock samples.

3. Why was Neil Armstrong's walk on the moon so important?
  Ⓐ It was the first time a human had stood on the moon.
  Ⓑ People everywhere felt pride.
  Ⓒ There was very little gravity on the moon.
  Ⓓ It was carried live on television.

4. What was the *Eagle*?
  Ⓐ the spacecraft that was built on the moon
  Ⓑ machine that took the astronauts to the moon's surface
  Ⓒ a place on the moon
  Ⓓ one of the three experiments

5. It was easy for the astronauts to walk and run on the moon because
  Ⓐ there were two astronauts.
  Ⓑ they spent more than two hours.
  Ⓒ they were carrying a flag.
  Ⓓ there is less gravity on the moon.

Vocabulary

> Find each vocabulary word in the selection. The words and sentences around it will help you figure out its meaning.

Fill in the letter with the best definition of the underlined word.

1. President Kennedy promised a moon landing by the end of the <u>decade</u>.
  Ⓐ year   Ⓒ dream
  Ⓑ ten years   Ⓓ rocket flight

2. President Kennedy <u>fulfilled</u> his promise.
  Ⓐ ended   Ⓒ carried out
  Ⓑ filled up   Ⓓ emptied

3. The moon's <u>gravity</u> makes it easy to walk on.
  Ⓐ rocks and craters   Ⓒ without wind
  Ⓑ being small in size   Ⓓ force that pulls down

4. The moon landing was a <u>historic</u> moment.
  Ⓐ important event
  Ⓑ having happiness
  Ⓒ state of confusion
  Ⓓ worthy of being on air

5. The *Apollo 11* flight was <u>launched</u> on July 16, 1969.
  Ⓐ sent up into space   Ⓒ forgotten
  Ⓑ given something to eat   Ⓓ lost

Hi-Lo Nonfiction Passages for Struggling Readers: Grades 6–8 • Scholastic Inc.

Name_____ Date_____

Word Work

> **Synonyms** are words that have similar meanings. For example, *little* and *small* are synonyms.

> To form the **past tense** of most verbs, add **-ed**. If the verb ends in *e*, drop the *e* and add *-ed*. If the verb ends in *y*, drop the *y* and add *-ied*.

Fill in the letter of the word that means the same or about the same as the underlined word.

1. It is <u>easy</u> to run on the moon.
  Ⓐ tiring   Ⓒ difficult
  Ⓑ simple   Ⓓ silly

2. You can <u>jump</u> high off the ground.
  Ⓐ bounce   Ⓒ leap
  Ⓑ fall   Ⓓ stumble

3. The astronauts <u>gathered</u> some moon rocks.
  Ⓐ saw   Ⓒ decorated
  Ⓑ threw   Ⓓ collected

4. They had a <u>chat</u> with the President.
  Ⓐ talk   Ⓒ snack
  Ⓑ meeting Ⓓ cat

5. We felt great <u>happiness</u> when the astronauts returned safely.
  Ⓐ hope   Ⓒ fear
  Ⓑ joy   Ⓓ panic

Read each sentence. Write the past tense of the word in dark type.

6. land   Yesterday, the *Eagle* _____ on the moon.

7. watch The world _____ it on their television sets.

8. walk   Astronaut Neil Armstrong _____ on the moon.

9. carry Then one astronaut _____ rock samples.

10. wave We watched as one astronaut _____ the American flag.

Write Now

Look at this chart about the moon landing.

- Plan to write your own news article about an important event that took place in your home, school, or community. First, make a chart like the one shown. Fill it in with the details of your important event.

- Write your news article. Remember to tell *who, what, where, when,* and *why.* Use your chart to help you.

Who:	the astronauts
What:	landed and walked
Where:	the moon
When:	July 16, 1969
Why:	to do it!

Rain-Forest Medicines

adapted by Jocelyn Piro

Set Your Purpose

Read this article to find out about medicines that come from rain forests.

A young boy is crying because his ear hurts. Then a man comes out of the forest. He carries some juice from a white fungus plant. Carefully, he drips the juice into the boy's ear. In some rain-forest villages of South America, that's how earaches are **cured**!

Rain-forest doctors, called shamans (SHAH-manz), use many kinds of plants as medicine. They make tea from one type of red vine. It cures stomachaches. Yellow flowers from another plant are used to treat snakebite. **Local** shamans have used the curing power of plants for thousands of years.

Learning from the Shamans

Today, scientists from all over the world want to learn what these shamans know about plant medicines. They are racing to find the secrets of the rain forest before the plants disappear for good. And the rain forests are disappearing fast. Every year, people cut down an area of rain forest as large as Florida. Sometimes they want to use the land for farms. Sometimes they cut down the trees and sell the wood.

Now the scientists travel by boat, air, and foot to tiny rain-forest villages. Then they spend long hours **trudging** through the steamy jungle with the local shamans. The shamans show the scientists which plants can be used as cures.

Saving the Rain Forest

One U.S. company has already found an important new medicine. It comes from a plant found in the rain forests of Ecuador. This medicine may soon be used to cure lung **infections** in kids.

Rain-forest plants might cure many bad **diseases**, such as cancer and AIDS. So medicine companies are working to save the rain forests. When people buy medicines made from the rain-forest plants, part of the money will go to help save the rain forests. If the rain forests survive, someday you may find cures in your home that were made from white fungus and red vines.

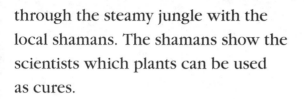

Think About It

What are some ways that scientists learn about new medicines?

Name _____   Date _____

Check Your Understanding

Fill in the letter with the best answer for each question.

1. What is the main idea of the first two paragraphs in this selection?

   Ⓐ Shamans can cure earaches.

   Ⓑ You can make tea from a red vine.

   Ⓒ There are rain forests in South America.

   Ⓓ Important medicines come from rain forests.

2. What is the main idea of "Learning from the Shamans" and "Saving the Rain Forest"?

   Ⓐ Scientists want to learn about rain-forest medicine before the plants disappear.

   Ⓑ Shamans are learning from scientists, and scientists are learning from shamans.

   Ⓒ Shamans are opening new schools.

   Ⓓ Scientists are destroying the rain forest.

3. Choose the detail that supports this idea: Shamans use many plants as medicine.

   Ⓐ Medicine companies are working to save the rain forests.

   Ⓑ Rain forests are rapidly disappearing.

   Ⓒ Yellow flowers from one plant are used to treat snakebite.

   Ⓓ One U.S. company has already found an important new medicine.

4. An important new medicine from a plant in the Ecuadorean rain forests may soon be used to

   Ⓐ ask for more government money.

   Ⓑ fight lung illnesses in young children.

   Ⓒ help rain forests survive.

   Ⓓ make local shamans more effective.

5. Another good title for the article is

   Ⓐ Jungle Cures.

   Ⓑ Snakebite Remedies.

   Ⓒ Buying Medicines.

   Ⓓ The Rain Forest Is Disappearing.

Vocabulary

> Find each vocabulary word in the selection. The words and sentences around it will help you figure out its meaning.

Fill in the letter with the best definition of the underlined word.

1. Earaches are sometimes <u>cured</u> by dripping plant juice into the ear.

   Ⓐ caught   Ⓒ caused

   Ⓑ made better   Ⓓ invented

2. <u>Local</u> rain-forest doctors use the curing power of plants.

   Ⓐ loud   Ⓒ worldwide

   Ⓑ nearby   Ⓓ room

3. Scientists spend long hours <u>trudging</u> through the jungle.

   Ⓐ waltzing   Ⓒ walking with effort

   Ⓑ jogging   Ⓓ jumping quickly

4. Lung <u>infections</u> in kids are cured by a special medicine.

   Ⓐ candies   Ⓒ inspections

   Ⓑ cuts, bruises   Ⓓ sicknesses caused by germs

5. Rain-forest plants might cure many bad <u>diseases</u>.

   Ⓐ illnesses   Ⓒ medicines

   Ⓑ dislikes   Ⓓ habits

Name_____   Date_____

Word Work

A **compound word** is made of two shorter words. To understand a compound word, separate it into the two shorter words and think about the meaning of those words.

ear + ache = earache

Read the definitions below. Join two words from each definition to make a compound word that fits the definition. Write the word. Look at the sample.

SAMPLE   definition: the **top** of a **tree**

compound word: **treetop**

Definitions

1. an ache in the head   _____

2. a book that tells how to cook   _____

3. the skin of a snake   _____

4. the light of the sun   _____

5. the bell by a door   _____

Look at the compound words below. Write the word that best completes each sentence. Then draw a line between the two shorter words that make up the compound word.

notebook   treetops   earache
rattlesnake   backpack

6. This rain-forest medicine can cure an _____.

7. Monkeys live in the _____.

8. An angry _____ can be very dangerous.

9. The scientist wrote notes in her _____.

10. She carried her materials in her _____.

Write Now

In "Rain-Forest Medicines," you read about a lot of interesting things scientists are learning about rain-forest plants. Pretend you are a news reporter who is assigned to write a news story about a new medicine found in a rain forest.

Who?	Who discovered the plant?
What?	What did the plant look like?
Where?	
When?	
Why?	
How?	

- Plan to write a news story. First, make a list of questions you think people would want answered. In their news stories, reporters always try to answer the questions in the chart above.

- Write a news story about the new rain-forest medicine. Write a newspaper headline, or title, for your article. Remember that reporters need to say a lot in a few words. A reporter usually states the main idea in the first few sentences. Additional details are given in the rest of the news story.

BASEBALL IS A HIT IN JAPAN

adapted by Patrick Lyle

Set Your Purpose

How is baseball in Japan like baseball in the United States? Read this article to find out.

The October air is crisp and cool. Leaves are on the ground. Inside the ballpark, fans are packed into the stands, watching a baseball game. Sounds like the World Series is under way, right?

Wrong! This game is being played in Japan! It is part of the Japan Series. That's the Japanese **version** of the World Series.

The Japanese have been playing baseball ever since Americans taught them the game in the 1870s. They have had professional baseball **leagues** since 1935. Millions of Japanese

Think About It

What are some of the differences between Japanese and American baseball?

attend ballgames every year. When they aren't watching baseball, many fans play the game. Among kids, baseball is Japan's most **prevalent** sport.

Baseball is played by the same basic rules as in the United States. It's a little different, though. In Japan, games can end in a **tie**. That's not true in the United States. And in Japan, fans must return foul balls. Like American fans, however, they get to keep home-run balls. And in both the U.S. and Japan, fans support their home teams.

Many Japanese **spectators** join an *oendan* (o-en-dahn). An *oendan* is a team's official group of fans. *Oendan* members sit together and cheer for their team. They show their support by yelling, blowing whistles, and banging drums. Fans also sing the team song and wave flags and pom-poms.

It seems that having fun is part of being a baseball fan. Masayasu Okada has been in an *oendan* for more than 20 years. "I'm just crazy about my team," he says. "You have to be crazy to act like this every night!"

Name _____   Date _____

Check Your Understanding

Fill in the letter with the best answer for each question.

1. The main idea of this selection is that
- Ⓐ Masayasu Okada is a baseball fan.
- Ⓑ baseball is a popular sport in Japan.
- Ⓒ Japanese fans belong to an *oendan*.
- Ⓓ the Japan Series is like the World Series.

2. How is Japanese baseball different from American baseball?
- Ⓐ Games can end in a tie.
- Ⓑ Fans get to keep home-run balls.
- Ⓒ Fans support their home teams.
- Ⓓ Fans have fun at games.

3. Japanese fans support their teams by
- Ⓐ joining an *oendan*.
- Ⓑ returning home-run balls.
- Ⓒ giving money to players.
- Ⓓ playing the game when not watching it.

4. What do members of an *oendan* do?
- Ⓐ keep home-run balls
- Ⓑ watch the World Series
- Ⓒ cheer, yell, bang drums, and wave flags and pom-poms for their team
- Ⓓ follow the rules of American baseball

5. Which of the following is an opinion?
- Ⓐ Millions of Japanese attend ballgames every year.
- Ⓑ Among Japanese kids, baseball is a popular sport.
- Ⓒ Japanese fans are more enthusiastic than American fans.
- Ⓓ In Japan, fans must return foul balls.

Vocabulary

Find each vocabulary word in the selection. The words and sentences around it will help you figure out its meaning.

Fill in the letter with the best definition of the underlined word.

1. The Japanese people have their own <u>version</u> of the World Series.
- Ⓐ different form of something
- Ⓑ something that is opposite
- Ⓒ one part of a poem or song
- Ⓓ type of game

2. Among kids, baseball is Japan's most <u>prevalent</u> sport.
- Ⓐ unpleasant   Ⓒ expensive
- Ⓑ unusual   Ⓓ common

3. Japan has had professional baseball <u>leagues</u> since 1935.
- Ⓐ equipment players use
- Ⓑ fans watching a sport
- Ⓒ television programs about sports
- Ⓓ sports teams that play each other

4. In Japan, games can end in a <u>tie</u>.
- Ⓐ long piece of fabric worn around the neck
- Ⓑ join with a bow or knot
- Ⓒ even score
- Ⓓ big traffic jam

5. Many <u>spectators</u> attend the games.
- Ⓐ people who watch a game
- Ⓑ people who play a game
- Ⓒ people who televise a game
- Ⓓ people from another country

Name _____   Date _____

Word Work

A **compound word** is made of two shorter words. Combining the meanings of the two shorter words often explains the meaning of the compound word.

playground = a **ground** where you can **play**

Combine each word on the left with a word on the right. Write the compound words.

1. base   glasses   _____

2. noon   shield   _____

3. wind   ball   _____

4. tooth   time   _____

5. sun   brush   _____

Look at the compound words below. Write the word that best completes each sentence. Then draw a line between the two shorter words that make up the compound word.

ballpark   flagpole
underfoot   ballgames   teammates

6. When the batter hit a home run, his _____ congratulated him.

7. The foul ball hit the _____.

8. The _____ was crowded with fans watching the game.

9. You can watch some _____ on TV.

10. The ball-field grass was soft _____.

Write Now

In "Baseball Is a Hit in Japan," you read similarities and differences between baseball in the United States and Japan. Look at the diagram below.

• Pretend that you are visiting Japan and have watched a baseball game there. Plan to write a postcard to a friend, telling about your experience. First, decide what would interest your friend most. Write down some ideas.

• Write your postcard. Use descriptive words and lively verbs to give your friend a clear picture of your experience.

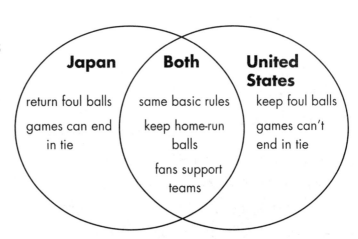

Japan
return foul balls
games can end in tie

Both
same basic rules
keep home-run balls
fans support teams

United States
keep foul balls
games can't end in tie

May You Have a Long Life

adapted by Sandra Reily

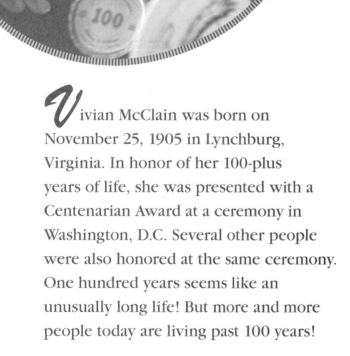

Set Your Purpose

Read this article to get some tips on how to live a long and healthy life.

*V*ivian McClain was born on November 25, 1905 in Lynchburg, Virginia. In honor of her 100-plus years of life, she was presented with a Centenarian Award at a ceremony in Washington, D.C. Several other people were also honored at the same ceremony. One hundred years seems like an unusually long life! But more and more people today are living past 100 years!

Why are we living longer now? There are many reasons. One reason is that medical care **continues** to improve. We have better medicine now. Many illnesses that used to make kids sick have been stopped with new vaccines.

If you want to live past 100, you have to take good care of yourself. That means eating **sensibly**, exercising your body and your mind, and staying involved with family and friends.

Eat Well! A healthy diet includes lots of vegetables, fruit, protein, and grains. Stay away from fat, sugar, and fast food.

How Long Will I Live?

In the 1700s, people could not expect to live much longer than 35 years. Look at the chart below. How long can people expect to live in the year 2100?

Date	Life Expectancy (years)
1700	35
1800	39
1900	47
2000	76

Get Moving! Exercise is great for people of all ages! It helps us sleep better. It improves our memory and makes us feel happier. People who exercise don't get sick as often. And remember, exercise doesn't have to be **vigorous**! Taking a walk with a friend is an excellent way to get exercise.

Chill Out! If you want to live longer, it's important to learn how to **cope** with stress. People who live longer generally don't let their problems get them down. "They are not quitters," says Lynn Adler, a volunteer who works with people over 100.

Be a Life-Long Learner! Keeping **mentally** active is also important. That means reading and learning new things.

Have Fun! And, finally, try to avoid being lonely. It's important to spend time with people who really care about you, like your family and friends.

So the next time your birthday rolls around, enjoy! Hopefully you'll have many, many more to come.

Think About It

What things can help you live a long and healthy life?

Name_____ Date_____

Check Your Understanding

Fill in the letter with the best answer for each question.

1. The main idea of the selection is: People can try to live longer by
- Ⓐ living in Canada, watching TV, and avoiding stress.
- Ⓑ eating lots of fast food and not exercising.
- Ⓒ eating well, exercising, and having fun with their friends.
- Ⓓ reading all the time, worrying, and eating fats.

2. Which of the following is a reason people are living longer?
- Ⓐ They are having more birthdays.
- Ⓑ They are younger.
- Ⓒ Parents keep children home from school.
- Ⓓ Medical care is better.

3. What is important to include in a healthy diet?
- Ⓐ fruits and vegetables
- Ⓑ candy and doughnuts
- Ⓒ french fries and milkshakes
- Ⓓ soda and cookies

4. Which of the following statements is an opinion?
- Ⓐ Keeping mentally active includes learning new things.
- Ⓑ You should never eat fried foods.
- Ⓒ People are generally living longer than before.
- Ⓓ Vivian McClain is more than 100 years old.

5. Which of the following sentences is not true?
- Ⓐ Having fun can help us stay healthy.
- Ⓑ Exercise improves our memory.
- Ⓒ People lived longer lives 100 years ago.
- Ⓓ Soon, many people will live to be more than 100 years old.

Vocabulary

Find each vocabulary word in the selection. The words and sentences around it will help you figure out its meaning.

Fill in the letter with the best definition of the underlined word.

1. One reason for longer life is that medical care continues to improve.
- Ⓐ goes on
- Ⓑ holds gently
- Ⓒ wants
- Ⓓ bends easily

2. By eating sensibly, a person can be healthy.
- Ⓐ with lots of feeling
- Ⓑ in an intelligent way
- Ⓒ on time
- Ⓓ a lot

3. Exercise doesn't have to be vigorous.
- Ⓐ lazy
- Ⓑ light
- Ⓒ forceful
- Ⓓ occasional

4. It's important to learn how to cope with stress.
- Ⓐ wear
- Ⓑ handle
- Ⓒ change
- Ⓓ avoid

5. Keeping mentally active is also important.
- Ⓐ in an unhealthy way
- Ⓑ in a hurried way
- Ⓒ having to do with the mind
- Ⓓ having to do with the body

Name_____ Date_____

Word Work

A **suffix** is a word part that comes at the end of a base word. The suffix **-ly** can be added to base words to form new words. For example:

soft + ly = softly

Write the base word for each of the following words.

1. officially _____

2. generally _____

3. quietly _____

4. mentally _____

5. finally _____

Add the suffix **-ly** to the base word in dark type to complete the sentence.

6. Vivian McClain has lived an **unusual**____ long life.

7. It is **hard**____ worth the risk of eating only fatty foods.

8. It's important to stay **physical**____ active.

9. **Actual**____, it is also important to stay mentally active.

10. Spend time with people who **real**____ care about you.

Write Now

In "May You Have a Long Life," you learned about different things people can do to help them live long and healthy lives. Look at the chart below. Use ideas from the article to fill it out.

Diet	Exercise	Stress	Keeping Active
eat grains	helps us sleep	don't be a quitter	read and learn

- Plan to write a short advice column for your school about ways to live longer. Feel free to add your own ideas for living longer. Use the chart above to help you organize your thoughts.

- Write your advice column. Use your chart to help you write. Add details to make your column interesting. Give it a title that will get people's attention!

The Truth About AIDS

by E. J. Kisslinger

Set Your Purpose

Hydeia, a girl with AIDS, teaches others about her disease. Read this article to learn about AIDS.

What do you first think when you find out someone has AIDS? Hydeia Broadbent was born with the virus known as HIV. This virus causes the **incurable** disease called AIDS.

How does HIV affect Hydeia? She gets tired easily, gets sick often, and is smaller than most kids her age. Her sickness has taught her that people have a lot to learn about HIV and AIDS.

"Sometimes people are afraid of me because they don't know what HIV is," she says. Hydeia has become famous as an AIDS educator. She has been on TV talk shows like *Oprah*. She often speaks to groups of kids to help them understand more. Here are some of the questions they often ask her:

Why do people with HIV get sick so often?

HIV attacks people's immune systems, so their bodies can't fight infections very well. It is easier to catch many kinds of sicknesses.

Is HIV the same as AIDS?

No. Many people with HIV are strong and healthy. They don't have AIDS. Eventually, people with HIV develop certain major infections. When this happens, they have AIDS.

How do you get HIV?

You can't get HIV "from the air." Therefore, you can't catch it like you can a cold. You can't get HIV from a sneeze or a handshake. You also can't get it by playing with or hugging **infected** people. HIV can only survive in bodily **fluids**, like blood. To infect you, the virus must pass from an infected person's bodily fluids into your blood.

Does having AIDS mean you will die?

People with AIDS can't be cured yet. But they can live for a long time before their **immune** systems finally stop being able to fight off disease and they die.

Hydeia feels well, even though she has AIDS. Her mother says she is a fighter.

"Mostly I try to stay upbeat and do what I do best—just have fun and be a kid," says Hydeia.

Think About It

What new information did you learn about HIV and AIDS?

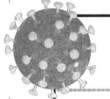

How HIV Is Different From Most Viruses

Infection by Most Viruses

1. When a virus gets into your blood, cells called helper T cells send out a chemical to "tell" killer cells to get ready to act to defend the body.

2. The killer cells then **release** a chemical that makes the virus powerless.

Infection by HIV

In the blood, HIV attaches to helper T cells. That stops the T cells from helping the killer cells fight the virus.

Name_____ Date_____

Check Your Understanding

Fill in the letter with the best answer for each question.

1. What is the main idea of this article?
   - (A) People are sometimes afraid of Hydeia, a young girl with AIDS.
   - (B) T cells help defend the body.
   - (C) Hydeia, a young girl with AIDS, teaches others about the disease.
   - (D) Hydeia, a young girl with AIDS, has appeared on Oprah Winfrey's talk show.

2. Which detail supports the main idea of this article?
   - (A) HIV survives in bodily fluids.
   - (B) Hydeia is small for her age.
   - (C) HIV attaches to helper T cells.
   - (D) Hydeia has become famous as an AIDS educator.

3. Most viruses
   - (A) help T cells kill other cells.
   - (B) cause helper T cells to "tell" killer cells to fight the virus.
   - (C) attach themselves to T cells.
   - (D) attach themselves to killer cells.

4. HIV stops
   - (A) T cells from helping the killer cells fight.
   - (B) killer cells from fighting T cells.
   - (C) certain major infections.
   - (D) a person from developing AIDS.

5. Why is it bad that HIV attaches itself to helper T cells?
   - (A) HIV shrinks the T cells.
   - (B) HIV then turns into AIDS.
   - (C) The T cells then cannot fight HIV.
   - (D) HIV makes the T cells multiply.

Vocabulary

Find each vocabulary word in the selection. The words and sentences around it will help you figure out its meaning.

Fill in the letter with the best definition of the underlined word.

1. Many people have died from an <u>incurable</u> disease called AIDS.
   - (A) hard to understand
   - (B) not able to be cured
   - (C) able to be cured
   - (D) curious

2. HIV attacks people's <u>immune</u> systems, so their bodies can't fight infections very well.
   - (A) disease-causing
   - (B) disease-fighting
   - (C) weight-gaining
   - (D) growing

3. You can't catch HIV from playing with or hugging <u>infected</u> people.
   - (A) virus-carrying
   - (B) free from the virus
   - (C) healthy
   - (D) strong

4. HIV can survive only in bodily <u>fluids</u>, like blood.
   - (A) illnesses
   - (B) small people
   - (C) difficult
   - (D) liquids

5. Killer cells <u>release</u> a chemical that makes a virus powerless.
   - (A) develop
   - (B) receive slowly
   - (C) send out
   - (D) attach to

Name _____ Date _____

Word Work

A **suffix** is an ending that changes the meaning of a word. The suffix **-able** means "capable of." The suffix **-ous** means "having." The suffix **-ness** means "the condition of."

us<u>able</u>	able to be used
poison<u>ous</u>	having poison
sick<u>ness</u>	the condition of being sick

Usually the final -e is dropped from the base word before adding the suffix *-able* or *-ous*.

adventure   **advent<u>ous</u>**

Write the base word for each of the following words. Remember, sometimes adding a suffix changes the spelling of the base word.

1. sickness   _____

2. famous   _____

3. dangerous   _____

4. lovable   _____

5. weakness   _____

Write a word that fits the definition by adding the suffix *-able*, *-ous*, or *-ness* to the base word.

6. able to be cured   cure_____

7. having danger   danger_____

8. the condition of being sad   sad_____

9. having fame   fame_____

10. able to be washed   wash_____

Things I Know About

1. being a twin

2. having asthma

3. taking care of rabbits

Write Now

In the article you read, Hydeia is able to teach people about AIDS because she knows what it is like to live with that illness. What is something you know about because of your life experiences? It could be something serious or fun. Look at the sample list above.

- Plan to make a poster that teaches others. First, write a list like the one above. Then choose the idea you like best. What are the most important things you can tell people about your experience so they will understand what it is like? Jot down some notes.

- Make your teaching poster. Use words and drawings to explain at least three important things about your topic.

Hail to the Chief!

by Neal Errett

The United States has had 43 presidents. Some stand as great. Some were weak or dishonest.

What does it take to be president? The U.S. Constitution says there are three **requirements** for presidents. They must be at least 35 years old. They must have been born in the United States. They must have **resided** in the United States for at least 14 years.

Set Your Purpose

People running for president make claims and promises. Whom should you believe? Read about how some voters judge.

However, the Constitution does not tell us how to pick a *good* president.

Look at our past presidents. Most have had significant experience in government. Fourteen of our presidents served first as vice president. Seventeen were former state governors. Twenty-three had served in Congress. So experience counts. You would not hire a ship's captain who had never been to sea.

Another thing we want is leadership. A leader **inspires** others to follow. We vote for presidents, not kings. That means our leader has to work with Congress and the people. And there will surely be times when they don't agree. That's when leadership is needed.

Still another issue is good character. Former President Jimmy Carter stressed honesty and strength. He also believed a president should stand for the rights of *all* the people. Former President Gerald Ford emphasized hard work and **integrity**. People often don't agree about what good character means. Can John Doe be president if he once cheated on a test? Can Jane Doe be elected if she has unpaid parking tickets? How perfect do our presidents have to be?

There's a fourth issue. Because of TV, personal charm now plays a big role in our elections. Voters now have to decide whether this is good or bad. How much should appearance count?

One class of middle-school students was asked what made a good president. They wanted someone who was well educated. They thought concern for others was important, too. They wanted someone who could take **criticism** well. And they thought a president should not back away from tough decisions.

What qualities do *you* think a president should have? In a few years, your vote will be very important to our nation's future.

Think About It

Who is the current U.S. president? What qualities does he or she have?

Name _____ Date _____

Check Your Understanding

Fill in the letter with the best answer for each question.

1. The main idea of the selection is what
- Ⓐ the Constitution requires of a president.
- Ⓑ middle-school students look for in a president.
- Ⓒ makes a weak or dishonest president.
- Ⓓ makes a good president.

2. Which detail does <u>not</u> support the main idea?
- Ⓐ A president must be at least 35 years old.
- Ⓑ A president must be a good leader.
- Ⓒ Experience counts.
- Ⓓ Former presidents cite the importance of character.

3. What kind of experience have most of our presidents had?
- Ⓐ They have taught middle-school students.
- Ⓑ They have held high-level government offices.
- Ⓒ They have been to sea.
- Ⓓ They have lived overseas for at least 14 years.

4. A president's personality and appearance have become more important in modern times because
- Ⓐ many early presidents were grouchy.
- Ⓑ we can now see them on television.
- Ⓒ people who don't pay their parking tickets shouldn't be president.
- Ⓓ appearance is a good way to judge a person's character.

5. Why does the author think the issues discussed in the selection are important to you?
- Ⓐ Someday you will be a voter, making decisions about who will lead our nation.
- Ⓑ Someday you may need to hire a ship's captain.
- Ⓒ The United States is the greatest nation in the world.
- Ⓓ In the past there have been presidents who looked bad on television.

Vocabulary

> Find each vocabulary word in the selection. The words and sentences around it will help you figure out its meaning.

Fill in the letter with the best definition of the underlined word.

1. The U.S. Constitution says there are three <u>requirements</u> for presidents.
- Ⓐ written tests
- Ⓑ things that are necessary
- Ⓒ things that are unimportant
- Ⓓ laws that are not obeyed

2. Presidents must have <u>resided</u> in the U.S. for at least 14 years.
- Ⓐ lived
- Ⓒ farmed
- Ⓑ visited
- Ⓓ made peace

3. Former President Gerald Ford emphasized hard work and <u>integrity</u>.
- Ⓐ long hours
- Ⓒ strength
- Ⓑ equal rights
- Ⓓ honesty

4. A leader <u>inspires</u> others to follow.
- Ⓐ asks
- Ⓒ influences
- Ⓑ orders
- Ⓓ wants

5. They wanted someone who could take <u>criticism</u> well.
- Ⓐ positive comments
- Ⓒ loud comments
- Ⓑ negative comments
- Ⓓ meaningless words

Name _____   Date _____

Word Work

Some words have more than one meaning. You can figure out the meaning of a word by looking at how the word is used in a sentence.

1. hail (*verb*) – to greet with enthusiasm

We all *hail* the president.

2. hail (*noun*) – small bits of ice that fall from the sky

Hail fell during the thunderstorm.

Read the sentences. Decide if each underlined word has meaning A or B. Fill in the letter with the correct answer.

1. Look at all our <u>past</u> presidents.
   Ⓐ having already served as an official
   Ⓑ going close to and then beyond

2. Seventeen presidents were former <u>state</u> governors.
   Ⓐ to express in words
   Ⓑ one of the main units of government

3. Former President Jimmy Carter discussed strength of <u>character</u>.
   Ⓐ the traits of a person
   Ⓑ a key person in a story

4. He <u>stressed</u> honesty and integrity.
   Ⓐ caused mental tension
   Ⓑ emphasized

5. How much should appearance <u>count</u>?
   Ⓐ to include in a tally
   Ⓑ to be under consideration

The **long-e** sound can be spelled several different ways.

e as in *sh<u>e</u>*   **ea** as in *h<u>ea</u>l*

ee as in *tr<u>ee</u>*

ie as in *br<u>ie</u>f*   **y** as in *fort<u>y</u>*

Circle the word in each group that has the long-e sound.

6. Jefferson   Monroe   Kennedy

7. cleaver   certain   clever

8. equal   spread   weigh

9. wreck   serve   freedom

10. pledge   president   shield

Write Now

In the article "Hail to the Chief!" you read about the importance of leadership. Think of someone in your life whom you admire as a leader.

• Plan to write a profile of this leader, describing her or his leadership qualities. Use this organizer to arrange your thoughts.

• Write your profile. Remember to explain exactly what it is about the person that shows leadership.

Leader's name:	Jimmy Carter
Experience:	former President of the United States
Qualities:	stressed honesty, strength of character

Set Your Purpose

What does it mean to be multiracial? Read this article to find out about some famous multiracial people.

Not Just Black or White

 by Louise Lampi

Mariah Carey

Black, white, **Hispanic**, Asian, or Native American? These days, most people give **credence** to the idea that people can belong to more than one race. Those who have a black father and a white mother can identify themselves as either black or white—or both. A person can be Hispanic and Asian or Native American and European. When people call themselves multiracial, it means they honor and accept more than one **ethnic** group as part of their heritage.

Singer Mariah Carey's mother is white and Irish. Her father is black and Venezuelan. Actress Halle Berry, golf star Tiger Woods, and actor Keanu Reeves are all multiracial. Derek Jeter, the New York Yankees ballplayer, is multiracial, too. His father is African American, his mother is white and Irish.

Jeter remembers that some of his high school classmates were perplexed. White students thought he was black. Black students presumed he was white. Others would walk up to him and start speaking Spanish.

"I'm biracial," Jeter says. "People ask if I'm black or white. I'm both. I'm not one race."

Devon Sutherland, 13, faced myriad questions from classmates about his race. They would ask him in the cafeteria of his middle school in Montclair, New Jersey. "They're just confused," says Devon, who has a white mother and a black father.

At least two million multiracial people live in the United States today. There may be as many as six million. As that number grows, the idea that every person has to be of just one race is being **surpassed** by the multiracial concept.

"Not all people fit neatly into one little box," say Ramona Douglas. She leads a group that supports multiracial Americans. "People should have the choice to identify themselves as they **perceive** themselves, not as others do."

Jeter was asked which he would choose if he had the choice of being all black or all white. He said he would choose both. "I wouldn't change a thing. I have the best of both worlds."

Think About It

What does Derek Jeter mean when he says he has the best of both worlds?

Derek Jeter

Name _____ Date _____

Check Your Understanding

Fill in the letter with the best answer for each question.

1. According to the article, being multiracial means

   Ⓐ enjoying the best of both worlds.

   Ⓑ being a member of more than one race.

   Ⓒ not wanting to change who you are.

   Ⓓ confusing friends and strangers.

2. The main idea of this article is that

   Ⓐ multiracial people face great difficulties.

   Ⓑ being multiracial is nothing special.

   Ⓒ more people in the United States now consider themselves multiracial.

   Ⓓ many celebrities are of mixed heritage.

3. Which detail does <u>not</u> support the main idea of this article?

   Ⓐ There are millions of multiracial people in the United States today.

   Ⓑ Derek Jeter is both African American and Irish.

   Ⓒ Devon Sutherland is in middle school.

   Ⓓ Attitudes about racial identity are changing.

4. Why might people identify themselves as multiracial?

   Ⓐ They are proud of their ancestry.

   Ⓑ There aren't enough multiracial people living in the United States.

   Ⓒ The law requires them to do so.

   Ⓓ They don't know who their ancestors are.

5. What is the author's purpose?

   Ⓐ to inform

   Ⓑ to entertain

   Ⓒ to express an opinion

   Ⓓ all of the above

Vocabulary

> Find each vocabulary word in the selection. The words and sentences around it will help you figure out its meaning.

Fill in the letter with the best definition of the underlined word.

1. Are you of <u>Hispanic</u>, Asian, or Native American heritage?

   Ⓐ Latin American   Ⓒ Greek

   Ⓑ Japanese   Ⓓ Canadian

2. Most people give <u>credence</u> to the idea that people can be multiracial.

   Ⓐ grief   Ⓒ acceptance

   Ⓑ comfort   Ⓓ lip service

3. Multiracial means that more than one <u>ethnic</u> group is part of a person's heritage.

   Ⓐ relating to a group of people with the same race or country of origin

   Ⓑ relating to a group of athletes

   Ⓒ relating to a group of students

   Ⓓ relating to a group of famous people

4. The idea of a single heritage is being <u>surpassed</u> by the multiracial concept.

   Ⓐ imitated   Ⓒ left out

   Ⓑ overtaken   Ⓓ repeated

5. People should identify themselves as they <u>perceive</u> themselves, not as others do.

   Ⓐ respect   Ⓒ write about

   Ⓑ see   Ⓓ present

Name _____ **Date** _____

Word Work

> **Number prefixes** come at the beginning of a word. They give clues about the meaning of the word. The prefix **bi-** means "two." The prefix **multi-** means "many."
>
> A **biracial** commission is composed of people representing **two races.**
>
> A **multiracial** neighborhood is composed of people of **many races**.

Read the words with the number prefixes *bi-* or *multi-*. Then write the word that best completes each sentence.

multiple   multilingual   multiculturalism
biannual   bilingual

1. To honor the many diverse cultures in this country is to respect _____.

2. There are _____ benefits to being a member of more than one ethnic group.

3. If people grow up speaking two languages, they are _____.

4. A _____ report is one that comes out every two years.

5. If a person is fluent in many languages, he or she is considered _____.

> The **long-i** sound can be spelled several different ways.
>
> un**i_te**   **i**dea   m**igh**t   tr**y**

Write the word in the sentence that has the long-*i* sound. Then underline the letters that spell the sound in each word.

6. Derek Jeter's high school classmates asked about his heritage.

7. What is Mariah Carey's family background?

8. She has a white mother and a black father.

9. Many people identify themselves as multiracial.

10. Tiger Woods and Keanu Reeves are both multiracial.

Write Now

In the article "Not Just Black or White," you read that millions of people in the United States are multiracial and the number is growing. What can people do to celebrate the racial diversity of the United States?

- Plan to design a poster that will celebrate our multiracial culture. Copy and complete a chart like the one shown to help organize your thoughts. First, list some facts about multiracial people. Then, suggest reasons for celebrating racial and cultural diversity.

- Create your poster. Don't forget to add a picture or drawing to add visual interest to the poster.

Facts about multiracial people	Reasons to celebrate racial and cultural diversity
Millions of people _____	To show that diversity is accepted
Multiracial people have contributed _____	We can learn a lot from our differences

The Real Dracula

adapted by Barb Kelly

Set Your Purpose

Read this article to find out how writer Bram Stoker got the idea for his famous character, Dracula.

Five hundred years ago, a man called Dracula lived in a huge stone castle in the mountains of Transylvania. It was said that strange things happened in that castle. Cries were heard in the night. Lights flashed on and off. People **mysteriously** disappeared.

Does this sound like the plot of a cheesy horror movie? Maybe. But this Dracula wasn't the villain in a story or movie. He was a real man. He was a prince who ruled part of the area we now know as Romania. History tells us that he was a **cruel** ruler who terrorized his people.

If it hadn't been for Bram Stoker, an Irish writer, people probably would not have known about Prince Dracula.

One day, Stoker heard about the legend of the evil Prince Dracula. Stoker was fascinated. He went to the library and read all he could about the real-life Dracula and his castle in Transylvania. What he discovered convinced him that Dracula would be a wonderful fictional villain.

In 1897, Stoker published his **masterpiece**, *Dracula*. The novel is about Jonathan, an Englishman who journeys to Transylvania. There, in a dark stone castle, he meets the strange Count Dracula. Jonathan soon learns that the count is a vampire—a monster that does not exist in real life.

The book was a great success. Thanks to Stoker, vampires became the world's most popular monster. Stoker's *Dracula* has inspired dozens of books, plays, movies, and TV shows.

For Stoker, however, writing *Dracula* wasn't much fun. He was by nature a gentle man. But while working on *Dracula*, his **personality** changed. He became mean and critical. His **temper** grew violent. Maybe it was the spirit of the nasty Prince Dracula!

Fortunately, though, Stoker returned to his old sweet self when he finished the book.

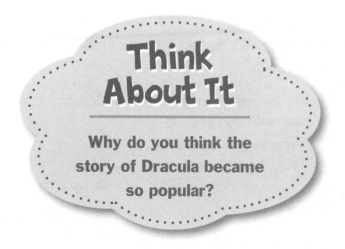

Think About It

Why do you think the story of Dracula became so popular?

Name _____ Date _____

Check Your Understanding

Fill in the letter with the best answer for each question.

1. The main idea of this article is that
- Ⓐ the real Prince Dracula was a horrible man.
- Ⓑ writers often base their stories on true events.
- Ⓒ the real Prince Dracula lived in Transylvania, just like Stoker's character.
- Ⓓ Bram Stoker based his famous character on stories told about a real Prince Dracula.

2. According to the story, why were people afraid of the real Prince Dracula?
- Ⓐ He made them have dinner with him.
- Ⓑ Strange things were rumored to happen at his castle.
- Ⓒ He was always yelling at people.
- Ⓓ They had read *Dracula* and so were afraid of him.

3. How did writing *Dracula* affect Stoker?
- Ⓐ He became very overweight.
- Ⓑ He began walking in his sleep.
- Ⓒ Stoker wasn't affected by the story at all.
- Ⓓ While writing the book, Stoker became mean and moody.

4. Another good title for this selection is
- Ⓐ Look Out for Vampires.
- Ⓑ Great Vampire Recipes.
- Ⓒ The True Story of Dracula.
- Ⓓ Dracula: The Movie.

5. *Dracula* may have been a success because
- Ⓐ people are fascinated by the strange and frightening.
- Ⓑ Stoker's friends bought it to please him.
- Ⓒ people didn't have any other books to read.
- Ⓓ the real Prince Dracula promoted it.

Vocabulary

Find each vocabulary word in the selection. The words and sentences around it will help you figure out its meaning.

Fill in the letter with the best definition of the underlined word.

1. People visiting Dracula's castle supposedly disappeared <u>mysteriously</u>.
- Ⓐ without explanation or reason
- Ⓑ with great caution
- Ⓒ without any clothing or supplies
- Ⓓ with great speed

2. The real Dracula was a <u>cruel</u> ruler who terrorized his people.
- Ⓐ true
- Ⓒ just
- Ⓑ mean
- Ⓓ gentle

3. *Dracula* is Bram Stoker's <u>masterpiece</u>.
- Ⓐ outstanding work
- Ⓒ boring story
- Ⓑ poor seller
- Ⓓ colorful picture

4. Bram Stoker's <u>personality</u> began to change.
- Ⓐ appearance
- Ⓒ handwriting
- Ⓑ way of behaving
- Ⓓ eating habits

5. Bram Stoker seldom lost his <u>temper</u> before starting *Dracula*.
- Ⓐ appetite
- Ⓒ love of writing
- Ⓑ sense of direction
- Ⓓ self-control

Fifty Nonfiction Passages for Struggling Readers, Grades 6–8 ▼ Scholastic Inc.

Name _____ Date _____

Word Work

A **possessive noun** is a noun that shows ownership. To make a singular noun possessive, add **'s**. To make a plural noun possessive, add an apostrophe after the (**s'**). Add **'s** to plural nouns that do not end in s.

vampire	⟶	vampire's
boys	⟶	boys'
children	⟶	children's

Fill in the letter of the correct possessive form of the phrase.

1. the books that belong to all the students
  Ⓐ the student's books
  Ⓑ the students' books

2. the skit put on by six girls
  Ⓐ the girls' skit
  Ⓑ the girl's skit

3. the pencil that belongs to my teacher
  Ⓐ my teacher's pencil
  Ⓑ my teachers' pencil

4. vacation time for my parents
  Ⓐ my parents' vacation time
  Ⓑ my parents vacation time

5. the talk given by the principal
  Ⓐ the principals' talk
  Ⓑ the principal's talk

Synonyms are words that have similar meanings. For example, *little* and *small* are synonyms.

Fill in the letter of the word or words that mean about the same as the underlined word.

6. Another word for <u>started</u> is
  Ⓐ continued.   Ⓒ began.
  Ⓑ stopped.   Ⓓ finished.

7. Something that is <u>strange</u> is
  Ⓐ familiar.   Ⓒ weary.
  Ⓑ odd.   Ⓓ wise.

8. Something that is <u>popular</u> is
  Ⓐ empty.   Ⓒ out-of-date.
  Ⓑ colorful.   Ⓓ well-known.

9. A <u>true</u> story is one that is
  Ⓐ real.   Ⓒ make believe.
  Ⓑ long.   Ⓓ short.

10. Another word for <u>terrifying</u> is
  Ⓐ sporty.   Ⓒ funny.
  Ⓑ frightening.   Ⓓ uneasy.

Write Now

In "The Real Dracula," you learned that Bram Stoker based his story *Dracula* on a real person. Both Stoker and the real Prince Dracula died long ago, but imagine you could interview one of them.

- Plan to write interview questions for Stoker or Prince Dracula. Copy the chart. Write the facts you learned from the selection in the "What I Know" column. Then write interview questions under the heading "What I Want to Know."

- Write three interview questions for Stoker or Prince Dracula. Choose your favorite ideas from your chart.

What I Know	What I Want to Know

Old Bones Dug Up

adapted by Ian Alexander

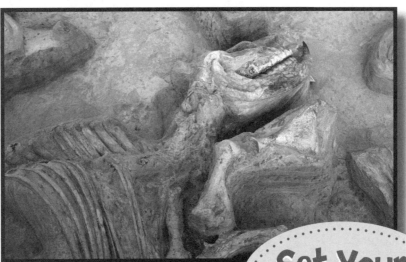

Long Ago

An **astounding** thing happened ten million years ago. A group of animals gathered at a watering hole near Royal, Nebraska. Barrel-bodied rhinoceroses, 15-foot giraffe camels, and other creatures came to drink. Then a volcano erupted 1,000 miles away. Wind carried the volcanic **ash** great distances. The ash rained down over the animals and buried them.

Set Your Purpose

What unusual discoveries have scientists made about animals that lived long ago? Read this article to find out.

More Recent Times

Dr. Michael Voorhies grew up in Nebraska. As a boy, he thought that he would have to visit Africa to see rhinos and camels. Then, in 1971, a strange thing happened.

He found a baby rhino skull in Nebraska! He dug around it. It was still attached to its skeleton. He kept digging and found five more rhino skeletons. At this point, he knew that he had discovered a special place. It was to become the find of a lifetime!

Treasures in Ash

So far paleontologists (pail-ee-on-TOL-o-jists), or fossil scientists, have found more than 240 **complete** animal skeletons near Royal, Nebraska. They even discovered the remains of a tiny three-toed horse. The ash preserved the bones almost perfectly. Many skeletons stayed whole.

The Whole Story

Finding so many whole skeletons in one place is very unusual. Usually bones are **scattered** far apart. This happens because wind blows them or waves pull them out to sea. Other animals can drag them away to eat. But the animals at this site lay just as they fell. Volcanic ash buried them so quickly that their skeletons never moved.

Prehistoric Habits

Scientists have learned a lot from the fossils. They found more than 100 rhinos together at this site. This means that **ancient** rhinos may have lived in big groups. Today most rhinos live alone. The scientists also found grass seed inside one rhino. Now they know more about what the animals ate. Scientists are still digging to find even more bones. This site has become the Ashfall Fossil Beds State Park. Here, visitors can watch the scientists uncover and study the fossils.

Think About It

What is the most important thing you learned about ancient animals?

Name _____ Date _____

Check Your Understanding

Fill in the letter with the best answer for each question.

1. What is the main idea of the first paragraph?
   - Ⓐ Volcanic ash buried rhinoceroses at an ancient watering hole.
   - Ⓑ Volcanic ash buried giraffe camels at an ancient watering hole.
   - Ⓒ Volcanic ash buried a group of animals at an ancient watering hole.
   - Ⓓ Scientists have discovered the bones of a tiny, three-toed horse.

2. What is the main idea of the third paragraph?
   - Ⓐ Dr. Voorhies grew up in Nebraska.
   - Ⓑ Dr. Voorhies found a baby rhino skull near Royal, Nebraska.
   - Ⓒ Dr. Voorhies dug around the baby rhino skull.
   - Ⓓ Dr. Voorhies had made the find of a lifetime.

3. What is the main idea of the fifth paragraph?
   - Ⓐ The wind can blow bones away.
   - Ⓑ Finding many whole skeletons in one place is unusual.
   - Ⓒ Waves can drag bones out to sea.
   - Ⓓ Animals sometimes drag bones away to eat.

4. Scientists who study fossils are called
   - Ⓐ voorhies.
   - Ⓑ visitors.
   - Ⓒ paleontologists.
   - Ⓓ rhinoceroses.

5. Paleontologists were surprised to learn that
   - Ⓐ visitors like to watch them uncover fossils.
   - Ⓑ today, most rhinos live alone.
   - Ⓒ ancient rhinos may have lived in groups.
   - Ⓓ ancient animals drank water.

Vocabulary

Find each vocabulary word in the selection. The words and sentences around it will help you figure out its meaning.

Fill in the letter with the best definition of the underlined word.

1. An <u>astounding</u> thing happened ten million years ago.
   - Ⓐ very loud
   - Ⓑ surprising
   - Ⓒ very dull
   - Ⓓ ordinary

2. Wind carried volcanic <u>ash</u> great distances.
   - Ⓐ rocks
   - Ⓑ trees
   - Ⓒ loud noise
   - Ⓓ powder that remains after something burns

3. Scientists have found more than 240 <u>complete</u> animal skeletons near Royal, Nebraska.
   - Ⓐ whole
   - Ⓑ partial
   - Ⓒ very small
   - Ⓓ irregular

4. Usually bones are <u>scattered</u> far apart.
   - Ⓐ in a circle
   - Ⓑ picked up
   - Ⓒ in a neat pile
   - Ⓓ spread out in different places

5. This means that <u>ancient</u> rhinos may have lived in big groups.
   - Ⓐ very new
   - Ⓑ very old
   - Ⓒ born today
   - Ⓓ very tall

Hi-Lo Nonfiction Passages for Struggling Readers Grades 6–8 • Scholastic Inc.

Name _____   Date _____

Word Work

Synonyms are words that have similar meanings. For example, *little* and *small* are synonyms.

Read the sentences and the words below. Write the word that means almost the same as the word in dark type.

whole   discovered   location

realized   covered

1. Dr. Voorhies **knew** that the watering hole was a very special place.

_____

2. Volcanic ash had preserved many **complete** skeletons.

_____

3. The skeletons were **buried** by the volcanic ash.

_____

4. He **found** rhino skeletons right here in Nebraska.

_____

5. Finding many skeletons in one **place** was very unusual. _____

The sound /**ow**/ can be spelled in several ways:

ow as in **cow**   **ou** as in **out**

The sound /**oy**/ can also be spelled in several different ways:

oi as in **coin**   **oy** as in **toy**

Each sentence below has an incomplete word. Add *ow*, *ou*, *oi*, or *oy* to complete the word.

6. It was **ast_____nding** to find the skeleton of a three-toed horse.

7. Dr. Voorhies **p_____nted** out where he discovered the baby rhino skull.

8. The soil **ar_____nd** the spot was soft and loose.

9. A grown male rhino is called a bull; a grown female rhino is called a **c_____**.

10. As a **b_____**, Dr. Voorhies dreamed of becoming a paleontologist.

Write Now

In the article "Old Bones Dug Up," you found out what unusual discoveries scientists have made about animals that lived long ago. Look at the chart. It shows a main idea and details from one paragraph in the article.

- Plan to write a postcard to a friend about a visit to Ashfall Fossil Beds State Park. Make a chart like the one shown. Think of how you would describe the experience in a postcard.

- Use your chart to help you write your postcard. State your main idea first. Then, list the most important detail first followed by other details.

Main Idea	Details
It is unusual to find many whole skeletons in one place.	The wind can blow bones away. Waves can drag bones out to sea. Animals sometimes drag bones away to eat.

Creatures of the Deep

adapted by
Paula Desmond

Set Your Purpose

Once people thought nothing lived at the bottom of the ocean. Read the article to find out what scientists have discovered.

Scientists have only just begun to explore the fascinating world of the ocean depths. At one time, they thought no life existed at the bottom of the sea. They knew it was dark and cold. Deep down, water pressures are enormous—measured in tons per square inch. However, about 100 years ago scientists began dragging heavy nets across the sea floor. They found crabs, worms, and some strange-looking fish. More recently, deep-sea submersibles—vehicles designed to explore the ocean floor—have helped scientists discover the surprising variety of life in this extreme environment.

The Gloomy Depths

There is little light below 600 feet (183 m). Total darkness begins at about 3,000 feet (914 m). No plant life exists in the deep **trenches**. This is because no sunlight reaches these depths. Yet not only do creatures live in this dark world, they are present in unexpected numbers and varieties. Some swim to the surface waters to feed. Still others hunt for food in their immediate surroundings. The main food source for deep-sea life, however, is the constant rain of plant and animal remains that drift down from above.

Glow-in-the-Dark Fish

Deep-sea creatures have **adapted** to survive the great water pressure and low temperatures of the depths. They have ways to find food in their dark world. Some fish have huge mouths to help them catch and eat anything that swims by. Some have elastic stomachs that stretch to hold whatever food they come across, even if it is larger than they are.

Many deep-sea animals glow in the dark! They have **luminous** organs on their bodies. The organs glow so the animals can attract their **prey**. These organs may also help fish identify each other and find mates. Deep-sea fish are dull in color—typically brown or black. However, their glowing organs can flash vivid colors.

Mini-Monsters

While animals of the coral reef are very colorful, deep-sea creatures are not. What sets creatures of the deep apart is their odd appearance. Most are quite small in size—often just a few inches in length. But these mini-monsters can be **fearsome** to see.

Much remains to be learned about the deep sea. Scientists now know one thing, though. Here in the darkness, beneath tons of icy water, life thrives.

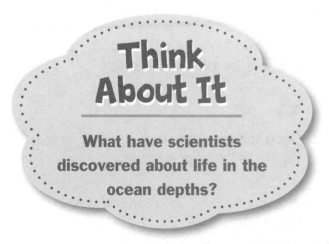

Think About It

What have scientists discovered about life in the ocean depths?

Name_____ Date_____

Check Your **Understanding**

Fill in the letter with the best answer for each question.

1. This selection explains what scientists have learned about
- Ⓐ life at the bottom of the sea.
- Ⓑ what deep-sea fish eat.
- Ⓒ glowing organs on fish.
- Ⓓ animals of the coral reef.

2. This article says that the ocean depths have
- Ⓐ no plant or animal life.
- Ⓑ low water pressure.
- Ⓒ no light.
- Ⓓ high temperatures.

3. Which detail supports the idea that deep-sea creatures have adapted to their environment?
- Ⓐ They have ways to find food in the dark.
- Ⓑ They are quite small in size.
- Ⓒ They look like mini-monsters.
- Ⓓ They are present in unexpected numbers.

4. Which sentence supports the idea that the bottom of the sea is difficult to explore?
- Ⓐ Scientists have only recently created vehicles that can reach ocean depths.
- Ⓑ They found crabs, worms, and some strange-looking fish.
- Ⓒ Animals glow in the dark.
- Ⓓ No plant life exists in the deep trenches.

5. The author of the selection wants to
- Ⓐ persuade scientists to explore the ocean depths.
- Ⓑ present information about deep-sea discoveries.
- Ⓒ learn more about fishing.
- Ⓓ live at the bottom of the ocean.

Vocabulary

Find each vocabulary word in the selection. The words and sentences around it will help you figure out its meaning.

Fill in the letter with the best definition of the underlined word.

1. No plant life exists in the deep <u>trenches</u> found at the bottom of the sea.
- Ⓐ puddles
- Ⓒ ditches
- Ⓑ weeds
- Ⓓ fish

2. Deep-sea creatures have <u>adapted</u> to survive in their harsh world.
- Ⓐ lighted
- Ⓑ changed to suit their environment
- Ⓒ not been able
- Ⓓ developed huge mouths

3. Some animals have <u>luminous</u> organs on their bodies.
- Ⓐ electric
- Ⓒ glowing
- Ⓑ loud
- Ⓓ unusual

4. The organs glow so the animals can attract their <u>prey</u>.
- Ⓐ people who fish
- Ⓑ plants that grow at the bottom of the sea
- Ⓒ friends
- Ⓓ animals hunted for food

5. Some deep-sea animals can be <u>fearsome</u> to see.
- Ⓐ frightening
- Ⓒ difficult
- Ⓑ beautiful
- Ⓓ amazing

Name _____ Date _____

Word Work

> **Connotation** is the emotional meaning of a word. The connotation of a word affects the tone or mood of the sentence. For example, in the sentences below, the word *stomped* conveys an angry mood. The word *skipped* conveys a happy mood.
>
> **Jesse *stomped* down the hall.**
>
> **Jesse *skipped* down the hall.**

1. Read the sentence. Circle the word that suggests deep-sea life is interesting.

Creatures of the ocean depths are _____ to see.

   boring   frightening   strange   fascinating

2. Read the sentence. Circle the word that suggests scientists' findings were surprising.

Scientists found an _____ variety of life in the depths

   unlimited   unexpected   unreal   uncertain

3. Read the sentence. Circle the word that suggests the conditions are uncomfortable.

Deep-sea creatures live in a _____ environment.

   harsh   pleasant   strange   special

4. Read the sentence. Circle the word that suggests that deep-sea creatures are odd.

Deep-sea creatures are remarkable for their _____ appearance.

   drab   colorful   small   unusual

5. Read the sentence. Circle the word that suggests that Robin is amazed.

"Look how that fish glows!" Robin said in _____.

   pain   wonder   fear   amusement

> A **compound word** is made of two shorter words. Combining the meanings of the two shorter words often explains the meaning of the compound word.
>
> **underwater** = **under** the surface of the **water**

Make compound words by combining each word on the left with a word on the right. Write the compound words.

6. sea   land   _____

7. water   fish   _____

8. wet   food   _____

9. jelly   house   _____

10. boat   fall   _____

Write Now

The web at right shows information from "Creatures of the Deep."

- Plan to write a journal entry from the point of view of someone exploring the ocean floor. First, brainstorm some ideas by copying and completing the web shown. Choose an unusual deep-sea creature to describe.

- Write your journal entry. Use colorful language to paint a picture of what you see.

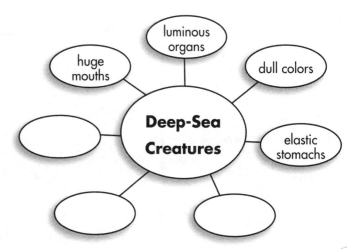

Recognizing Cause & Effect

❖ When reading a story or an article, it's helpful to think about events and what caused them.

- As you read, ask yourself: "**What happened?**" and "**Why?**"
- The answer to "**What happened?**" tells you the **effect**.
- The answer to "**Why?**" tells you the **cause**.

❖ Read this paragraph. Look for the answers to these **cause/effect** questions:

- What happened to penguins' colors?
- Why did this happen?

Effect
The first sentence tells you **what happened**: *Penguins developed a similar color pattern.*

Cause
This sentence tells **why**: *Their color pattern protects penguins from their enemies in the water.*

Why Penguins Wear Tuxedos

All species of penguin developed a similar color pattern. They have black or dark blue feathers on their backs and white feathers on their chests and stomachs. Scientists think that this basic pattern evolved because it protected penguins so well from their enemies, such as seals, in the water. From below, its white chest and stomach hide a penguin in the glare of sunlight. From above, its dark back makes a penguin hard to see against the darkness of the water.

❖ You could chart the **cause/effect** in this article like this:

Cause
A penguin's color pattern protects it from its enemies in the water.

Effect
All species of penguin developed the same color pattern.

Your Turn

❖ Read this story. Look for **causes** and **effects**. Make a chart like the one above.

Wild, Wild Snowstorm!

A blizzard is a wild snowstorm. It snows for hours and hours. Sometimes, it snows for days! The air is freezing cold. Strong gusts of wind make trees sway and cause high snowdrifts. These drifts can bury cars. It might take days, even weeks, to uncover them!

Swirling snows cause whiteouts. That's when the sky and ground look like a big white sheet! It's easy to get lost in a whiteout.

Protect yourself and your pets during a blizzard. Stay inside until the snow stops. Then go out and have some fun!

One Cool-Looking COWHAND

by Carol Domblewski

Set Your Purpose

The cowhands of the Old West were pretty cool characters. Read this article to find out what a cowhand wore.

Picture a cowhand riding the **range**. The sky stretches for miles above the open plains. The horse breaks into a gallop, and the herd of cows picks up its pace.

Cowhands, another name for cowboys and cowgirls, were important workers in the Old West. They drove **herds** of cattle across the plains to railroad stations. At the railroad station, the cattle were loaded onto trains and taken to market. Cowhands spent many long weeks riding the range. But do you know what they wore and why?

STARTING AT THE TOP

A cowhand always wore a big hat. Hats kept out the dirt and shaded the cowhand from the sun. A cowhand might also use a hat to carry water. Cowhands touched their hats to say hello, and they waved their hats to show they were happy.

Cowhands wore bandannas to keep dust out of their mouths. Bandannas also came in handy in cold weather because they **doubled** as scarves. In a pinch, they could even be used as a bandage.

KEEPING COVERED

Cowhands wore long-sleeved shirts and vests. The first cowhands wore wool pants. But once jeans showed up in the markets, cowhands wore jeans. Over their jeans, cowhands wore chaps. Chaps are covers for pants, often made of leather. Why did cowhands wear them? They rode through **brush** and rough country. And back then, it was embarrassing to have big holes in your pants.

USING THEIR FEET

On their feet, cowhands wore tall boots, **protecting** their feet and shins. The boots were high enough to keep out dust, dirt, stones, and water. There were spurs on the backs of the boots. Cowhands used spurs to give their horses the message: "Get a move on" or "Go faster."

How cool was a cowhand? In summer, a cowhand was definitely not very cool. Think about all those clothes. Riding the range in the summer was a hard, hot job!

Think About It

What pieces of clothing did cowhands wear, and why did they wear them?

Name _____   Date _____

Check Your Understanding

Fill in the letter with the best answer for each question.

1. One reason why cowhands wore hats was to
- Ⓐ keep dirt out of their hair.
- Ⓑ be seen more easily.
- Ⓒ make their horses go faster.
- Ⓓ keep their heads from getting hurt.

2. One reason why cowhands wore bandannas was to
- Ⓐ keep something red on their bodies for cows to see.
- Ⓑ protect the tops of their shirts.
- Ⓒ keep dust out of their mouths.
- Ⓓ keep their necks cool.

3. One reason why cowhands wore high boots was to
- Ⓐ cover up their short pants.
- Ⓑ protect their chaps.
- Ⓒ climb onto their horses more easily.
- Ⓓ keep stones and dirt from their feet.

4. The job of a cowhand was to
- Ⓐ ride a horse.
- Ⓑ take care of horses.
- Ⓒ move cattle where they needed to go.
- Ⓓ keep the West safe.

5. Cowhands, like people today, sometimes used their hats to
- Ⓐ show they were in danger.
- Ⓑ shade their heads from the sun.
- Ⓒ show they were fans of a certain person or team.
- Ⓓ give them a certain fashion look.

Vocabulary

Fill in the letter with the best definition of the underlined word.

1. Picture a cowhand riding the <u>range</u>.
- Ⓐ large grassy area of open land
- Ⓑ top of an oven
- Ⓒ stretch across a large area
- Ⓓ western horses

2. They drove <u>herds</u> of cattle across the plains to railroad stations.
- Ⓐ loud sounds
- Ⓑ large groups of animals
- Ⓒ truckloads
- Ⓓ train cars

3. Bandannas <u>doubled</u> as scarves.
- Ⓐ served the same purpose
- Ⓑ made to look alike
- Ⓒ were not very good
- Ⓓ were doubted

4. They rode through <u>brush</u> and rough country.
- Ⓐ forests
- Ⓑ streams
- Ⓒ dry bushes and weeds
- Ⓓ tool for smoothing hair

5. Cowhands wore boots, <u>protecting</u> their feet and shins.
- Ⓐ keeping warm
- Ⓑ hurting
- Ⓒ drawing attention to
- Ⓓ keeping safe

Name _____ Date _____

Word Work

Some words have more than one meaning. You can often figure out the meaning of a word by looking at how the word is used in a sentence. For example, the word *range* has several different meanings.

1. range (*noun*)—group of mountains

2. range (*noun*)—open area over which animals roam and feed

An **idiom** is a group of words used in a way that has a special meaning. This meaning is different than the usual meanings of those words.

Read each sentence. Decide if each underlined word has meaning A or B. Fill in the letter of the correct answer.

1. They <u>drove</u> the cattle north.
   Ⓐ rode in a car
   Ⓑ herded and moved animals

2. My dog <u>pants</u> after a long run.
   Ⓐ breathes quickly and heavily
   Ⓑ clothing worn over the lower body

3. Mei Ling shivered because the morning air was <u>cool</u>.
   Ⓐ in fashion
   Ⓑ not warm; chilly

Write the letter of the definition that matches the idiom in dark type.

Idioms	Definitions
___ **4.** looking cool	**A.** get going
___ **5.** hold your horses	**B.** looking fashionable
___ **6.** hold your tongue	**C.** fall asleep
___ **7.** get a move on	**D.** keep quiet
___ **8.** in a pinch	**E.** say no to
___ **9.** nod out	**F.** if necessary
___ **10.** turn down	**G.** calm down, be patient

Write Now

In "One Cool-Looking Cowhand," you read about what cowhands wore and why. Look at this chart to see some examples.

- Plan to write a paragraph telling what a certain group of people wear and why. Who, besides cowhands, needs to dress in a special way for work? Think of one group. Make a chart showing what they wear and why they wear it.

- Write your paragraph. Explain what each piece of clothing does. Use your chart to help you organize your thoughts.

Clothing Item	Why Cowhands Wore It
hat	to keep out the sun; to carry water
bandanna	to keep dust out; to use as a scarf in cold weather
chaps	to protect pants while riding through brush

Americans Discover TV

by Pat Cusick

Set Your Purpose

When did TV become an important part of American life? Read this article to find out.

In the 1940s, TV was still new. Early TV sets had small screens. The pictures were slightly greenish. There weren't many programs. Most people **amused** themselves in other ways. They listened to the radio. They went to the movies. They read books, and they played games. On special nights, they went out to restaurants and dance halls. TV was not very popular in those early days.

Then, in 1948, all that changed. A man named Milton Berle got his own TV show. He was a stand-up **comic**. He wore funny clothes. He twisted his mouth into strange shapes. He had pies thrown in his face. He acted out funny skits. Milton Berle made the whole country laugh.

Soon, new TV comedy shows, such as *I Love Lucy*, appeared. These shows were also **entertaining**. More families bought TV sets. Grown-ups rushed home from work to catch their favorite show. Children rushed home from school. America was in love with TV!

Suddenly, there was less time to cook after the workday was done. No one wanted to miss the evening shows. Families bought precooked dinners. Stores called them TV dinners. People ate their dinners on small tables in front of their TV sets.

TV **dramatically** changed our way of life. Americans spent less time reading. Bookstores sold fewer books. Many restaurants, dance halls, and movie houses closed down. Everyone was at home, watching TV.

The change was here to stay. TV became a **fixture** in most American homes. People saw the world from their living rooms as they watched TV news. They met candidates for president on their TV screens. They watched movies in their homes. TV changed the way America lived.

Think About It

Why do you think TV became so popular?

Name _____ **Date** _____

Check Your **Understanding**

Fill in the letter with the best answer for each question.

1. The first TV sets were not much fun to watch because

   Ⓐ the picture was poor.

   Ⓑ the sets were too large to fit into most homes.

   Ⓒ there were too many programs to pick from.

   Ⓓ the sound was not as good as the sound on radio.

2. People watched Milton Berle's show because

   Ⓐ he had good ideas.

   Ⓑ he was funny.

   Ⓒ he was the only person with a TV show.

   Ⓓ he was a great storyteller.

3. Instead of cooking, people began buying TV dinners because

   Ⓐ they needed to save money on food.

   Ⓑ TV dinners took less time to cook.

   Ⓒ they wanted to eat different kinds of food.

   Ⓓ they wanted to lose weight.

4. After reading this article, you can conclude that TV caused people to spend more time

   Ⓐ at work.   Ⓒ at home.

   Ⓑ on the streets.   Ⓓ playing sports.

5. The first successful TV shows were

   Ⓐ comedy shows.   Ⓒ news shows.

   Ⓑ dramatic shows.   Ⓓ sports shows.

Vocabulary

Find each vocabulary word in the selection. The words and sentences around it will help you figure out its meaning.

Fill in the letter with the best definition of the underlined word.

1. People <u>amused</u> themselves in different ways.

   Ⓐ entertained; enjoyed   Ⓒ lined up

   Ⓑ were thoughtful   Ⓓ worked for money

2. Milton Berle was a stand-up <u>comic</u>.

   Ⓐ someone who tells jokes

   Ⓑ someone who sings songs

   Ⓒ someone who dances

   Ⓓ someone who tells scary stories

3. Milton Berle's show was <u>entertaining</u>.

   Ⓐ difficult   Ⓒ enjoyable

   Ⓑ strange   Ⓓ serious

4. TV <u>dramatically</u> changed our way of life.

   Ⓐ in a small way   Ⓒ slowly

   Ⓑ in an important way   Ⓓ partly

5. TV became a <u>fixture</u> in the home.

   Ⓐ something lasting   Ⓒ something ugly

   Ⓑ something funny   Ⓓ something new

Name _____ Date _____

Word Work

A **noun** names a person, place or thing. A **plural noun** names more than one person, place, or thing. Most nouns are made plural by adding **-s** or **-es**. If a noun ends in a consonant and *y*, change the *y* to *i* and add *-es*. If a noun ends in a vowel and *y*, just add *-s*.

baby ⟶ **babies**

toy ⟶ **toys**

Write the plural of each word.

1. monkey _____

2. fly _____

3. day _____

4. party _____

5. supply _____

A **prefix** is a word part that comes at the beginning of a base word. The prefix **pre-** means "before" or "in advance." The prefix **sub-** means "under" or "below."

precook   to cook in advance

subway   a road or way under the ground

Read the definitions below. Add the suffix *pre-* or *sub-* to the base word to make a new word that fits the definition.

6. an early view of something, before the real thing _____**view**

7. to pay in advance _____**pay**

8. below the set standard _____**standard**

9. the age before the teenage years _____**teen**

10. a vessel that goes under the water, into the marine world _____**marine**

Write Now

In the selection "Americans Discover TV," you learned how TV first became a part of American life. TV is probably part of your life today. Which TV show do you like best? Why?

- Plan to write a letter to a friend describing your favorite TV show and explaining why you like it. Look at the questions on the chart. Answer these questions in your letter.

- Write your letter. Try to convince your friend that this show is worth watching.

What is the name of the show?

Who are the main characters?

What kind of things happen in the episodes?

Why do you like the show so much?

Do you think it is an educational show? Why or why not?

Collectors $trike It Rich!

by Amy Deckard

Set Your Purpose

Can you imagine selling one of your small racing cars and making a fortune? Read this article to find out how some toys are selling for thousands of dollars.

How can a small plastic toy that once cost 30 cents be sold for more than $4,000 forty years later? It is because not many were made, and now lots of people want them. This plastic toy is a **collectible**.

Collectibles are objects that people like and want to keep for a long time. A true collectible is **rare**, or hard to find. Comic books, plastic miniature toys, baseball cards, and dolls are a few examples of collectibles. Some people collect objects to **earn** a living. But for most people, collectibles are a **hobby**. "People want to collect things that make them happy," said Mark McMahon, owner of a collectibles shop in New York City.

The small stuffed animals called Beanie Babies® are collectibles. One Beanie Baby is particularly **valued** by collectors. It is Brownie the Bear. Brownie was one of the first Beanie Babies. In 1993, a few hundred thousand of these bears were created. They were sold for $4.95. A year later, the company that made Brownie retired him, so no more Brownies were made. In 1995, Brownie was being sold for as much as $600. One year later, Brownie could have cost a collector $1,300.

Rare comic books can also be extremely valuable. Recently, a New York comic shop sold a copy of the comic book that introduced Superman. The price was $150,000! In 1938, when the comic book first hit the shelves, it cost only 10 cents.

To be truly valuable, a collectible item must be in great condition, almost like brand-new. For example, a copy of the comic book that introduced Lois Lane is worth $2,000 if it's in perfect condition. The same comic book with one page torn might be worth only $175.

The toys and games you play with today may be worth a lot of money someday—so take good care of them! You never know what the next hot collectible will be!

Think About It

Were you surprised to find out how much Brownie the Bear is worth? If you owned Brownie the Bear, would you sell it or keep it?

Name _____ Date _____

Check Your **Understanding**

Fill in the letter with the best answer for each question.

1. What happened when a particular Beanie Baby was no longer made?

Ⓐ It became valuable.

Ⓑ People were no longer interested in it.

Ⓒ It was sold in card shops for several more years.

Ⓓ A year later, more were made.

2. Why are some old comic books so valuable?

Ⓐ They are made out of a very rare paper.

Ⓑ Comic books are sold only in New York.

Ⓒ Very few of them still exist.

Ⓓ The first comic books sold for 10 cents.

3. What happens if a collectible is scratched or damaged?

Ⓐ It makes no difference.

Ⓑ It becomes more valuable.

Ⓒ It becomes less valuable.

Ⓓ It is exchanged for another one.

4. Why do most people start collecting?

Ⓐ to have a hobby

Ⓑ to earn a living

Ⓒ to meet new people

Ⓓ to find something they need

5. Which statement best describes a collector?

Ⓐ Collectors like to spend a great deal of money.

Ⓑ Collectors are bored and need to keep busy.

Ⓒ Collectors only want money.

Ⓓ Collectors have fun collecting objects and sometimes make some money selling them.

Vocabulary

Find each vocabulary word in the selection. The words and sentences around it will help you figure out its meaning.

Fill in the letter with the best definition of the underlined word.

1. This old plastic toy is a <u>collectible</u>.

Ⓐ objects that are given away

Ⓑ objects people like and want to keep

Ⓒ objects that are delivered by mail

Ⓓ objects that are spread out

2. A true collectible is <u>rare</u>.

Ⓐ hard to find   Ⓒ well-liked

Ⓑ easy to find   Ⓓ shared with many people

3. Some people collect objects to <u>earn</u> a living.

Ⓐ spend   Ⓒ lose

Ⓑ waste   Ⓓ gain

4. For most people, collectibles are a <u>hobby</u>.

Ⓐ favorite activity

Ⓑ way to shop for objects

Ⓒ way to make good grades

Ⓓ sporting event

5. One Beanie Baby is especially <u>valued</u> by collectors.

Ⓐ thought important   Ⓒ talked about

Ⓑ lazy   Ⓓ cheerful

Name _____ Date _____

Word Work

> **Synonyms** are words that have the same meaning. For example, *hard* and *difficult* are synonyms.

Fill in the letter with the synonym of the underlined word.

1. Another word for <u>hobby</u> is
   Ⓐ fun.   Ⓒ a chore.
   Ⓑ pastime.   Ⓓ games.

2. To <u>collect</u> is to
   Ⓐ wonder.   Ⓒ sell.
   Ⓑ gather.   Ⓓ enjoy.

3. Something that is <u>rare</u> is
   Ⓐ beautiful.   Ⓒ unusual.
   Ⓑ new.   Ⓓ old.

4. Another word for <u>valuable</u> is
   Ⓐ free.   Ⓒ expensive.
   Ⓑ condition.   Ⓓ secret.

5. Another term for <u>extremely</u> is
   Ⓐ popular.   Ⓒ unsafe.
   Ⓑ somewhat.   Ⓓ very great.

> A **suffix** is an ending that changes the meaning of a base word. Knowing the meaning of a suffix helps you figure out the meaning of the whole word. The suffix *-ible* means "capable of." Here are some suffixes and their meanings.
>
> **-ible** capable of   **-ness** the quality of
>
> **-ful** full of   **-ish** to some degree

Read each word. Add a suffix from the box above to the word in dark type. Write the word that completes the sentence.

6. collect   A rare Beanie Baby is a _____.

7. hope   I'm _____ that I can find one to buy.

8. fool   To pay too much money for an old toy is somewhat _____.

9. care   Please be _____ with that comic book.

10. soft   Children love the stuffed bear because of its _____.

Write Now

Does the selection "Collectors Strike It Rich!" make you want to collect something special? Think of something you might like to collect. It doesn't have to be anything you buy. You could collect rocks from places you've been or stamps from letters your family receives.

- Plan to write a letter to a friend to tell him or her about your new collecting hobby. First, brainstorm ideas for a collection, using the idea web shown. Then choose the one you like best.

- Now write your letter to your friend. Try to persuade him or her to start collecting the same thing, too.

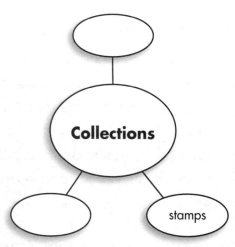

Victory at Sea

by Joe White

Set Your Purpose

From the title, you know the story is about a battle at sea. But who won? Who was defeated? Read this article to find out!

The year was 1588, and King Philip of Spain was angry at England. For twenty years, English pirates had been attacking Spanish treasure ships. The pirates had also raided Spanish towns in the New World. Philip had complained to Queen Elizabeth of England. The queen, however, had ignored his messages. In fact, she had rewarded the men who attacked the Spanish ships!

Philip decided he would stop complaining and start fighting. He made plans to **invade** England. Because England was an island nation, it was difficult to attack. But Philip believed he could succeed. He **assembled** an army of thousands of soldiers and sent them marching north to France. He also gathered a **fleet** of 130 warships. The fleet, called an armada, would carry more soldiers. It would also carry food, cannons, and other weapons the army would need for the attack. The army and the armada would meet, and together they would conquer England.

The leader of the English navy, Sir Francis Drake, learned of King Philip's plans and prepared to fight. The English were good sailors, and their ships were very fast. However, the English had fewer ships than the Spanish did. These 90 ships were also smaller and carried fewer soldiers. Many people in England feared their fleet would be defeated.

The fight began when the Spanish armada sailed into view of the English navy. The Spanish ships were not ready to fight yet. They first needed to meet their army and get them on board. The English navy immediately attacked the Spanish armada, but they could not sink the Spanish ships. The Spanish ships fought back, but they could not catch the faster English ships.

Then Sir Francis Drake, the English commander, had a brilliant idea. He ordered his men to set fire to some abandoned ships. Then he sent the burning **vessels** toward the Spanish fleet. The Spanish panicked, and their ships rushed to escape. Many ships crashed together and were damaged in the confusion. The Spanish armada turned and fled north, **intending** to sail around Ireland and head back to Spain. Unfortunately, they ran into a violent storm. Terrible winds and waves sank many of the Spanish ships. Only 65 ships made it back to Spain. King Philip's attack on England had failed.

Think About It

How did the English navy win a victory at sea? How could King Philip have prevented his defeat?

Name _____ Date _____

Check Your Understanding

Fill in the letter with the best answer for each question.

1. King Philip decided to attack England because
   - Ⓐ English pirates had attacked his ships.
   - Ⓑ he wanted more land.
   - Ⓒ he didn't like Queen Elizabeth.
   - Ⓓ he wanted to invade an island.

2. The Spanish armada was the key to attacking England because
   - Ⓐ it would surprise the English.
   - Ⓑ it would frighten the English.
   - Ⓒ it would carry the supplies and soldiers needed to invade an island.
   - Ⓓ it would carry treasure from the New World.

3. The Spanish armada failed because
   - Ⓐ it wasn't big enough.
   - Ⓑ the English were better sailors.
   - Ⓒ the Spanish sailors were not ready to fight.
   - Ⓓ the Spanish army did not follow orders.

4. Only 65 Spanish ships returned to Spain because
   - Ⓐ they were frightened by the English navy.
   - Ⓑ the rest were damaged by fire or sunk by storms.
   - Ⓒ the others fled to the New World.
   - Ⓓ they carried heavy cannons.

5. The main topic of this selection is
   - Ⓐ why King Philip wanted to invade England.
   - Ⓑ the battle between the English navy and the Spanish armada.
   - Ⓒ the reason the Spanish army marched through Europe.
   - Ⓓ the difficulty of attacking an island nation.

Vocabulary

Find each vocabulary word in the selection. The words and sentences around it will help you figure out its meaning.

Fill in the letter with the best definition of the underlined word.

1. Philip made plans to <u>invade</u> England.
   - Ⓐ assist
   - Ⓒ interfere
   - Ⓑ attack
   - Ⓓ insist

2. He <u>assembled</u> an army of thousands of soldiers.
   - Ⓐ gathered
   - Ⓒ fooled
   - Ⓑ destroyed
   - Ⓓ insulted

3. He also gathered a <u>fleet</u> of 130 warships.
   - Ⓐ group of hotels
   - Ⓒ assembly of kings
   - Ⓑ group of soldiers
   - Ⓓ group of ships

4. The British set fire to the abandoned <u>vessels</u>.
   - Ⓐ cannons
   - Ⓒ soldiers
   - Ⓑ ships
   - Ⓓ sailors

5. The ships were <u>intending</u> to head back to Spain.
   - Ⓐ refusing
   - Ⓒ planning
   - Ⓑ asking
   - Ⓓ threatening

Name_____   Date_____

Word Work

> **Antonyms** are words that have opposite meanings. For example, *night* and *day* are antonyms.

> A **prefix** comes at the beginning of the word and changes the meaning of the word. The prefix **re-** means "again." The prefix **un-** means "not."
>
> **reassemble**   to assemble again
>
> **unable**   not able

Read each sentence. Fill in the letter with the antonym of the word in dark type.

1. The invasion did not **succeed**.
   - Ⓐ happen
   - Ⓒ overcome
   - Ⓑ triumph
   - Ⓓ fail

2. The Spanish **assembled** many ships.
   - Ⓐ scattered
   - Ⓒ burned
   - Ⓑ joined
   - Ⓓ gathered

3. It was a **terrible** storm.
   - Ⓐ horrifying
   - Ⓒ frightening
   - Ⓑ rain
   - Ⓓ wonderful

4. The English burned **abandoned** ships.
   - Ⓐ battle
   - Ⓒ in use
   - Ⓑ no longer used
   - Ⓓ ignored

5. The Spanish began to **panic**.
   - Ⓐ frighten
   - Ⓒ relax
   - Ⓑ worry
   - Ⓓ flee

Add the prefix *re-* or *un-* to the word in dark type to make a new word that fits the sentence.

6. defeated   When the Spanish attack failed, England remained _____.

7. send   To attack again, Spain would have to _____ its army.

8. ready   Without the army on board, the Spanish ships were _____ to fight.

9. friendly   Queen Elizabeth was _____ to King Philip.

10. invade   To _____ England with fewer ships would have meant another defeat for Spain.

Write Now

In "Victory at Sea," you read about a dispute between King Philip of Spain and Queen Elizabeth of England. Read the chart. It shows one of the reasons King Philip was angry with Queen Elizabeth.

- Plan to write a letter to Queen Elizabeth explaining King Philip's point of view. First, copy the chart and add details from the selection.

- Write a letter to Queen Elizabeth. Tell her what your complaints are, and persuade her that they can be peaceably settled. Sign your letter "King Philip."

> **Reasons King Philip Was Angry With Queen Elizabeth:**
>
> 1. English pirates had attacked Spanish ships.
>
> 2.
>
> 3.

The Earth Heats Up

adapted by Pam Halloran

Set Your Purpose

Why is the Earth's temperature rising? Read this article to find out.

The Adélie penguins of Antarctica have nowhere to go. These penguins live on the ice near the South Pole. But the temperature is continuing to rise, and the ice is disappearing. So are the penguins' homes. Why is their ice melting? An overall increase in the Earth's temperature may be to blame. Scientists call it **global** warming.

Getting Warmer

Ice melting at the South Pole is only one of the many problems caused by global warming. The melting ice may cause the sea level to rise several feet.

That would mean that in many countries people who live along the coast would have to move. Global warming may also cause unusual heat waves and dangerous storms.

How does global warming happen? Some warming happens naturally. Earth's temperatures rise when sunlight hits it. Then little drops of water and carbon dioxide and other gases trap most of the heat within Earth's **atmosphere**. (The atmosphere is a layer of gases

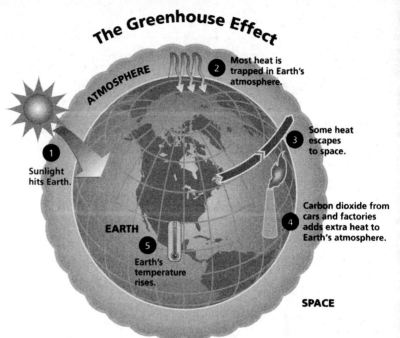

The Greenhouse Effect

ATMOSPHERE

2 Most heat is trapped in Earth's atmosphere.

3 Some heat escapes to space.

1 Sunlight hits Earth.

EARTH

4 Carbon dioxide from cars and factories adds extra heat to Earth's atmosphere.

5 Earth's temperature rises.

SPACE

surrounding the Earth.) This is like glass trapping **solar** heat from the sun in a greenhouse. Scientists sometimes call this **situation** "the greenhouse effect." (See diagram at right.)

What's the Problem?

The greenhouse effect isn't a bad or unnatural thing. Without the trapped heat, Earth would be 60 degrees colder than it is now. And we'd all be freezing! The problem **occurs** when there is too much carbon dioxide in Earth's atmosphere. Then too much heat gets trapped, and the planet gets too warm.

How do we get too much carbon dioxide in the air? We create carbon dioxide when we burn fossil fuels such as coal, oil, and gas. We burn fossil fuel to keep our factories running. We also burn fossil fuel when we drive cars and turn on the heat, air conditioner, or lights in our homes. As you might guess, we burn a lot more fossil fuel now than we did 100 years ago!

How Hot Is It?

Earth is now one degree warmer than it was 100 years ago. Some scientists predict that temperatures will go up two to six degrees by the year 2100. That may not sound like much, but it's more than temperatures have risen in 10,000 years.

What can we do to slow down global warming? Countries and businesses can do their part by controlling the amount of carbon dioxide and other gases their factories produce. Ordinary people can also help. Walk, ride a bike, or take the bus instead of riding in your car. Turn off lights when you leave a room. And when you're cold, don't turn up the heat. Instead, put on a warm sweater and help Earth cool off.

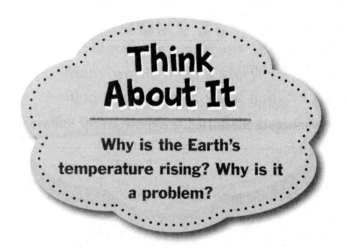

Think About It

Why is the Earth's temperature rising? Why is it a problem?

Name _____ Date _____

Check Your **Understanding**

Fill in the letter with the best answer for each question.

1. Which of the following is <u>not</u> an effect of the melting ice in Antarctica?

Ⓒ Penguins are losing their homes.

Ⓓ Sea levels are rising.

Ⓔ More fossil fuels are being burned.

Ⓕ The amount of ice around the South Pole is decreasing.

2. What can cause global warming?

Ⓒ melting ice in Antarctica

Ⓓ riding a bike

Ⓔ too much carbon dioxide in the atmosphere

Ⓕ unusual weather patterns near the South Pole

3. What could increase the amount of greenhouse gases being released in the atmosphere?

Ⓒ More factories burning fossil fuels.

Ⓓ More people turning off lights when leaving a room.

Ⓔ More people taking the bus instead of driving.

Ⓕ More people growing plants in greenhouses.

4. Which statement is <u>not</u> correct?

Ⓒ Ice melting in Antarctica causes the temperatures on Earth to increase.

Ⓓ Carbon dioxide and other gases trap heat within the Earth's atmosphere.

Ⓔ When too much heat gets trapped within Earth's atmosphere, the planet gets warmer.

Ⓕ Burning fossil fuels creates carbon dioxide in the atmosphere.

5. Which statement explains why the greenhouse effect is <u>not</u> a bad or unnatural thing?

Ⓒ Earth is now one degree warmer than it was 100 years ago.

Ⓓ Temperatures could go up two to six degrees by the year 2100.

Ⓔ Greenhouse gases cause Earth to cool off.

Ⓕ Without trapped heat, Earth would be 60 degrees colder than it is now.

Vocabulary

Fill in the letter with the best definition of the underlined word.

1. Scientists call it <u>global</u> warming.

Ⓒ shaped like a ball

Ⓓ map

Ⓔ large

Ⓕ including the whole Earth

2. Gases trap most of the heat within Earth's <u>atmosphere</u>.

Ⓒ the air that surrounds the Earth

Ⓓ a kind of gas

Ⓔ a mood

Ⓕ carbon dioxide

3. This is like glass trapping <u>solar</u> heat in a greenhouse.

Ⓒ warm

Ⓓ from the sun

Ⓔ the only

Ⓕ high-tech

4. Scientists sometimes call this <u>situation</u> "the greenhouse effect."

Ⓒ a location

Ⓓ a job

Ⓔ an assignment

Ⓕ a condition at a given time

5. The problem <u>occurs</u> when there is too much carbon dioxide.

Ⓒ solves

Ⓓ asks

Ⓔ hides

Ⓕ happens

Name _____ Date _____

Word Work

> Some words have more than one meaning. You can often figure out the meaning of a word by looking at how the word is used in a sentence. For example, *row* can mean "a line" or "to paddle."

> A **compound word** is made of two shorter words. Combining the meanings of the two shorter words often explains the compound word.
>
> **wrist + watch = wristwatch**

Decide if each underlined word has meaning A or B. Fill in the letter with the correct answer.

1. Fossil fuels keep our factories <u>running</u>.
  Ⓐ operating
  Ⓑ jogging or racing

2. Global warming can cause rising sea <u>levels</u>.
  Ⓐ tools used to help adjust the position of a surface
  Ⓑ heights of a body of water

3. Gases <u>trap</u> the heat within Earth's atmosphere.
  Ⓐ to catch an animal
  Ⓑ to hold in place

4. The temperature of Earth is one <u>degree</u> warmer than it was 100 years ago.
  Ⓐ a rank given to a person who completes college
  Ⓑ a unit of measure on a scale

Read the definitions below. Join two words from each definition to make a compound word that fits the definition. Write the compound word.

SAMPLE definition: **work** that you do at **home**
  compound word: **homework**

Definitions

5. ground where people camp _____

6. piece of glass that is a shield from the wind _____

7. list of items you can check off _____

8. game in which a ball is hit with the hand _____

9. box for holding mail _____

10. light that comes from the sun _____

Write Now

Burning fossil fuels creates carbon dioxide. Too much carbon dioxide in the atmosphere can cause global warming. Here is the beginning of a list of ways you and your family use fossil fuels every day.

- Plan to write a poster telling your family members how to cut down on the amount of fossil fuels that you use. First, make a list of the ways fossil fuels are used in your home.

- Write your poster. Use your list to suggest ways of cutting the amount of fossil fuels that you use. Remember that your poster must convince family members to change.

1. Heat our house
2. Cook our food
3.
4.

FIRE IN THEIR EYES

adapted by Chris Kirejczyk

Set Your Purpose

What do smokejumpers do? Read this article to find out.

Deep in the Montana wilderness, a cloud sweeps across the sky. Its heavy gray shadows indicate smoke, and it's coming from Morrell Mountains.

The fire management officer, Maggie Doherty, watches from a fire tower. She has to decide—and quickly. Should she put the fire out or let it burn? In a year with more rain, Doherty might let it burn. It could clean out leaves and fallen trees that feed even bigger fires. But since the forest is so **arid**, she doesn't want to take a chance that it could spread beyond the wilderness.

Wilderness fires often burn far from roads, so Doherty called in smokejumpers. These firefighters parachute down from airplanes to put out fires.

The smokejumpers' **routine** begins with digging a fire line to clear a wide path around the fire. If that doesn't work, they'll change plans. They will try to confine the fire to the forest floor and keep it out of the treetops by clearing away low-hanging branches. Flames can climb these branches and speed along overhead. It might take several days to cut enough branches, but it will help control the fire.

Next, the smokejumpers dig through the burned area with *Pulaskis* (puh LASS kees), tools that are a combination of axes and hoes. They dig up cool dirt and work it into the forest floor to **smother** the fire.

The smokejumpers' final task is to crawl through the area. They feel the ground to make sure it isn't hot. Fires that appear to be out can sometimes start again.

In wilderness areas, lightning starts most fires. Human carelessness also causes fires. Sometimes, though, fire experts start fires **intentionally**.

Fire can rid the forest floor of debris and clear space for new growth. Just as a doctor **prescribes** medicine, land managers sometimes "prescribe" fire.

When it is carefully controlled by experts, fire can be a useful tool for preserving open spaces and untamed lands. When fires rage out of control, however, the smokejumpers will be there, ready to fight.

Think About It

What might be the hardest thing about being a smokejumper?

Pulaski

Name _____ Date _____

Check Your Understanding

Fill in the letter with the best answer for each question.

1. When the forest is dry
- Ⓐ trees don't grow as quickly.
- Ⓑ fires are easier to control.
- Ⓒ fires can spread out of control more easily.
- Ⓓ airplanes are used to put out fires.

2. What effect does clearing low-hanging branches away from the forest floor have?
- Ⓐ It helps keep the fire on the forest floor.
- Ⓑ It's not as difficult to walk through the forest.
- Ⓒ It makes it easier to dig through the burned area.
- Ⓓ Trees will grow back more quickly.

3. What is the most likely cause of a fire in a wilderness area?
- Ⓐ careless firefighters
- Ⓑ fire experts
- Ⓒ lightning
- Ⓓ lack of rain

4. The last thing the smokejumpers do to make sure the fire is out is to
- Ⓐ feel the ground.
- Ⓑ dig a fire line.
- Ⓒ cut down low-hanging branches.
- Ⓓ stir cool dirt into the forest floor.

5. Land managers may "prescribe" a fire to
- Ⓐ keep campers out of the forest.
- Ⓑ prune low-hanging tree branches.
- Ⓒ give smokejumpers practice.
- Ⓓ rid the forest floor of debris.

Vocabulary

Find each vocabulary word in the selection. The words and sentences around it will help you figure out its meaning.

Fill in the letter with the best definition of the underlined word.

1. Since the forest is <u>arid</u>, Doherty doesn't want the fire to spread beyond the wilderness.
- Ⓐ dark
- Ⓑ crowded
- Ⓒ wet
- Ⓓ dry

2. The smokejumpers' <u>routine</u> begins with digging a fire line.
- Ⓐ way of doing a job
- Ⓑ time spent in the field
- Ⓒ interest
- Ⓓ equipment and gear check

3. They dig up cool dirt and work it into the forest floor to <u>smother</u> the fire within.
- Ⓐ suppress
- Ⓑ intensify
- Ⓒ heat up
- Ⓓ dry out

4. Sometimes fire experts start fires <u>intentionally</u>.
- Ⓐ angrily
- Ⓑ purposely
- Ⓒ accidentally
- Ⓓ neglectfully

5. Just as a doctor <u>prescribes</u> medicine, land managers sometimes "prescribe" fire.
- Ⓐ tries out
- Ⓑ orders
- Ⓒ describes
- Ⓓ issues warnings about

Name_____   Date_____

Word Work

Connotation is the emotional meaning of a word or phrase. Sometimes we use a polite or gentle phrase to talk about something unpleasant. For example, "They *paid no attention* to the warnings" can be a polite way of saying "They *ignored* the warnings."

Read the following sentences. Fill in the letter of the word or words that show the plain meaning of the underlined words.

1. The park rangers are <u>always reminding</u> us about putting out campfires.
   - Ⓐ fooling
   - Ⓒ surprising
   - Ⓑ writing
   - Ⓓ nagging

2. I caught the <u>smell</u> of smoke first.
   - Ⓐ look
   - Ⓒ idea
   - Ⓑ stench
   - Ⓓ air

3. The firefighter <u>spoke loudly</u> to call attention to the fire.
   - Ⓐ arrived
   - Ⓒ shouted
   - Ⓑ whispered
   - Ⓓ strutted

4. None of the firefighters appeared <u>unwilling to try hard</u>.
   - Ⓐ lazy
   - Ⓒ busy
   - Ⓑ lost
   - Ⓓ proud

5. Five minutes with a runaway fire seems like a <u>lifetime</u>.
   - Ⓐ a year
   - Ⓒ a minutes
   - Ⓑ an eternity
   - Ⓓ a second

The **long-*a*** sound can be spelled in three main ways:

a__e as in **n<u>a</u>m<u>e</u>**

ai as in **p<u>ai</u>nt**

ay as in **h<u>ay</u>**

Read the following sentences. Circle the words that have the long-*a* sound and underline the letters that stand for that sound.

6. We dread the day that a forest fire is spotted.

7. It takes a special kind of person to be a smokejumper.

8. Smokejumpers will come to the aid of trapped campers.

9. Jumping from an airplane into a forest fire is my idea of courage.

10. Smokejumpers must be sure that all flames have been put out.

Write Now

In the article "Fire in Their Eyes," you read about the specialized skills of smokejumpers. Many occupations require specialized skills. Can you think of some?

- Plan to write a job description about a smokejumper or another specialized job. Make a chart like the one shown to help you organize your thoughts.

- Write the job description based on your chart.

Job	Smokejumper
Qualifications	able-bodied
	_____
	_____
Training	parachute jumping
	_____
	_____

Hi-Lo Nonfiction Passages for Struggling Readers: Grades 6–8 • Scholastic Inc.

119

Children at Work

by Nora Samuels

Set Your Purpose

What if all you did all day, every day, was work? Read to find out about kids who do nothing else.

The tags on your clothing say where your clothes were made. What they don't say is who made them. Many people believe they should. These people are concerned that the clothing was made by child **laborers**.

Lots of kids work. Many work delivering newspapers, baby-sitting, or walking dogs. They go to school all day and work only part-time—a few hours a week. Working is a good way to become more **responsible**. Other children, however, work full-time.

For more than 250 million children **worldwide**, work isn't something done for school or after school. It's something done instead of school. They work between 12 and 14 hours a day. Most are only 5 to 14 years old. They are very young, but they work very hard.

Some work in coal mines. Others work on **construction** sites. Still others harvest crops. Thousands work to make clothing and things like soccer balls.

These children don't work this hard by choice but because they must. Many work to help their families earn enough money to pay for food, clothing, and shelter. Most child laborers do not go to school.

There are laws against child labor. Unfortunately, it still happens. There are child laborers all over the world, including the United States. Between 2 ½ and 3 ½ million children work in this country. There are many reasons why some companies hire children to work. But it is still against the law.

There are groups that are trying to help child laborers. Organizations like the United Nations Children's Fund (UNICEF) and the International Labor Organization (ILO) work to increase public **awareness** of the problem. Now many people and major companies won't do business with factories that employ children.

Think About It

Why might working so long and hard be dangerous and unhealthy for young children?

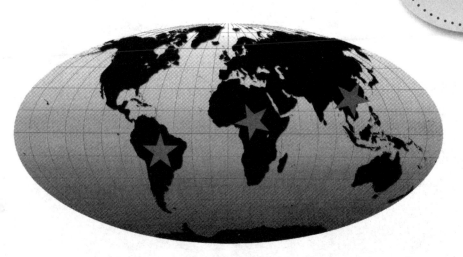

This map indicates the three continents that allow child labor: South America, Asia, and Africa.

Name _____ Date _____

Check Your **Understanding**

Fill in the letter with the best answer for each question.

1. Most children are forced to work because

Ⓐ there aren't any schools for them to attend.

Ⓑ other kids will make fun of them if they don't.

Ⓒ their families need the money they earn.

Ⓓ their brothers and sisters say they must.

2. One effect of the work done by UNICEF and the ILO is that

Ⓐ many companies won't do business with factories using child labor.

Ⓑ factory owners have started paying children more.

Ⓒ conditions for child laborers have gotten worse.

Ⓓ more people are buying things made by child laborers.

3. What information would many people like to see added to clothing tags?

Ⓐ where it was made   Ⓒ the size

Ⓑ who made the clothes   Ⓓ the cost

4. Besides working very hard, what's another disadvantage faced by child laborers?

Ⓐ They have to wear ugly uniforms.

Ⓑ The factory owners don't feed them.

Ⓒ Their families spend all of their money.

Ⓓ Because they can't go to school, they can't learn how to improve their lives.

5. Putting a description of who made a product on the tag might help stop child labor because

Ⓐ factory owners don't want to spend extra money on the labels.

Ⓑ people might not buy a product if they knew it was made with child labor, and the factory might lose money.

Ⓒ children might quit if they were described on the labels.

Ⓓ adult workers would quit because their names weren't being used, too.

Vocabulary

Find each vocabulary word in the selection. The words and sentences around it will help you figure out its meaning.

Fill in the letter with the best definition of the underlined word.

1. Child <u>laborers</u> work long hours every day.

Ⓐ teachers   Ⓒ workers

Ⓑ coaches   Ⓓ students

2. Working is a good way to become more <u>responsible</u>.

Ⓐ concerned   Ⓒ employed

Ⓑ hardworking   Ⓓ trustworthy and dependable

3. Millions of children <u>worldwide</u> work very hard.

Ⓐ other world   Ⓒ in a wide way

Ⓑ very wide   Ⓓ all over the world

4. Many young children work on <u>construction</u> sites hauling materials.

Ⓐ painting   Ⓒ teaching

Ⓑ building   Ⓓ sleeping

5. Fortunately, public <u>awareness</u> of the problem is increasing.

Ⓐ knowledge of something

Ⓑ hours a person works

Ⓒ money people are paid

Ⓓ number of days a person gets off from work

Name _____   **Date** _____

Word Work

> A **contraction** is two words joined to make one. One or more letters have been left out. The apostrophe shows where the letters were left out.

Read each sentence. Write the contraction that can be formed by the two underlined words.

1. The thought of young children working so hard <u>is not</u> a pleasant one. _____

2. Many child laborers <u>do not</u> go to school. _____

3. People feel that they <u>are not</u> doing enough to solve the problem. _____

4. <u>It is</u> a big problem, but things are changing for the better. _____

5. <u>That is</u> a big step in the right direction. _____

Read each sentence. Look at the underlined contraction. Write the two words that have been joined together to form the contraction.

6. Monya <u>can't</u> go to the game tomorrow. _____

7. <u>She's</u> attending a lecture on child labor laws. _____

8. Apparently, <u>there'll</u> be speakers there from around the world. _____

9. We <u>would've</u> gone also, but it was already sold out. _____

10. Next time, <u>we'll</u> look into getting tickets earlier. _____

Write Now

In the article "Children at Work," you learned about the millions of children who must work all day. You learned that some people feel we shouldn't buy clothes or rugs or toys made by factories that use child labor.

- Plan to create a radio public service announcement informing people about the dangers of child labor. Use an idea web like the ones shown to brainstorm ideas.

- Write a public service announcement telling about child labor and what people can do to work against it. Use the information from your idea web to help you.

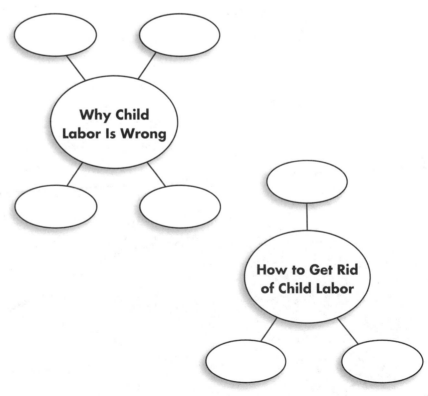

The California GOLD RUSH

adapted by Pearl Trudeau

In 1848 *gold* was a magic word. The discovery of gold in California that year started one of the most important events in U.S. history: *The California Gold Rush*.

The gold rush started in Coloma, a small town not far from Sacramento. A carpenter named James Marshall was building a sawmill on the banks of the American River. The mill belonged to John Sutter.

Set Your Purpose

Did you know that the discovery of gold changed the United States forever? Read this article to find out how.

Marshall was inspecting the mill's water channel. Suddenly he saw something **glistening** in the stream. He stooped for a closer look. It was gold! Within just a few months, the rush was on. By the end of the year, thousands of miners were digging for gold near Sutter's Mill.

In 1849, the **zeal** for gold swept the nation and the world. Workers left their jobs. Soldiers left their posts. People sold everything for the trip west. To the "forty-niners," nothing mattered except gold.

Getting to California was a challenge. The Panama Canal wasn't built until 1914. There were only three ways to get to California, and all of them were **treacherous**. Travelers could make the five-month trip by ship around the stormy tip of South America. They could sail the Atlantic Ocean to Panama, cross the **isthmus** by mule, and wait for a Pacific Ocean ship to take them to San Francisco. Or they could ride across the country by wagon. This was the fastest route, but it came with scorching deserts, towering mountains, and **ambushes** by outlaws.

Despite the dangers, tens of thousands of people traveled these routes. They risked their lives for a chance to find gold. Almost overnight, the quiet village of San Francisco became a bustling town. The gold rush captivated the hearts and minds of everyone looking to "strike it rich."

Think About It

Would you take a risky journey for the chance to find gold or other treasures? Why or why not?

Name _____ Date _____

Check Your Understanding

Fill in the letter with the best answer for each question.

1. What caused thousands of people to move to California in 1849?

Ⓐ the opening of the American West

Ⓑ the discovery of gold at Sutter's Mill

Ⓒ the building of the Panama Canal

Ⓓ the development of San Francisco into a city

2. One effect of the gold rush was

Ⓐ the founding of Sacramento.

Ⓑ San Francisco became a big, bustling town.

Ⓒ outlaws ambushed fewer travelers.

Ⓓ that Sutter's Mill was never built.

3. Which was <u>not</u> an effect of the discovery of gold in California?

Ⓐ Workers left their jobs to move West.

Ⓑ San Francisco became a bustling town.

Ⓒ James Marshall built a mill on the banks of the American River.

Ⓓ Tens of thousands of people risked their lives to go to California.

4. Although the trip was dangerous, people went to California because they

Ⓐ had sold everything for the trip.

Ⓑ were determined to find gold.

Ⓒ liked long trips.

Ⓓ wanted to get to Panama.

5. The author's main purpose was to

Ⓐ tell the story of the California gold rush.

Ⓑ encourage people to search for gold.

Ⓒ explain how people traveled before the Panama Canal was built.

Ⓓ explain the routes to California from the East Coast.

Vocabulary

Fill in the letter with the best definition of the underlined word.

1. Suddenly Marshall saw something <u>glistening</u> in the stream.

Ⓐ stuck   Ⓒ sparkling

Ⓑ interesting   Ⓓ swimming

2. In 1849, the <u>zeal</u> for gold swept the nation and the world.

Ⓐ boredom   Ⓒ enthusiasm

Ⓑ confusion   Ⓓ hatred

3. There were only three ways to get to California, and all of them were <u>treacherous</u>.

Ⓐ funny   Ⓒ dull

Ⓑ confusing   Ⓓ dangerous

4. They could sail the Atlantic Ocean to Panama, cross the <u>isthmus</u> by mule, and wait for a Pacific Ocean ship to take them to San Francisco.

Ⓐ long stretch of desert

Ⓑ raging river

Ⓒ narrow strip of land between two bodies of water

Ⓓ lake

5. This was the fastest route, but it came with <u>ambushes</u> by outlaws.

Ⓐ accidents   Ⓒ assistance

Ⓑ attacks   Ⓓ answers

Name _____   Date _____

Word Work

> Some words have more than one meaning. You can figure out the meaning of a word by looking at how the word is used.
>
> **1. saw** (*noun*)—a cutting tool
>
> **2. saw** (*verb*)—see in the past

Read each sentence below. Decide if the underlined word has meaning A or B. Fill in the letter with the correct answer.

1. The craze for gold was <u>sweeping</u> the country.
   Ⓐ using a broom to clean
   Ⓑ carrying along forcefully

2. James Marshall discovered gold on the <u>bank</u> of the river.
   Ⓐ a mound raised above the surface
   Ⓑ a place to save money

3. He decided to <u>stoop</u> down for a closer look.
   Ⓐ resort to low tactics
   Ⓑ bend forward

4. Soldiers left their <u>posts</u> to search for gold.
   Ⓐ places at which soldiers are stationed
   Ⓑ wooden stakes in the ground

5. The route to California included a stretch of <u>desert</u>.
   Ⓐ a large dry area
   Ⓑ to run away from

> A **possessive noun** shows ownership. To make a singular noun possessive, add **'s.** To make a plural noun possessive, add an apostrophe after the *s* (**s'**).
>
> the **ship's** owner   the owner of one ship
> the **ships'** owner   the owner of more than one ship

Rewrite the following phrases using possessive nouns.

6. the mill that belonged to Sutter _____

7. the water channel of the mill _____

8. the growth of San Francisco _____

9. the importance of these events _____

10. the wagons that belonged to the forty-niners _____

Write Now

In the article "The California Gold Rush," you read about people who journeyed across the United States in order to search for gold.

- Plan to make a travel poster advertising three ways to get to California for the gold rush. Copy and complete a chart like the one shown. Explain the route for each kind of transportation.

- Write your travel poster, using information from your chart. Try to make any would-be travelers excited about the trip!

OFF to CALIFORNIA

Transportation	Route
• Ship	_____
	_____
• Ship – mule – ship	_____
	_____
	_____
• Wagon	_____
	_____

DEBORAH SAMSON, *Secret Soldier*

by Jake Whitehead

Set Your Purpose

Read this article to find out what one young woman did during the American Revolution.

In 1776, the American colonies began a war against Britain. The colonies wanted their independence. Many great men served in that war. But did you know that several women fought as well?

One of the most famous was a woman named Deborah Samson. Deborah wanted to help the colonies win their freedom. But at that time, women were not allowed to fight. So, in 1778, Deborah **disguised** herself as a young man. She joined the army under the name Robert Shirtliffe.

Deborah thought she would be discovered after a few weeks. Instead, she served in the army for three years! She was even **wounded** twice. Once she was hit in the head with a sword. Later, a bullet struck her shoulder. Doctors bandaged her wounds, but no one discovered her secret.

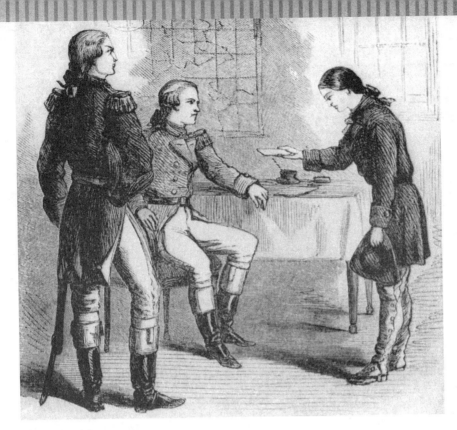

Deborah Samson presents her message to General George Washington.

Years passed, and Deborah continued to fight for the colonies. But after three years she became very ill. She was sent to a doctor, who finally discovered the truth. Imagine his surprise when he learned that Robert Shirtliffe was **actually** a woman!

The kind doctor did not reveal Deborah's secret right away. He took her into his home until she recovered. Then the doctor spoke to Deborah's commanding officer. Soon, "Robert Shirtliffe" was ordered to carry a message to General George Washington. She was told to hand it to him personally.

Deborah knew that the message would reveal her secret. She **trembled** with fear as Washington read the note. She thought he would be angry with her for tricking her fellow soldiers and her **commanding** officers. Instead, Washington released her from her service in the army. Then he gave her enough money to get home.

The colonies won the war, and George Washington became the first President of the United States. Soon after that, Deborah received a letter inviting "Robert Shirtliffe" to visit the capital. During her stay, Deborah was given money as a reward for her years of service. Maybe President Washington realized an important fact. "Robert Shirtliffe" may have been a lie, but there was nothing false about Deborah's courage.

Think About It

If you had been Deborah Samson, would you have put on a disguise and joined the army? Why or why not?

Name _____   Date _____

Check Your **Understanding**

Fill in the letter with the best answer for each question.

1. Why did Deborah Samson disguise herself as Robert Shirtliffe before she joined the army?

Ⓐ She didn't like her own name.

Ⓑ Men got paid more money.

Ⓒ Women were not allowed to join the army.

Ⓓ She was playing a joke.

2. One effect of Deborah's disguise was that

Ⓐ she was able to fight in the war for three years.

Ⓑ she was wounded twice.

Ⓒ she was sent to a doctor.

Ⓓ she chose the name Robert Shirtliffe.

3. How was Deborah's secret finally discovered?

Ⓐ She was wounded by a sword.

Ⓑ She was shot.

Ⓒ She became ill and went to a doctor.

Ⓓ General Washington noticed her.

4. The best word to describe Deborah Samson is

Ⓐ foolish.   Ⓒ timid.

Ⓑ brave.   Ⓓ angry.

5. How would you explain General Washington's lack of anger at Deborah's secret?

Ⓐ He knew of many women who dressed as men so they could fight.

Ⓑ He understood that she only wanted to help the colonies.

Ⓒ He was too busy fighting the war.

Ⓓ He thought she was still sick.

Vocabulary

Find each vocabulary word in the selection. The words and sentences around it will help you figure out its meaning.

Fill in the letter with the best definition of the underlined word.

1. Deborah <u>disguised</u> herself as a young man.

Ⓐ dressed in a captain's uniform

Ⓑ wore a costume that hid her identity

Ⓒ wore a kind of party dress

Ⓓ carried a false identity card

2. She was <u>wounded</u> twice during the war.

Ⓐ fed   Ⓒ hurt

Ⓑ comforted   Ⓓ tickled

3. The doctor saw that Robert was <u>actually</u> a woman.

Ⓐ in an actor's way   Ⓒ totally

Ⓑ in fact   Ⓓ in part

4. Deborah <u>trembled</u> with fear as Washington read the note.

Ⓐ shook   Ⓒ smiled

Ⓑ laughed   Ⓓ growled

5. She thought he would be angry because she tricked her <u>commanding</u> officers.

Ⓐ in control of a group   Ⓒ colorful

Ⓑ shouting   Ⓓ caring and gentle

Name _____   Date _____

Word Work

A **suffix** is an ending that changes the meaning of a base word. Knowing the meaning of a suffix helps you figure out the meaning of the whole word. The suffix **-ish** means "to some degree." The suffix **-ness** means "the quality of." The suffix **-ly** means "in a manner or way." The suffix **-ful** means "full of."

Write a word that fits the definition by adding the suffix -ish, -ness, -ly, or -ful to the base word.

1. in a secret manner   secret_____

2. a fool to some degree   fool_____

3. in a personal way   personal_____

4. full of hope   hope_____

5. the quality of being sad   sad_____

Each word on the left contains a base word and a suffix. Complete the definition by writing the correct form of the base word.

6. really   in a _____ way

7. truthful   full of _____

8. meanness   the quality of being _____

9. freely   in a _____ manner

10. reddish   _____ to some degree

Write Now

If you were the secret soldier in this selection, how would you record your experiences? One way is to keep a diary. Here is an example of a diary entry that Deborah Samson might have written.

- Plan to write a diary entry. First, brainstorm some ideas by imagining what it would be like to be a secret soldier like Deborah. Make a list of imaginary events and how you might have felt when they happened.

- Write your diary entry on the day that your identity is about to be revealed. Use your list to help you get started.

> Dear Diary,
>   Today, I am meeting with General George Washington. I'm supposed to give him this letter from my doctor. I know that it will reveal my secret. What will he do to me? I'm scared.
>   Deborah

Identifying Problem & Solution

❖ When you read a story or an article, it's helpful to think about what the problem is, what steps could be taken to solve the problem, and how the problem is resolved.

- As you read, ask yourself: "What is the problem in the story?"
- Next, ask: "What steps are taken to solve the problem?"
- Finally, ask: "How was the problem solved?"

❖ Read this article. Look for the answers to these **problem/solution** questions:

- What is the problem in this article?
- How did they try to solve the problem?
- How was the problem finally solved?

Problem
These sentences identify the **problem**: *A ship sailing from New York to California took several months!*

Steps
These sentences tell you the **steps** taken to solve the problem.

Solution
This sentence tells the **solution**: *In 1914, workers finished the Panama Canal—a 7,000-mile shortcut for ships!*

The Panama Canal

In the 1800s, a ship traveling from New York to California had to go around the southern tip of South America before sailing northward to California. The trip took several months! A faster route was needed, and Panama seemed the best choice.

The Panama Canal is only about 50 miles long. But it took ten years to build! Workers had to dig all across Panama. They hauled away tons of dirt. It was not easy to dig through jungles, hills, and swamps. Insects were a big problem. Some spread yellow fever and other diseases. To kill the insects, workers drained swamps and cleared brush. It was a hard job, but it worked! In 1914, workers finished the canal—a 7,000-mile short-cut for ships!

❖ You could chart the **problem** and **solution** in this article like this:

Problem	Steps	Solution
A ship sailing from New York to California took several months!	Workers had to dig through jungles, hills, and swamps across Panama; haul away tons of dirt; and battle insects that caused diseases.	In 1914, workers finished the Panama Canal—a 7,000-mile shortcut for ships!

Your Turn

❖ Read this story. Look for the **problem**, the **steps** taken to solve the problem, and the **solution**.

Save Our Wetlands

Wetlands are low, wet places like marshes and swamps. They are flooded with water at least part of the time.

People used to think that wetlands were useless. They thought that they were just soggy places. Now we know that's not true. Wetlands are home to many birds and other animals. Some of them are endangered species. That means that very few of them are left on Earth. How can we make sure that they don't disappear?

One way is to protect the places where wildlife lives. Laws now make it illegal to use wetlands as garbage dumps. Also, roads can't be built through wetlands. If we're careful, wetland animals will be around for a long time.

STORIES THAT REACH TOWARD THE SKY

adapted by Adrienne Hathoway

Set Your Purpose

How do the Gitxsan Indians keep records of their tribal history? Read this article to find out.

Can an artwork prove a fact in a court of law? One piece of art did. It was a totem pole that belonged to the Gitxsan (GIT-san) Indians.

The Gitxsans have always told their stories on totem poles. A totem pole is a post carved and painted with symbols. One tall Gitxsan totem pole tells an important story. It tells how the tribe came to live in what is now known as Canada. This totem pole stands in the center of their village in Canada.

Not long ago, the Gitxsan totem pole became an important part of Canadian history. In fact, it was used in a **ruling** by the Canadian Supreme Court. First, the court listened as the totem-pole stories were explained. The stories offered proof that the tribe has lived on the land for many **generations**. Then the court accepted the stories as valid proof. The court declared that the land where the Gitxsans live rightfully belongs to them.

In the past, the courts have always required **documents** to prove that a tribe owned the land. This was a big problem. Most Indian tribes don't keep such papers. Instead, they listen to stories told by their ancestors. They carve pictures of these stories on totem poles. The Gitxsan people **record** their history in their own way.

This Supreme Court ruling is important because it gives ownership rights back to the tribe. Now the Gitxsan people can **profit** from the land. Lumber and mining companies must pay for the right to use Gitxsan land.

Neil Sterritt, Jr., a tribe leader, praised the decision. "This ruling is the most major decision for any native people anywhere in the world. We have our rights back."

The Gitxsans now have what belongs to them, and it's all thanks to a totem pole!

Think About It

How do you think it would feel to be fighting for your own land? How would you prove that it was yours?

Name _____   Date _____

Check Your Understanding

Fill in the letter with the best answer for each question.

1. What was the main problem the Gitxsan people faced?

ⓐ They wanted more totem poles.

ⓑ They wanted to move to new land.

ⓒ They needed to prove that they owned their land.

ⓓ They needed to stop the lumber companies.

2. How did the Gitxsan people solve their problem and prove they owned their land?

ⓐ They called a detective.

ⓑ They explained the totem-pole stories to the Canadian Supreme Court.

ⓒ They took a vote.

ⓓ They looked it up in their files of important papers.

3. How did the stories on the totem pole help solve the problem?

ⓐ The carvings explained the tribe's history.

ⓑ The carvings were very old.

ⓒ The stories were broadcast on TV.

ⓓ The stories were fun to read.

4. How do the Gitxsan people earn money, now that the land is legally theirs?

ⓐ by showing their totem poles to tourists

ⓑ by telling their stories

ⓒ by charging lumber and mining companies that use Gitxsan land

ⓓ by teaching others how to carve

5. Neal Sterritt, Jr., mentions a "most major decision." What is that decision?

ⓐ the decision to be a tribal leader

ⓑ the decision to carve totem poles

ⓒ the decision that stories on totem poles may be used as proof

ⓓ the decision that people can profit from their land

Vocabulary

> Find each vocabulary word in the selection. The words and sentences around it will help you figure out its meaning.

Fill in the letter with the best definition of the underlined word.

1. The Canadian Supreme Court used a totem pole in a <u>ruling</u>.

ⓐ ancient story

ⓑ official decision

ⓒ magic carving

ⓓ special friend

2. The tribe has lived on the land for many <u>generations</u>.

ⓐ old friends

ⓑ good friends

ⓒ series of lifetimes

ⓓ animal spirits

3. Courts have always required <u>documents</u> to prove land ownership.

ⓐ important papers that prove things

ⓑ board games

ⓒ arguments about freedom

ⓓ decisions

4. The Gitxsan people <u>record</u> their history in their own way.

ⓐ keep track

ⓑ destroy

ⓒ play music

ⓓ win a race

5. The Gitxsans can <u>profit</u> from their land by charging fees to those who use it.

ⓐ prove a point

ⓑ use unfairly

ⓒ give away

ⓓ earn money

Name _____   Date _____

Word Work

A **compound word** is a word of two shorter words. Combining the meanings of the two shorter words often explains the compound word.

weekend = end of the **week**

Make compound words by combining each word on the left with a word on the right. Write the compound word that best completes each sentence.

bath	way
book	tub
class	yard
barn	glasses
eye	room
drive	worms

1. The _____ is very noisy with the sounds of chickens, pigs, cows, and horses.

2. Be careful not to slip on the soap in the _____.

3. People who read a great deal are sometimes called _____.

4. My teacher likes us to keep the _____ neat and tidy.

5. Park your car in the _____.

6. I wear _____ so that I can see better.

Read the definitions below. Join two words from each definition to make a compound word that fits the definition. Look at the sample.

SAMPLE   definition: a **house** for a **bird**

compound word: **birdhouse**

Definitions

7. a pen to play in   _____

8. a large box full of sand   _____

9. a ring to wear in your ear   _____

10. a room with your bed   _____

Write Now

If the Gitxsans had kept a written list of events in their history, what would be included in the list? The beginning of the list might look like this.

- Plan to write a story about a special event in your family's history. First, brainstorm and write a list of events. Choose one special event. It could be one that took place long before you were born.

- Write your story. Use your list to help you. Maybe the story you write will become an important family document!

1. The Gitxsan tribe come to live in what is now Canada.

2. The tribal leader marries a maiden.

3. The tribal leader's children are born.

A Bridge to a New World

by Margo Usher

Set Your Purpose

Who were the real first settlers in the Americas? Read this article to find out.

Where they may have walked then, there is ocean today. Most likely, they didn't set out to discover anything. They were just following their next meal as their ancestors had done for **centuries**.

It probably all began innocently enough. Slowly, people started moving east across what is now Asia, traveling in groups of several families. The weather was cold, but thick furs of wolf, caribou, and bear kept them warm. Their clothing was sewn with bone needles and rawhide thread.

Their tools were of bone or wood or stone. Their spear points were long and sharp. Food was heated by placing it into skin bags with hot stones. Around the fire, they told jokes, sang, and made tools or scraped animal **hides**. The children played games and cuddled the pups too young to stand guard. The hunting dogs kept watch nearby.

They were a people of the seasons. When winter came, they made camp. In some sunny spot, they built **sturdy** huts of brush and skins. They ate dried meat, roots, berries,

and seeds stored up from the summer. Hopefully, there also would be fresh meat.

Come spring, flowers bloomed, and bears came out of their dens. The caribou, musk ox, and moose had their calves. There were fresh greens to eat and birds' eggs to gather. It was time to move on.

Years passed. The people probably followed the wandering herds farther and farther east. One day, they may have crossed over to the land we call Alaska. Most likely, it was not a great **event**. The people probably just went on walking.

Today, scientists try to re-create their journey. It's not easy. The scientists have different theories about whether the first people in the Americas crossed over a land bridge from Asia or came there another way. As we study the bits of bones and fragments of huts and **belongings** these people left behind, we can only imagine their world and the lives they led.

Tool used by the first people in the Americas

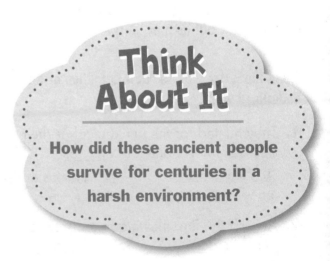

Think About It

How did these ancient people survive for centuries in a harsh environment?

Name _____ **Date** _____

Check Your Understanding

Fill in the letter with the best answer for each question.

1. What were two ways the ancient hunters solved the problem of staying warm?

Ⓐ They wore fur and ate berries.

Ⓑ They joked and told stories.

Ⓒ They wore fur and used fire.

Ⓓ They had dogs and used fire.

2. How did they cook without pots?

Ⓐ They ate their food raw.

Ⓑ They heated food in skin bags with hot stones.

Ⓒ They cooked in ovens.

Ⓓ They warmed food between their hands.

3. How did they kill game for food?

Ⓐ They used bows and arrows.

Ⓑ They used bone needles.

Ⓒ They threw stones.

Ⓓ They used spears with sharp stone points.

4. What was the main reason the people kept dogs?

Ⓐ The dogs were great pets.

Ⓑ The dogs woke them up in the morning.

Ⓒ The people used the dogs for hunting and protection.

Ⓓ The people used them to carry their children.

5. The reason the author doesn't call these people by name is probably because

Ⓐ the author forgot their name.

Ⓑ no one knows what they called themselves.

Ⓒ no one is allowed to say their name.

Ⓓ the name is too long to print.

Vocabulary

> Find each vocabulary word in the selection. The words and sentences around it will help you figure out its meaning.

Fill in the letter with the best definition of the underlined word.

1. They hunted for their next meal as their ancestors had done for <u>centuries</u>.

Ⓐ a few months　　　Ⓒ hundreds of years

Ⓑ cents and dimes　　Ⓓ thirty days

2. Around the fire, they made tools or scraped animal <u>hides</u>.

Ⓐ to beat　　　　　　Ⓒ animal noises

Ⓑ to stay out of sight　Ⓓ animal skins

3. In some sunny spot, they built <u>sturdy</u> huts of brush and skins.

Ⓐ too large　　　　Ⓒ made quickly

Ⓑ strongly made　　Ⓓ built in a square

4. Most likely, coming to Alaska was not a great <u>event</u>.

Ⓐ way to hunt animals　Ⓒ land bridge

Ⓑ happening　　　　　Ⓓ scientist's idea

5. Scientists study the <u>belongings</u> these people left behind.

Ⓐ animal bones　　Ⓒ things owned

Ⓑ bells and whistles　Ⓓ sciences

Hi-Lo Nonfiction Passages for Struggling Readers Grades 6–8　•　Scholastic Inc.

Name _____   Date _____

Word Work

> **Antonyms** are words that have opposite meanings. For example, *hot* and *cold* are antonyms.

Read the sentences and the words below. Write the word that means the opposite of the word in dark type.

die   descendants   sturdy

clumsy   celebrated

1. flimsy   To prepare for winter, the hunters built _____ huts.

2. accomplished   At first, the children were _____ at making tools, but they learned fast.

3. ancestors   Elders were expected to pass on their wisdom to their _____.

4. grieved   When spring came, everyone _____.

5. survive   If members of the group did not work together, they might all _____.

Read each sentence. Fill in the letter of the antonym of the underlined word.

6. Scientists are <u>confused</u> by the different evidence they are finding.

Ⓐ certain of   Ⓒ quiet
Ⓑ embarrassed   Ⓓ colorful

7. They used to <u>believe</u> people came to the Americas over a land bridge from Asia.

Ⓐ trust   Ⓒ disbelieve
Ⓑ shout   Ⓓ scold

8. Then the people <u>gradually</u> moved down through North America and into South America.

Ⓐ slowly   Ⓒ carefully
Ⓑ quickly   Ⓓ noisily

9. But scientists found settlements in South America that are too <u>old</u> for that theory to work.

Ⓐ damaged   Ⓒ recent
Ⓑ clean   Ⓓ ancient

10. Now they believe some early people used boats to sail along the <u>coast</u> of the Americas.

Ⓐ beach   Ⓒ waterline
Ⓑ shore   Ⓓ inland

Write Now

In "A Bridge to a New World," you read about the lives of early people who lived thousands of years ago. A word web like the one at right could be used to organize the information you learned in the selection.

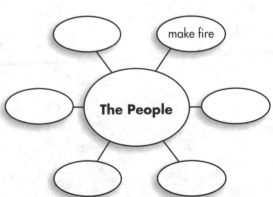

• Plan to write a description of the daily life of an early hunter family. Copy the word web and complete it with information from the selection. Make a note if something happens only in a certain season.

• Write a description of a day in the life of an early hunter family. Tell what they do in the morning, afternoon, and night. Be sure to tell what season it is. Use the details from your word web to help write your story.

SAVING THE SPHINX

by Gina Giddeon

Set Your Purpose

What is the Sphinx? Why does it need to be saved? Read this article to find out.

What has the body of a lion and the head of a man? It is the Sphinx in the Giza desert. This huge stone creature has guarded the famous Egyptian pyramids for 4,000 years. The Sphinx does not look like it did 4,000 years ago. It has **weathered**. Wind, water, pollution, and people have slowly aged the Sphinx. Sand, blown by the desert wind, acts like sandpaper. Water and pollution make softer rock flake off and blow away. People have also removed pieces of the Sphinx to keep as treasures.

Scientists are now trying to **restore** the Sphinx. They want it to look like it did when it was first built. They are also looking for ways to keep it from **deteriorating** more than it has.

Fixing the Sphinx is not an easy job. It took four years of planning before the work began. Each stone in the Sphinx was carefully measured. Scientists used computers to help figure out the size and shape of each stone. Each old stone was given a number. Then, one by one, replacement stones are carved by hand, just like people did long ago. Each new stone is carved to the exact size and shape as an old stone. Worn stones are removed and replaced, as each new stone is ready.

Scientists are worried about how to keep the Sphinx from falling apart again. Instruments have been placed on the Sphinx to monitor **moisture**, pollution, and wind speed. Scientists have talked about building a wall around the Sphinx to protect it from the wind and sand. Perhaps completely covering the Sphinx with a glass pyramid would work. Some think that burying part of it in the sand would protect it from the wind, sand, and pollution. One scientist suggested building a movable shelter. This shelter could protect the Sphinx at night and during bad weather. During the day, the walls of the shelter could be **retracted** into the ground. Visitors could see the Sphinx without the protective walls. There are no easy solutions.

The one thing that is agreed upon is that something needs to be done.

Think About It

Should something be done to protect the Sphinx? If so, what?

Name _____ Date _____

Check Your Understanding

Fill in the letter with the best answer for each question.

1. How do the people restoring the Sphinx know exactly where to place each new stone block?

  Ⓐ It did not matter where they placed them.
  Ⓑ They numbered each stone.
  Ⓒ They made a plastic mold of the Sphinx.
  Ⓓ They replaced every third limestone block.

2. What are scientists doing to keep track of the Sphinx's deterioration?

  Ⓐ They are taking photographs each day.
  Ⓑ There is nothing they can do.
  Ⓒ They measure wind, moisture, and pollution.
  Ⓓ They measure the temperature of the sand.

3. One way scientists might protect the restored Sphinx is to

  Ⓐ paint it.
  Ⓑ bury part of it in the sand.
  Ⓒ build another one on top of the existing one.
  Ⓓ cover it with a mixture of sand, salt, and water.

4. What is another possible title for this selection?

  Ⓐ History of the Sphinx
  Ⓑ Treasures of the Sphinx
  Ⓒ Time Takes Its Toll on the Sphinx
  Ⓓ How to Build a Pyramid

5. In which book might you find this selection?

  Ⓐ Traveling Around the World
  Ⓑ Pharaohs and Kings
  Ⓒ How to Build a Sand Castle
  Ⓓ Protecting Ancient Structures

Vocabulary

> Find each vocabulary word in the selection. The words and sentences around it will help you figure out its meaning.

Fill in the letter with the best definition of the underlined word.

1. The Sphinx looks <u>weathered</u>.

  Ⓐ worn   Ⓒ mean
  Ⓑ stormy   Ⓓ brand new

2. Scientists are now trying to <u>restore</u> the Sphinx.

  Ⓐ purchase   Ⓒ uncover
  Ⓑ rebuild   Ⓓ display

3. They want to keep it from <u>deteriorating</u>.

  Ⓐ being seen   Ⓒ getting wet
  Ⓑ being photographed   Ⓓ falling apart

4. Instruments monitor <u>moisture</u> and pollution.

  Ⓐ wetness   Ⓒ windiness
  Ⓑ television   Ⓓ loneliness

5. The walls can be <u>retracted</u> into the ground.

  Ⓐ secured   Ⓒ drawn back
  Ⓑ set wide   Ⓓ built

Hi-Lo Nonfiction Passages for Struggling Readers Grades 6–8 • Scholastic Inc.

Name _____   Date _____

Word Work

Antonyms are words that have opposite meanings. For example, *before* and *after* are antonyms.

Read each sentence. Fill in the letter of the antonym of the word in dark type.

1. The workers **removed** the stone.
   - Ⓐ replaced
   - Ⓒ measured
   - Ⓑ cleaned
   - Ⓓ ignored

2. A new stone was **carefully** carved.
   - Ⓐ slowly
   - Ⓒ carelessly
   - Ⓑ neatly
   - Ⓓ soon

3. There are many **problems**.
   - Ⓐ worries
   - Ⓒ questions
   - Ⓑ solutions
   - Ⓓ mysteries

4. How can we **protect** the Sphinx?
   - Ⓐ guard
   - Ⓒ create
   - Ⓑ monitor
   - Ⓓ attack

5. We don't want the Sphinx to fall **apart**.
   - Ⓐ another
   - Ⓒ together
   - Ⓑ somewhat
   - Ⓓ alone

The **long-e** sound can be spelled several different ways. Look at these examples: **gri<u>e</u>f   s<u>ee</u>d   l<u>ea</u>f   mayb<u>e</u>**

Circle all the words in each sentence that have a long-*e* sound. Then underline the letters that spell the long-*e* sound in each word.

6. I believe it would be fun to see experts work on the Sphinx.

7. We feel so small near the Sphinx.

8. It seems like it would not be easy to fix the Sphinx.

9. It will be a great treat for others to see it when it is fixed.

10. We pleaded with our teacher to let us meet at the feet of the statue.

Write Now

In the selection, you read about how scientists are trying to save the Sphinx. Here is a chart of the steps they have taken.

Step 1	Step 2	Step 3
Figure out the size and shape of each stone.	Carve new stones in the exact same size and shape as the old stones.	Remove worn stones and replace them with new stones.

- Plan to write a flier that can convince people to help save the Sphinx. First, brainstorm some ideas such as learning more about the Sphinx and being careful when visiting the pyramids. Then make a step-by-step chart like the one shown.

- Create your flier. If you have time, include a drawing of the Sphinx. Use your chart to help you.

Scum Energy

adapted by Doug Gregory

Set Your Purpose

Can you think of a good use for pond scum? Read this article to find out how this green slime might improve your life.

Imagine a running car with gas made from pond scum! That's what Tasios Melis hopes to do. Melis is a plant biologist. He is trying to make a better fuel for cars. He believes that pond scum may be the answer. If Melis succeeds, he'll be a hero. The green scum could churn out endless supplies of hydrogen gas. When burned as fuel, hydrogen doesn't produce any pollution. Its only by-product is water.

Hydrogen gas can be manufactured. But the process is difficult and costly. Usually, hydrogen is **extracted** from natural gas. This process **generates** pollution. It also **depletes** our natural gas supply. Melis is searching for a better way to produce hydrogen gas. In his **quest**, he has turned his lab into a "scum station."

Pond scum is made up mostly of green algae (AL jee). Green algae are very tiny plants that have a special ability. They can **convert** water and sunlight into hydrogen.

In his lab, Melis grows green algae in a container. He gives the plants sunlight, water, and nutrients. Millions of new algae cells form. Then, he covers the container with an airtight lid to cut off the supply of oxygen. This forces the green algae to produce hydrogen gas bubbles. Melis sucks out those bubbles with a needle.

How much hydrogen can green algae produce? Imagine an algae-filled pond the size of an average swimming pool. That much algae could fuel ten cars for a week. But don't get too excited just yet! You won't see a scum station anytime soon. It could take another few years for Melis to perfect his scummy process.

Think About It

Do you think using pond scum for fuel is a good idea? Why or why not?

Did You Know?

Some scientists think algae could help solve the world hunger problem. They are trying to make food from the plants, too.

Name _____   Date _____

Check Your Understanding

Fill in the letter with the best answer for each question.

1. What problem is Tasios Melis trying to solve?
    - Ⓐ the difficulty of removing scum from ponds
    - Ⓑ the high cost of fast cars
    - Ⓒ the need for non-polluting fuel
    - Ⓓ the lack of recognition of heroic plant biologists

2. Why does Melis think that pond scum is the solution to the problem?
    - Ⓐ Algae can make hydrogen from water and sunlight.
    - Ⓑ Algae can make sunlight from hydrogen.
    - Ⓒ Algae can make gasoline from water.
    - Ⓓ Algae is found everywhere in the world.

3. Hydrogen gas is not used for fuel in cars because
    - Ⓐ it can be found only in outer space.
    - Ⓑ people refuse to buy hydrogen gas.
    - Ⓒ there is a shortage of water and sunlight on Earth.
    - Ⓓ extracting it from natural gas is difficult and costly.

4. Which is the last step in Melis's process?
    - Ⓐ Millions of new algae cells form.
    - Ⓑ Melis collects the hydrogen bubbles.
    - Ⓒ The algae's oxygen supply is cut off.
    - Ⓓ The algae produce hydrogen bubbles.

5. The author wrote "Scum Energy" to
    - Ⓐ persuade people to use less gas.
    - Ⓑ make fun of Tasios Melis's idea.
    - Ⓒ compare hydrogen and natural gas.
    - Ⓓ explain how pond scum may one day be useful.

Vocabulary

Find each vocabulary word in the selection. The words and sentences around it will help you figure out its meaning.

Fill in the letter with the best definition of the underlined word.

1. Hydrogen usually is <u>extracted</u> from natural gas.
    - Ⓐ disguised
    - Ⓑ hidden
    - Ⓒ removed
    - Ⓓ stored

2. The usual process for making hydrogen <u>generates</u> pollution.
    - Ⓐ stops
    - Ⓑ produces
    - Ⓒ weakens
    - Ⓓ cleans up

3. Making hydrogen from natural gas <u>depletes</u> our natural gas supply.
    - Ⓐ increases
    - Ⓑ uses up
    - Ⓒ strengthens
    - Ⓓ manufactures

4. In his <u>quest</u>, Melis has turned his lab into a scum station.
    - Ⓐ search
    - Ⓑ spare time
    - Ⓒ home
    - Ⓓ game

5. Green algae can <u>convert</u> water and sunlight into hydrogen.
    - Ⓐ push
    - Ⓑ pull
    - Ⓒ grow
    - Ⓓ change

Name _____   Date _____

Word Work

Some words have more than one meaning. You can often figure out the meaning of a word by looking at how the word is used in a sentence. For example, the word *plant* has different meanings.

Algae is a kind of *plant*. (noun)
I will *plant* peas in the garden. (verb)

Read the sentences below. Decide if each underlined word has meaning A or B. Fill in the letter with the correct answer.

1. After the hike, I <u>long</u> for a soft bed.
Ⓐ not short
Ⓑ to want very much

2. My horse is in his <u>stall</u>.
Ⓐ a section in a stable
Ⓑ to hold off or delay

3. When I'm sick I <u>tire</u> easily.
Ⓐ an air-filled rubber tube
Ⓑ to make or become weary

4. I'll clean up when the company <u>leaves</u>.
Ⓐ flat, thin parts of a plant
Ⓑ goes away

5. The pain was so bad that I couldn't <u>bear</u> it.
Ⓐ a large, heavy animal
Ⓑ to endure

A **compound word** is made of two shorter words. The meanings of the shorter words will help you understand the meaning of the compound word.

sun + light = sunlight

Make compound words by combining each word on the left with a word on the right. Write the compound word.

6. smoke   top   _____

7. air   town   _____

8. day   stack   _____

9. down   tight   _____

10. tree   light   _____

Write Now

In the article "Scum Energy," you read about Tasios Melis's attempts to produce hydrogen gas from pond scum. What more would you like to know about his work or background?

• Plan to write a letter to Tasios Melis. First tell what you know about his work. Then ask him questions that the article raised in your mind. Use a graphic organizer like the one shown to help you plan your letter.

• Write your letter. Use the format for a friendly letter. Be sure to include a salutation and a closing.

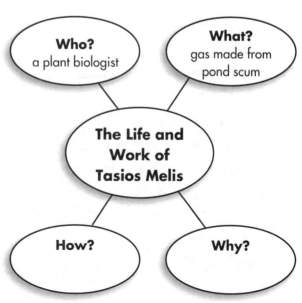

Condor Comeback

adapted by Pam Messer

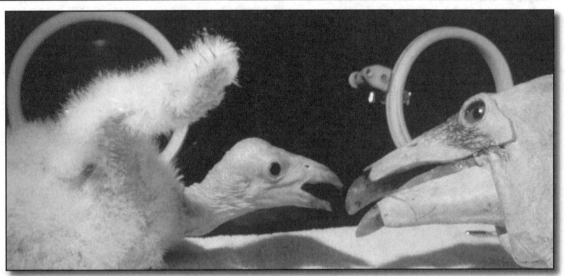

A baby condor is fed using a hand puppet.

Thousands of years ago, California condors crowded North America's skies. Then humans began hunting the condors. By 1985, only nine California condors were left in the world.

This called for drastic action. The U.S. government approved a plan for saving the species. Scientists took the nine condors into **captivity**. They planned to breed and raise the birds in a safe, controlled environment. Hopefully, they could increase the species' numbers.

They were right. By 1996, there were 120 condors in captivity. Scientists decided it was time to return them to their former habitats, or homes. The first group was **released** in California that summer. These condors had never lived in the wild.

Set Your Purpose

How did people work together to save the California condor? Read this article to find out.

The scientists attached radio tags to the condors' wings so they could keep track of them.

The condor release was a success. California condors adjusted well to life in the wild. The next step of the plan was to rebuild the condor population in Arizona and Utah. But **residents** of those states objected violently to the plan. The scientists were shocked. Why would the people object to the return of the condors? They met with the objectors to find out what the problem was.

The people of Arizona and Utah explained their position. Years ago, the peregrine falcon was endangered. The U.S. government passed laws to protect the dwindling falcon population. The laws made it illegal to cut down trees in forests where the falcon lived. The peregrine falcon lived in forests in parts of Arizona and Utah. The lumber industry in those areas was badly hurt. Sawmills closed down. People lost their jobs. Many people still felt angry. They felt that the government had no right telling them what they could or could not do with their land.

The scientists on the condor project **assured** the people that this program was quite different. The California condor wasn't a threat to them or their land. But people were still nervous. How could they be certain the condor situation wouldn't be the same as that of the peregrine falcon?

Fortunately, the two sides were able to reach a **compromise**. Scientists would set the condors free. The people of Arizona and Utah would continue living as they always had, as long as they didn't try to hurt the condors on purpose.

The California condor project is a good example of how the government and landowners can work together to save a species. Scientists believe that the program will successfully rebuild the condor population. Hopefully, trust between citizens and the federal government will be rebuilt as well.

Think About It

How did the government and the residents of Arizona and Utah work together to save the condor?

Name _____ Date _____

Check Your Understanding

Fill in the letter with the best answer for each question.

1. The California condor's biggest problem was

   Ⓐ government control.   Ⓒ extinction.

   Ⓑ captivity.   Ⓓ radio tagging.

2. Scientists saved the condor by

   Ⓐ taking the remaining nine condors into captivity.

   Ⓑ releasing the last nine condors in Arizona.

   Ⓒ banning people from cutting forests.

   Ⓓ taking them off the endangered species list.

3. What problem did scientists saving the condor face in Arizona and Utah?

   Ⓐ The condors didn't like living in those areas.

   Ⓑ The people in these states didn't want the condors back.

   Ⓒ Scientists lost track of the condors.

   Ⓓ The government was reluctant to let condors go free in those states.

4. Why didn't people in Arizona and Utah want to save the condor?

   Ⓐ People thought the condor was a dangerous species.

   Ⓑ They worried that laws protecting the condors would change their way of life.

   Ⓒ Scientists studying the condor are not good neighbors.

   Ⓓ The condors are harmful to the environment in Arizona and Utah.

5. It is sometimes difficult to help endangered species because

   Ⓐ the endangered species doesn't want help from humans.

   Ⓑ scientists are busy working on other projects.

   Ⓒ people don't know which species are endangered.

   Ⓓ humans and the species have to share limited space and resources.

Vocabulary

> Find each vocabulary word in the selection. The words and sentences around it will help you figure out its meaning.

Fill in the letter with the best definition of the underlined word.

1. Scientists took nine condors into <u>captivity</u>.

   Ⓐ type of scientific study

   Ⓑ form of government

   Ⓒ condition of being under another's control

   Ⓓ way of tracking birds

2. The condors were <u>released</u> in California.

   Ⓐ born   Ⓒ tagged

   Ⓑ captured   Ⓓ let go

3. The <u>residents</u> didn't want the condors.

   Ⓐ scientific instruments

   Ⓑ people living in a place

   Ⓒ places to go on vacation

   Ⓓ rules for the government

4. The scientists <u>assured</u> the people that the condor was not a threat to them.

   Ⓐ promised   Ⓒ greeted

   Ⓑ warned   Ⓓ proved

5. The government and the people reached a <u>compromise</u>.

   Ⓐ way of tracking animals

   Ⓑ type of sawmill

   Ⓒ small home

   Ⓓ type of agreement

Name_____ Date_____

Word Work

> A **contraction** is a word that is formed by putting two words together and replacing one or more letters with an apostrophe.
>
> **would + not = wouldn't**

Read each sentence. Write the contraction that can be formed by the two underlined words.

1. If scientists <u>had not</u> taken the condors into captivity, they might be extinct by now. _____

2. Landowners <u>do not</u> like the government telling them what to do with their land. _____

3. However, they do realize <u>it is</u> important for people to protect endangered species. _____

4. <u>There is</u> a good chance that the California condor will make a complete recovery. _____

5. By recycling paper products, <u>you are</u> helping to save animals' homes. _____

Fill in the letter of the contraction formed by the two words in dark type.

6. was not
- Ⓐ we'll
- Ⓑ won't
- Ⓒ wasn't
- Ⓓ weren't

7. should not
- Ⓐ couldn't
- Ⓑ wouldn't
- Ⓒ shall
- Ⓓ shouldn't

8. were not
- Ⓐ weren't
- Ⓑ wasn't
- Ⓒ we're
- Ⓓ we'll

9. that is
- Ⓐ that's
- Ⓑ that'll
- Ⓒ they're
- Ⓓ they'll

10. do not
- Ⓐ won't
- Ⓑ don't
- Ⓒ didn't
- Ⓓ wouldn't

Write Now

In the selection "Condor Comeback," you learned that it isn't always easy to balance the needs of animals and people. This chart outlines a problem described in the selection.

- Plan to write a conversation between a scientist and a landowner in Arizona or Utah. Copy the chart shown on a piece of paper. What might a scientist say to convince the residents to allow the condors in their state? What might the residents say to explain their point of view? Complete the chart.

- Write a conversation between the scientist and the landowner. Try to present both sides of the condor issue in a lively, interesting way. Use your chart to help you remember details.

Problem	Points of View
Scientists wanted to rebuild the condor population in Arizona and Utah.	Scientists:
Residents in Arizona and Utah didn't want the condors released in their states.	Residents:

Exploring Jupiter

by S. Chang

Set Your Purpose

How can humans safely learn about faraway planets? Read this article to find out.

Did you hear? There's a storm **raging**. Its wind speeds are up to 250 miles per hour! And this is weird—the storm looks like a giant red spot.

Don't worry. You don't need to run for cover. The big storm is not on Earth. It's on Jupiter—two planets and millions of miles away. You might wonder how we know about weather on a planet way out in space. After all, it would be difficult to send humans to explore a place like Jupiter.

The trip would be dangerous for people. An explorer would need **protection** from Jupiter's poisonous gases. Since Jupiter is mostly made of gas, there isn't any ground for a spaceship to land on. It would take years to get there, so explorers would have to pack enough food and air for a round trip. That's a lot of food and air!

Scientists have a **solution** to these problems. They explore Jupiter and other planets using robots. Scientists stay safely on Earth and send electronic messages far away to **robotic** spacecraft. The messages tell spacecraft to orbit around planets or to land and explore. It's less expensive to send a robot than it is to send humans into space, too. For one thing, robots don't need food or air.

The robotic spacecraft *Galileo* took six years to get to Jupiter. Its 11 instruments collected information. Then *Galileo* beamed the information, including pictures, back to Earth. The spacecraft has helped scientists discover strong winds, lightning, and tornadoes on Jupiter. The spacecraft has studied some of Jupiter's moons, too.

One exciting bit of news was about Jupiter's icy moon, called Europa. There may be an ocean underneath the ice surface! For a long time, scientists thought Earth was the only planet with water. Some scientists think that where there is liquid water, there is the **possibility** of finding life!

Galileo is not the first spacecraft to help scientists learn about other planets. In 1997, the *Mars Pathfinder* and its robot passenger, Sojourner Rover, sent back pictures from the Red Planet. In September of 1998, the spacecraft *Cassini* was traveling toward Saturn at over 50,000 miles per hour. Where will robotic spacecraft take us next? What planet would you like a closer look at?

Think About It

What do you think is the biggest problem humans face when trying to find out about other planets?

Spacecraft *Galileo* at Kennedy Space Center before it was launched to the planet Jupiter.

Name _____ Date _____

Check Your Understanding

Fill in the letter with the best answer for each question.

1. Which is not a problem for human explorers?

Ⓐ poisonous gases

Ⓑ dangerous weather

Ⓒ how to fly a spacecraft

Ⓓ how to bring enough food and air

2. Which is the best solution that keeps people safe, yet still lets scientists gather information about other planets?

Ⓐ send people who don't mind poisonous gas

Ⓑ send robotic spacecraft to collect information

Ⓒ use powerful telescopes to see planets

Ⓓ send animals to collect information

3. Which is not a reason for sending robotic spacecraft instead of humans?

Ⓐ It is more expensive to send humans.

Ⓑ Robots weigh less than humans.

Ⓒ Robots don't need to take food and air.

Ⓓ Robots don't care about danger.

4. What did the spacecraft *Galileo* do?

Ⓐ orbit the sun

Ⓑ take passengers to Jupiter

Ⓒ send electronic messages to other robots

Ⓓ collect information and beam it back to Earth

5. Why do you think it took *Galileo* six years to get to Jupiter?

Ⓐ Its instruments did not work properly.

Ⓑ Jupiter is millions of miles away from Earth.

Ⓒ It got lost and went to Mars instead.

Ⓓ It was busy gathering and beaming information on the moon.

Vocabulary

Find each vocabulary word in the selection. The words and sentences around it will help you figure out its meaning.

Fill in the letter with the best definition of the underlined word.

1. There's a storm raging.

Ⓐ tearing into strips   Ⓒ going out of control

Ⓑ leaving   Ⓓ smiling

2. An explorer would need protection from the poisonous gases of Jupiter.

Ⓐ type of lotion

Ⓑ run away

Ⓒ something that guards or shields against harm

Ⓓ something that wakes you up

3. Scientists have a solution to these problems.

Ⓐ mixture   Ⓒ question

Ⓑ experiment   Ⓓ answer

4. Scientists on Earth send electronic messages far away to robotic spacecraft.

Ⓐ like a machine controllable from a distance

Ⓑ able to replace humans on Earth

Ⓒ dangerous

Ⓓ electronic messages from space

5. There is a possibility of life on other planets!

Ⓐ reaction to something

Ⓑ idea

Ⓒ something that will not happen

Ⓓ something that could happen

Name_____   Date_____

Word Work

> A **suffix** is an ending that changes the meaning of a base word. Knowing the meaning of a suffix helps you figure out the meaning of the whole word. The suffix **-ous** means "having." The suffix **-ful** means "full of." The suffix **-less** means "without."
>
> **care<u>less</u>**   without care

Write a word that fits the definition by adding the suffix -ous, -ful, or -less to the base word.

1. having poison   **poison**_____
2. without air   **air**_____
3. having danger   **danger**_____
4. full of wishes   **wish**_____
5. full of hope   **hope**_____

Add the suffix -ous, -ful, or -less to the base word in dark type to complete the sentence.

6. Scientists cannot be **care**_____ when collecting information.
7. To go to the moon on *Galileo* would be a **wonder**_____ experience.
8. Is there a way humans could live on a **water**_____ planet?
9. I wonder how it feels to be **weight**_____.
10. Daring to go where no one has gone before is a **courage**_____ feat.

Write Now

In "Exploring Jupiter," the writer presents problems and their solutions. The chart shows an example.

- Plan to write about a fictional trip. It could be to any place—a high mountain, the bottom of the ocean, or even space. Make your own problem-and-solution chart by listing some problems you might run into on your way. Think about how you might solve them.

- Write a few paragraphs describing your fictional trip. Explain some of the problems that you expected and how you came up with solutions to those problems.

Problem	Solution
how to explore Jupiter, which is mostly made up of poisonous gas	use robots

Categorizing

❖ When reading a story or an article, it's helpful to categorize information, or notice what certain things have in common. Categorizing helps you remember important information.

- As you read, think about what things have in common.
- Think about how you would group these things together.
- Think of a title or label for each group.

❖ Read this paragraph. Look for things that are alike in some way. How can you **categorize** them?

A Gourd for Every Reason

Gourds, a fruit that grows on long vines, have a hard outer shell when they dry out. Hollowed out, gourds have many uses. In some parts of Africa, they are used <u>in the home</u> to store grain, scoop water, and serve food and drinks. Gourds are also used to create <u>musical instruments</u>, such as drums and rattles. Carved and painted, gourds become <u>works of art</u>. Artists turn gourds into wall decorations and masks worn by actors in plays.

Categories
The paragraph presents three ways in which gourds are used.

❖ You could **categorize** these uses like this:

Uses in the Home	Uses as Musical Instruments	Uses as Works of Art
Store grain, scoop water, serve food and drinks	Drums, rattles	Wall decorations, masks

Your Turn

❖ Read this passage. Look for ways the information can be **categorized**. Make a chart like the one above.

Celebrations and Festivals

Around the world many people hold celebrations and festivals at the same time of year.

Spring is an important time in many parts of the world. Christians celebrate Easter at that time. In Iran, the arrival of spring is heralded with the *Noruz* (noh-ROOZ) festival, when families do many special things together. In Thailand, everyone has fun splashing water on people to celebrate *Songkran* (SONG-krahn), or New Year.

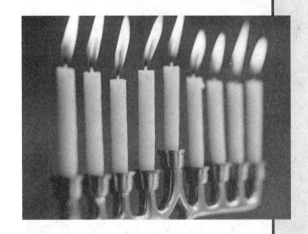

Fall is another time when people of many cultures celebrate the harvest as well as the changing seasons. Thanksgiving is a time for feasting in the United States. The Jewish New Year, *Rosh Hashanah*, comes in the fall. In India, people place lighted lamps everywhere to celebrate *Diwali* (dee-WAH-lee), the Festival of Lights.

Light is also a part of many festivals held in midwinter, such as Hanukkah, Christmas, Kwanzaa, and the Swedish festival of *Luciadagen* (loo-SEE-ah-dah-gen).

The King's Things

by Carol Domblewski

Set Your Purpose

When King Tut of Egypt died, what do you think the ancient Egyptians placed in his tomb? Read the article to find out.

King Tut was known as the "boy king." He was just 16 when he died. Although he didn't live long, he did live well. In fact, his **tomb** tells us he was one very rich and famous young man.

The ancient Egyptians believed that there was life after death. Wealthy Egyptians packed items they would need for this afterlife in their tombs. When Tut died, people couldn't do enough to make him happy in the afterlife. They seemed to think of everything.

What was in Tut's tomb? Of course, there was **dazzling** jewelry. Much of it was gold. There was plenty of food, too. Raisins, dates, goat, duck, beef, and other meat were all stored there. For those late-night snacks, there were baskets of bread, garlic, fruit, and honey. No king could be without his shaving kit in the afterlife, so one was packed. The good packers did not forget the eye makeup either. (Are you surprised?)

Tut might like to hunt in the next life, so boomerangs were placed in the tomb. There were also bows, arrows, knives, and leather **armor**. War chariots were put in, too, although they had to be taken apart in order to fit inside.

What king could be without a trumpet? And of course he also needed thrones. Three of those were packed. There were also six beds!

No great king could be seen without **fashionable** clothes. There were many pairs of sandals, shirts, caps, gloves, and more. There was even a dummy for hanging clothes on. To ward off **boredom** in the afterlife, there were game boards, model boats, paper, pens, and ink. Can you imagine what King Tut must have had when he was alive?

Think About It

Which of these items did you guess would be found in Tut's tomb? Which were surprises?

Name _____ **Date** _____

Check Your Understanding

Fill in the letter with the best answer for each question.

1. The items King Tut was buried with fall into all of these categories except
- Ⓐ food.
- Ⓑ clothing.
- Ⓒ pets.
- Ⓓ personal care.

2. In which category does the boomerang belong?
- Ⓐ clothing
- Ⓑ sports
- Ⓒ jewelry
- Ⓓ food

3. In which category does the throne belong?
- Ⓐ furniture
- Ⓑ games and hobbies
- Ⓒ snacks
- Ⓓ war

4. Which of these best describes King Tut?
- Ⓐ the first king of Egypt
- Ⓑ the king who wore eye makeup
- Ⓒ an Egyptian king who was rich
- Ⓓ an Egyptian boy king with an important burial chamber

5. What do the items people were buried with show about their idea of the afterlife?
- Ⓐ A person's clothes did not matter in the afterlife.
- Ⓑ The afterlife was much like the present.
- Ⓒ People did not need food in the afterlife.
- Ⓓ There was no way to plan for the afterlife.

Vocabulary

Find each vocabulary word in the selection. The words and sentences around it will help you figure out its meaning.

Fill in the letter with the best definition of the underlined word.

1. King Tut's <u>tomb</u> tells us he was very rich.
- Ⓐ photograph
- Ⓑ newspaper article
- Ⓒ fancy clothes
- Ⓓ building for holding a body

2. Inside the tomb, there was <u>dazzling</u> jewelry.
- Ⓐ amazingly beautiful
- Ⓑ heavy and expensive
- Ⓒ old and dull
- Ⓓ Egyptian

3. The packers included leather <u>armor</u>.
- Ⓐ wild animal found in Egypt
- Ⓑ dried fruit
- Ⓒ protective clothing worn during battle
- Ⓓ a liquid soap

4. No great king could be seen without <u>fashionable</u> clothes.
- Ⓐ fattening
- Ⓑ stylish
- Ⓒ robe-like
- Ⓓ fitting

5. Games were packed to ward off <u>boredom</u>.
- Ⓐ kingdom
- Ⓑ dull times
- Ⓒ anger
- Ⓓ happiness

Name_____ Date_____

Word Work

> A **contraction** is a word that is formed by putting two words together and replacing one or more letters with an apostrophe.
>
> ### do + not = don't

Fill in the letter of the contraction formed by two words in dark type.

1. was not
- Ⓐ weren't
- Ⓒ won't
- Ⓑ wasn't
- Ⓓ wouldn't

2. could not
- Ⓐ couldn't
- Ⓒ cannot
- Ⓑ can't
- Ⓓ won't

3. did not
- Ⓐ don't
- Ⓒ doesn't
- Ⓑ weren't
- Ⓓ didn't

4. you have
- Ⓐ you'll
- Ⓒ you've
- Ⓑ you'd
- Ⓓ you're

5. are not
- Ⓐ aren't
- Ⓒ won't
- Ⓑ you're
- Ⓓ don't

6. I will
- Ⓐ I'm
- Ⓒ I'll
- Ⓑ I've
- Ⓓ I'd

Read each sentence. Write the contraction that can be formed by the two underlined words.

7. <u>I have</u> been reading about King Tut for hours. _____

8. No king <u>could have</u> been treated better. _____

9. <u>Would not</u> it be great to discover a tomb like that? _____

10. I know I <u>have not</u> ever seen anything like it. _____

Write Now

In "The King's Things," you read about what people packed inside King Tut's tomb. What do you think Egyptians would send along if King Tut were a 4th grader going to school now?

- Plan to write a paragraph about the things packed with a modern King Tut in his tomb. First, brainstorm a list. Use a chart like the one below.

toys	clothes	furniture	food

- Write your paragraph. Illustrate your paragraph if you wish.

What's It Like to Live in CHINA?

by Michela Marfisi

Set Your Purpose

Have you ever wondered what life is like in other countries? Read this article to learn a little about life in China.

How would you like to live in the same building as your school? In China, some children do. Some apartment buildings include stores and a school. For these children, classes are only an elevator ride away. Many other children walk or bike to nearby schools.

Chinese students work hard in school. They work on homework until late at night. All that reading, writing, and studying can be hard on the eyes. Twice a day at school, everyone takes a break. For five minutes, students do eye exercises to rest and **strengthen** their eyes. They listen to music as they exercise their eyes. Students take a break to exercise their bodies, too. They do jump-ups and toe-touches together.

In China, apartments are very small. Families often eat, sleep, study, read, and watch TV in the same room. The room is **organized** carefully. Everything has its place. There is very little **privacy**. Most families do not have their own kitchen, bathroom, or telephone. These things are shared. You might meet your friends in the bathroom while brushing your teeth in the morning!

China's population is very large. There is a shortage of housing. People worry about a **shortage** of food. To deal with these problems, the government has a "one child only" rule. Almost every child in China today is an only child. It is rare to have a brother or a sister.

Chinese families have very close relationships. Grandparents and grandchildren often spend a great deal of time together. Parents and grandparents do their best to **advise** children about tough decisions. They want to help their children any way they can.

Like people everywhere, the Chinese love having pets. You won't see many St. Bernard dogs, though. Usually pets are pretty small. Song birds and crickets are two favorites. To keep their cricket warm during the winter, a family might use a hot-water bottle. They don't want their pet to catch a cold. Bird owners in the city often take their birds for morning outings. They carry the birds in cages with covers pulled down. When they get to the park, they meet other bird owners. The people hang the cages from branches and take off the covers. The birds hop around and sing together.

Think About It

How is school and family life in China different from your life? How is it similar?

Name_____ Date _____

Check Your **Understanding**

Fill in the letter with the best answer for each question.

1. This selection gives information about life in China today. It includes information about

Ⓐ food, housing, and pets.

Ⓑ school, housing, and names.

Ⓒ school, housing, and pets.

Ⓓ families, names, and clothing.

2. Which category would include information about apartment living?

Ⓐ housing   Ⓒ clothing

Ⓑ food   Ⓓ pets

3. Most families in China have

Ⓐ many children.   Ⓒ just one child.

Ⓑ large homes.   Ⓓ pet dogs.

4. Why does China have a "one child only" rule?

Ⓐ because the Chinese don't like children

Ⓑ because the country is very crowded

Ⓒ because they like to have tough rules

Ⓓ because school is very hard

5. What do people often do with their pet birds?

Ⓐ They let them fly free in the park.

Ⓑ They give them hot-water bottles.

Ⓒ They take them in cages to the park.

Ⓓ They take them for walks on leashes.

Vocabulary

Find each vocabulary word in the selection. The words and sentences around it will help you figure out its meaning.

Fill in the letter with the best definition of the underlined word.

1. Students do eye exercises to <u>strengthen</u> their eyes.

Ⓐ make stronger   Ⓒ be strong

Ⓑ make less strong   Ⓓ lose strength

2. The small room is <u>organized</u> carefully.

Ⓐ messed up   Ⓒ cleaned

Ⓑ decorated   Ⓓ arranged

3. Living together in a small space doesn't allow for a lot of <u>privacy</u>.

Ⓐ separateness   Ⓒ singing

Ⓑ group activity   Ⓓ Chinese building

4. In China, there is a <u>shortage</u> of housing.

Ⓐ lot   Ⓒ system

Ⓑ lack   Ⓓ building

5. Parents and grandparents do their best to <u>advise</u> children about life.

Ⓐ do homework

Ⓑ punish

Ⓒ try to sell something

Ⓓ offer help and suggestions

Name _____ Date _____

Word Work

Some words have more than one meaning. You can often figure out the meaning of a word by looking at how the word is used in a sentence. For example, the word *desert* has two different meanings:

1. **desert** (*DES ert*) – a large dry area
   We traveled across the *desert*.

2. **desert** (*de SERT*) – to run away from
   Why did he *desert* the army?

Read the sentences below. Decide if each underlined word has meaning A or B. Fill in the letter with the correct answer.

1. We <u>live</u> in a small apartment.
   Ⓐ live (*līv*) – the opposite of dead
   Ⓑ live (*liv*) – to have your home somewhere

2. <u>Live</u> birds are more interesting than stuffed birds.
   Ⓐ live (*līv*) – the opposite of dead
   Ⓑ live (*liv*) – to have your home somewhere

3. <u>Wind</u> up the toy, then watch it move.
   Ⓐ wind (*wīnd*) – to twist an object in one direction
   Ⓑ wind (*wind*) – moving air, a strong breeze

4. The children <u>bow</u> when they greet their teacher.
   Ⓐ bow (*bō*) – a knot with loops
   Ⓑ bow (*bou*) – to bend at the waist as a sign of respect

A **suffix** is a word part that comes at the end of a base word. The suffixes **-ment, -en**, and **-ship** can be added to base words to form new words.

govern + **ment** = **government**
strength + **en** = **strengthen**
relation + **ship** = **relationship**

Add the suffix *-ment, -en*, or *-ship* to each base word below to make a new word. Write the entire word.

5. arrange _____

6. friend _____

7. soft _____

8. enjoy _____

9. weak _____

10. apart _____

Write Now

Home	
School	
Family	

In the article you learned about Chinese homes, schools, and family life. How would you describe your home, school, and family to a child in China?

• Plan to write a letter to a Chinese pen pal. First, make a chart like the one shown. Jot down some interesting details about your home, school, and family.

• Write a letter to a pen pal in China. Use the notes from your chart to describe what your home, school, and family are like here in the United States.

Unsolved Mysteries

adapted by Paul Mores

Set Your Purpose

Everyone loves a mystery. Read this article to find out about some famous ones that have never been solved.

Wanted: Proof of Bigfoot

It is human or beast? Is it dangerous or gentle? Does it exist at all? These and other questions surround the mystery of Bigfoot. Native American legends tell of a giant creature called Sasquatch that roamed the mountains of the Pacific Northwest and western Canada. Some people believe that a large, hairy creature—Bigfoot—still lives there. They claim to have seen him or his footprints. His foot measures 16 inches (41 cm) long and 6 inches (15 cm) wide! Scientists are not convinced that Bigfoot is real. But those who claim to have seen him were convinced enough to run!

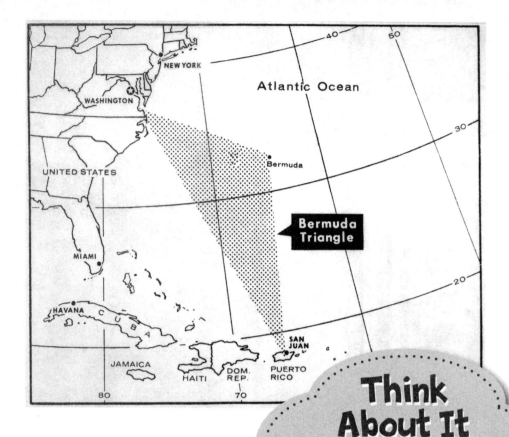

The Bermuda Triangle Puzzle

Strange things are happening in the Bermuda Triangle. Or are they? Planes, ships, and people seem to vanish into thin air in this **triangular** area of ocean. More **disappearances** happen in this part of the world than anywhere else.

Some people think that **supernatural** forces are at work here. Others say that the strange events are just accidents. They are caused by natural conditions in the area. The water is rough, and storms come up without warning. Some people are afraid to travel through the Bermuda Triangle. Others laugh and think this mystery is a bunch of nonsense. What is the truth?

Think About It

Do you think that any of these mysteries are based on fact? Why or why not?

Nessie Is Still at Large

What **lurks** in the deep, dark waters of Loch (lok) Ness? Some people say that a monster lives underwater in this lake in Scotland. **Blurry** photographs show a small head. But Nessie, as some people call her, hides from view. No one can prove that she exists.

Some scientists suggest that Nessie may be a kind of dinosaur. Others say that people just imagine they have seen the Loch Ness Monster. What do you think?

Name _____ Date _____

Check Your Understanding

Fill in the letter with the best answer for each question.

1. In which category could the Loch Ness Monster, the Bermuda Triangle, and Bigfoot all be placed?

Ⓐ Things That Are Unexplained
Ⓑ Scary Beasts
Ⓒ Puzzles That Have Been Solved
Ⓓ Dangerous Places

2. Which unsolved mystery does <u>not</u> belong in the category "Strange Creatures"?

Ⓐ the Loch Ness Monster
Ⓑ the Bermuda Triangle
Ⓒ Bigfoot
Ⓓ Sasquatch

3. Which statement is true of all three unsolved mysteries?

Ⓐ No one can prove them to be true.
Ⓑ They are all caused by natural conditions.
Ⓒ No sane person believes them.
Ⓓ Scientists have explanations for all of them.

4. At the end of the article, why does the author ask, "What do you think?"

Ⓐ The author is scared and wants to be calmed.
Ⓑ The author thinks the reader knows the real answer.
Ⓒ The author wants the reader to form his or her own opinion.
Ⓓ The author cannot think of anything else to say.

5. Which of the following statements is an opinion?

Ⓐ Strange forces are at work in the Bermuda Triangle.
Ⓑ Planes, ships, and people have disappeared in the Bermuda Triangle.
Ⓒ The Bermuda Triangle is a triangular patch of ocean.
Ⓓ Some people are afraid to travel through the Bermuda Triangle.

Vocabulary

Fill in the letter with the best definition of the underlined word.

1. Strange <u>disappearances</u> happen in the Bermuda Triangle.

Ⓐ unhappy things
Ⓑ times when things vanish
Ⓒ returns
Ⓓ disappointing things

2. Planes and ships vanish in this <u>triangular</u> area of ocean.

Ⓐ having three corners
Ⓑ having sharp corners
Ⓒ unusual
Ⓓ dangerous

3. Vanishing into thin air is too unusual. It must be caused by <u>supernatural</u> forces.

Ⓐ extremely loud
Ⓑ much better than usual
Ⓒ outside the laws of nature
Ⓓ unusually sensitive

4. What <u>lurks</u> in the deep, dark waters of Loch Ness?

Ⓐ suddenly appears
Ⓑ watches
Ⓒ lies hidden
Ⓓ leads into danger

5. It is hard to see what is in the <u>blurry</u> photographs.

Ⓐ sharp
Ⓑ colorful
Ⓒ mysterious
Ⓓ unclear

Name _____ **Date** _____

Word Work

A **compound word** is made of two shorter words. Combining the meanings of the two shorter words often explains the compound word.

weekend = end of the **week**

Read the definitions below. Join two words from each definition to make a compound word that fits the definition. Look at the sample.

SAMPLE   definition: the **wreck** of a **ship**

compound word: **shipwreck**

Definitions

1. the prints of a foot   _____

2. the side of a hill   _____

3. a storm with thunder   _____

4. the light of the moon   _____

5. a paper that contains news _____

Look at the compound words below. Write the word that best completes each sentence. Then draw a line between the two shorter words that make up the compound word.

downpour   airport   underwater
takeoff   skywriting

6. One day, three planes took off from a Florida _____.

7. The goal was to do a short _____ job.

8. Less than two hours after _____ the planes were in trouble.

9. The last message said, "We're in a heavy _____. We must ditch!"

10. Is it possible that the planes are now _____ in the Bermuda Triangle?

Write Now

The chart shows information from "Unsolved Mysteries."

- Plan to write a short paragraph explaining one of these mysteries. First, list the details you have read about the mystery.

- Write your paragraph. Use the details from the article and what you already know to help you.

Mystery	What It Is
The Loch Ness Monster	strange creature in Loch Ness, Scotland
The Bermuda Triangle	area of ocean where planes, ships, and people disappear
Bigfoot	giant, hairy creature in the Pacific Northwest

The Galápagos— Can They Survive?

by Patrick Lyle

Set Your Purpose

Some call the Galápagos Islands an endangered treasure. Read this article to find out about the islands.

More than three million years ago, volcanoes erupted deep in the Pacific Ocean. The lava from these volcanoes cooled and piled up, forming the Galápagos Islands. Over time, soil covered the bare volcanic rock. Then, across the water and through the air, life arrived. The islands' native animals and plants all come from species that swam, drifted, flew, or were blown here.

A Natural Wonderland

The Galápagos lie 600 miles (965 km) off the coast of South America. They are a natural wonderland. Cactus plants dot the dry lowlands. Moist, **dense** forests filled with trees grow higher up. Higher still, treeless upland areas are covered with ferns and grasses.

Unique animals, plants, and insects **abound**. Some 95 percent of the reptiles here are found nowhere else in the world! For instance, huge iguanas that look like colorful dragons bask on sunny rocks. Giant tortoises slowly **amble** along. These slow-moving reptiles weigh as much as 500 pounds (227 kg)! They can live for more than 100 years. Birds waddle by on bright blue, webbed feet. They look very **comical**. Their name is (of course) the blue-footed booby!

Rare creatures like these attract thousands of tourists each year. And that is part of the islands' problem.

Fighting for Survival

The Galápagos Islands have a fragile ecology. The balance of this unique environment can be destroyed easily. Today, the islands are in deep trouble for many reasons.

First, the islands have become a favorite among tourists. Some tourists trample plants and disturb the wildlife. The cruise ships that brought them dump garbage into the water.

Also, when more people came to settle in the islands, they arrived with their goats, pigs, cattle, cats, and dogs. These animals from other places disrupt the lives of native species. They compete for food, destroy habitat, and prey on the eggs and young of reptiles and birds. Dogs, in fact, have killed off most of the land iguanas on one island.

Finally, there are poachers who kill giant tortoises for their meat and fishers who overharvest the waters. Many species of sea creatures are caught illegally.

Can the Galápagos survive?

Preservation Efforts

Efforts to save the islands go back to 1934. Some islands were set aside then as wildlife **sanctuaries**. In 1959, most of the land— 97 percent of it—became a national park. In 1986, the ocean in and around the island group became a Marine Resources Reserve.

Today, environmental groups are working with the government of Ecuador. Their goal is to protect and preserve the islands. It may not be too late to save this special part of the world.

Think About It

What makes the Galápagos Islands so special, and how has this put them in danger?

Name _____   Date _____

Check Your Understanding

Fill in the letter with the best answer for each question.

1. This selection is an example of
- (A) short fiction.
- (C) an informational article.
- (B) a poem.
- (D) a biography.

2. Into which category do tortoises and iguanas fall?
- (A) mammals
- (C) insects
- (B) birds
- (D) reptiles

3. Which animals are causing problems for native species on the island?
- (A) fish and frogs
- (C) tortoises and iguanas
- (B) all kinds of birds
- (D) pigs, cats, and dogs

4. Tourists are drawn to the Galápagos Islands because the islands
- (A) are so far from anywhere.
- (B) are unlike any place in the world.
- (C) have a good climate.
- (D) don't have a national park.

5. Which of the following would <u>not</u> help protect the islands?
- (A) limiting tourism
- (B) stopping poaching
- (C) prohibiting cruise ships from dumping garbage
- (D) bringing in nonnative animals

Vocabulary

Find each vocabulary word in the selection. The words and sentences around it will help you figure out its meaning.

Fill in the letter with the best definition of the underlined word.

1. Moist, <u>dense</u> forests filled with trees grow higher up in the hills.
- (A) green
- (C) unusual
- (B) beautiful
- (D) thick

2. Several unique animals <u>abound</u> on the islands.
- (A) jump around
- (C) live in large numbers
- (B) arrive
- (D) grow large

3. Everywhere on the islands, giant tortoises slowly <u>amble</u> along.
- (A) walk slowly
- (C) sleep idly
- (B) eat slowly
- (D) swim leisurely

4. Many birds look so <u>comical</u> that they make us laugh.
- (A) scary
- (C) sleepy
- (B) funny
- (D) dangerous

5. Wild animals live safely in <u>sanctuaries</u>.
- (A) deep forests
- (C) protected areas
- (B) hidden places
- (D) zoos

Name _____   **Date** _____

Word Work

Many English words have Greek or Latin **roots**. For example, the root *vis* comes from a word that means "to see." The words *vision*, *visit*, and *visible* all relate to seeing. Here are four common roots:

spect	to look
rupt	to break
tract	to draw, to pull
port	to carry

Read each word. Write the root and the meaning of the root.

1. erupted _____

2. attract _____

3. spectator _____

4. disrupt _____

5. portable _____

Read each definition. Add the root word *spect*, *tract*, *rupt*, or *port* to complete the word.

6. a means of carrying people and goods   trans_____ation

7. take or draw away from   sub_____

8. breaking off or happening suddenly   ab_____

8. the act of looking closely   in_____ion

10. break in on   inter_____

Write Now

The chart at right contains information from "The Galápagos—Can They Survive?"

• Plan to create a poster with a slogan. A slogan is a quick and catchy statement that makes a point. First, brainstorm ideas for a slogan about the Galápagos Islands—their uniqueness or their problems, for example. Think about illustrations for the poster.

• Create your poster. Write your catchy slogan on it.

Unique Features	Problems
a natural wonderland	people damage environment
animals and plants found nowhere else in world	nonnative animals threaten wildlife
giant tortoises, huge iguanas	fishers and poachers catch and kill animals

WHAT'S THE WORD?

adapted by Pat Cusick

Set Your Purpose

Have you ever made up a new word? Americans invent many new words. Read this article to find out how this happens.

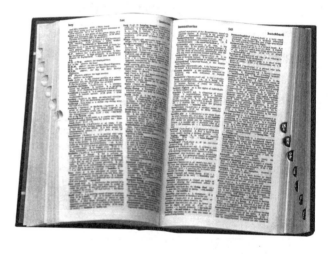

Next time you eat potato chips in the bathtub during a blizzard, think about this: *potato chips*, *bathtub*, and *blizzard* are all words that were born in the U.S.A.!

Americans have added thousands of words to the English language. "These words make up the story of America," says Allan Metcalf, co-author of a book called *America in So Many Words*.

"They show our goals, hopes, worries, and **attitudes** over time."

Need a Ride?

The word *carpool* was invented in 1962. Around that time, Americans were becoming more **aware** of the environment. To help protect the air, people began to share, or "pool," car rides.

Teen Idol

Can you wait to be a teenager? Eighty years ago, there was no such thing as a "teenager." Until the early 1900s, kids, age 13 or 14, were viewed as adults. At that age, many kids ended their schooling and went to work.

But new **regulations**, which ended child labor, required kids to finish high school. People in their teens were no longer children, but they weren't yet adults. So *teenager* was the perfect word to give these 13- to 19-year-olds an identity.

Words Get a New Look

Some words change their meaning over time. If you were hit by a blizzard in 1825, you wouldn't be shoveling snow. But, you might have a black eye. Back then, a blizzard meant a knockdown punch in boxing.

Through the years, the word **evolved**. Soon a knockdown snowstorm was called a *blizzard*.

Imagine trying to catch a skyscraper! In 1866, it was possible. At that time, fans **referred** to a high-flying baseball as a *skyscraper*. But when American cities started growing "up," the old term was given a new meaning. The tall buildings that appeared to scrape the skies became known as skyscrapers.

Words have a weird and wonderful way of changing. You never know when they'll change. In 50 years, you might be driving a hamburger to work!

Think About It

Many words have a story behind them. Which word had the most interesting story to you? Why?

Name _____ Date _____

Check Your Understanding

Fill in the letter with the best answer for each question.

1. Which words used to have another meaning?
- Ⓐ potato chips and bathtub
- Ⓑ blizzard and skyscraper
- Ⓒ teenager and carpool
- Ⓓ hamburger and baseball

2. Which word named a new trend?
- Ⓐ carpool
- Ⓑ blizzard
- Ⓒ growing up
- Ⓓ clean air

3. Which word was once a sports term?
- Ⓐ carpool
- Ⓑ bathtub
- Ⓒ potato chip
- Ⓓ blizzard

4. What conclusion can you draw from this selection?
- Ⓐ Before 1866, American cities did not have skyscrapers.
- Ⓑ Automobiles were invented in the early 1990s.
- Ⓒ Americans began driving to work in 1962.
- Ⓓ Before 1900, kids were required to finish high school.

5. This article would probably appear in a book about
- Ⓐ American heroes.
- Ⓑ weather patterns.
- Ⓒ language.
- Ⓓ sports and games.

Vocabulary

> Find each vocabulary word in the selection. The words and sentences around it will help you figure out its meaning.

Fill in the letter with the best definition of the underlined word.

1. People became more <u>aware</u> of the environment and started to carpool.
- Ⓐ watchful
- Ⓒ jealous
- Ⓑ tried
- Ⓓ scared

2. Through the years, the word <u>evolved</u> and gained a new meaning.
- Ⓐ turned in circles
- Ⓑ came to an end
- Ⓒ slowly changed over time
- Ⓓ exploded

3. New <u>regulations</u> ended child labor.
- Ⓐ laws
- Ⓒ storms
- Ⓑ adults
- Ⓓ words

4. New words show our goals, hopes, worries, and <u>attitudes</u>.
- Ⓐ test scores
- Ⓑ opinions and feelings about people and things
- Ⓒ height above sea level
- Ⓓ new clothes

5. Fans <u>referred</u> to a high-flying baseball as a "skyscraper."
- Ⓐ looked at
- Ⓑ spoke of
- Ⓒ read about
- Ⓓ heard of

Name _____ Date _____

Word Work

> A **compound word** is made of two shorter words. To understand a compound word, separate it into the two shorter words and think about the meaning of those words.
>
> ### bath + tub = bathtub

Combine each word on the left with a word on the right. Write the compound words.

1. car   storm   _____

2. knock   side   _____

3. space   pool   _____

4. snow   room   _____

5. class   down   _____

6. mountain   ship   _____

> Some words have more than one meaning. You can often figure out the meaning of a word by looking at how the word is used in a sentence. For example, the word *row* can mean "a line" or "to paddle."

Decide if each underlined word has meaning A or B. Fill in the letter with the correct answer.

7. The <u>view</u> of the blizzard from our upstairs window was incredible.

   Ⓐ opinion
   Ⓑ that which is seen

8. I have a strong <u>view</u> on carpooling to work.

   Ⓐ opinion
   Ⓑ that which is seen

9. The fighter delivered a knockdown <u>punch</u>.

   Ⓐ a blow delivered with a fist
   Ⓑ a sweet drink

10. The teenagers enjoyed some orange <u>punch</u> after playing tennis.

    Ⓐ a blow delivered with the fist
    Ⓑ a sweet drink

Write Now

Look at the list. It shows some words that have recently been added to the English language. Can you think of some other "new" words?

New Words in English		
snowboard	website	blading

- Plan to write some definitions of new words. Create a list, like the one shown, of words that are new to the English language. You can include slang words as well as words that have to do with new technologies, sports, trends, and so on.

- Select three words from your list and write definitions for them.

Who Dropped the Ball?

by Jessica Weiner

Sometimes the more serious people try to be, the funnier they are. That can certainly be true of athletes. They work hard to win the game. The last thing they want to do is turn into **comedians**. Nevertheless, hardworking athletes have created some of the funniest moments in the history of sports. Read these **anecdotes** and see if you agree!

Have you ever felt frustrated, sitting on the sidelines watching the action go by? Then you might sympathize with football player, Tommy Lewis. At the 1954 Cotton Bowl, Tommy was sitting on the bench, watching an **opposing** player race down the field, heading for a touchdown. It was too much for Tommy to bear. He jumped off the bench, ran onto the field,

Set Your Purpose

Can a serious athletic competition turn into a comedy of errors? Read this article to find out.

and tackled the player. At first the crowd was **flabbergasted**. Who was that mystery player? Where did he come from? Then, as they realized what had just happened, the crowd roared with laughter. The referee, on the other hand, did not have the same appreciation for Tommy's **unbridled** enthusiasm. He awarded the touchdown to the opposing team.

Baseball batter Dave Kingman had a bizarre experience at the Minnesota Metrodome. In a 1984 game, Kingman hit a pop-up. It soared up towards the fabric roof of the indoor stadium and disappeared into a drainage hole. The ball never came down! After some moments of stunned silence, the umpire awarded Kingman a ground-rule double for his mysterious disappearing shot.

Basketball player Charles Barkley went all out in his effort to rack up points for his team. In one 1987 game, Barkley attempted three slam dunks. Each time, the shots were foiled by his own head! Barkley slammed the ball through the net so hard that it bounced off his head and came back up through the hoop. Each time the referee ruled "no basket." It was not a good day for Charles Barkley!

High school athletes have also contributed their share of comic sports stories. In St. Cloud, Minnesota, basketball player Larry Nelson was looking the other way when his teammate passed him the ball. The basketball bounced off Larry's head, and then it neatly dove into the hoop, scoring two points for Larry's team.

Athletes may take their sports seriously, but sometimes their antics can be hilarious!

Think About It

Which mistake do you think would have been the most fun to have seen?

Name _____ Date _____

Check Your Understanding

Fill in the letter with the best answer for each question.

1. The events described in this selection all fit in the following category:
   Ⓐ athletes who do stand-up comedy.
   Ⓑ an amusing look at mistakes athletes make.
   Ⓒ an argument against watching athletics.
   Ⓓ an argument against baseball and basketball.

2. Tommy Lewis's tackle could best be classified as
   Ⓐ a good decision.
   Ⓑ an angry decision.
   Ⓒ an unfortunate mistake.
   Ⓓ a clever plan.

3. Charles Barkley's repeated failure to score on a slam dunk could best be classified as
   Ⓐ a frustrating mistake.   Ⓒ a skillful distraction.
   Ⓑ a foolish prank.   Ⓓ an annoying habit.

4. Larry Nelson's basket could best be described as
   Ⓐ a lucky accident.
   Ⓑ a foolish decision.
   Ⓒ an unfortunate mistake.
   Ⓓ a clever plan.

5. What happened to Dave Kingman when his ball disappeared into the ceiling?
   Ⓐ He had to buy a replacement ball.
   Ⓑ He was out.
   Ⓒ He had to search for the ball.
   Ⓓ The umpire ruled the hit a double.

Vocabulary

Find each vocabulary word in the selection. The words and sentences around it will help you figure out its meaning.

Fill in the letter with the best definition of the underlined word.

1. The last thing athletes want to do is to turn into <u>comedians</u>.
   Ⓐ people who play seriously
   Ⓑ people who make us laugh
   Ⓒ players who make mistakes
   Ⓓ players who lose

2. Read these amusing <u>anecdotes</u> to learn more.
   Ⓐ medicines   Ⓒ short, true stories
   Ⓑ arguments   Ⓓ jokes

3. Tommy watched the <u>opposing</u> player run down the field.
   Ⓐ from the other team   Ⓒ quick
   Ⓑ fast   Ⓓ friendly

4. The crowd was <u>flabbergasted</u> when Tommy tackled the player.
   Ⓐ upset   Ⓒ surprised
   Ⓑ loud   Ⓓ happy

5. In sports, <u>unbridled</u> enthusiasm is not always best.
   Ⓐ gentle   Ⓒ unpleasant
   Ⓑ wild   Ⓓ unfair

Name _____ Date _____

Word Work

Synonyms are words that have similar meanings. For example, *little* and *small* are synonyms.

Read each sentence. Fill in the letter of the synonym of the word in dark type.

1. The player **suddenly** turned around.
  Ⓐ slowly   Ⓒ joyfully
  Ⓑ quickly   Ⓓ annoyingly

2. We laughed at the ballplayer's **antics**.
  Ⓐ pranks   Ⓒ favors
  Ⓑ chores   Ⓓ habits

3. Dave Kingman had a **bizarre** experience.
  Ⓐ scary   Ⓒ boring
  Ⓑ unusual   Ⓓ nice

4. The crowd thought the mistake was **hilarious**.
  Ⓐ depressing Ⓒ annoying
  Ⓑ serious   Ⓓ funny

5. The player waved to the **cheering** crowd.
  Ⓐ applauding Ⓒ insulting
  Ⓑ mocking   Ⓓ delaying

A **noun** names a person, place, or thing. A **plural noun** names more than one person, place, or thing. To make the plural of most nouns, add -**s**. Add -**es** if the noun ends with *s, ss, x, sh, ch,* or *tch*.

class	→	class**es**
ax	→	ax**es**
dish	→	dish**es**

Read each sentence. Write the correct plural form of the word in dark type.

6. player The _____ went to the coach's birthday celebration.

7. box The table was filled with brightly wrapped _____.

8. match It took five _____ to light all the candles.

9. wish The coach decided to make three _____.

10. glass The players raised their _____ and toasted their coach.

Write Now

In "Who Dropped the Ball?" you read about mistakes made by some professional athletes.

I Made a Mistake		
something I misunderstood or messed up	something that made people laugh at me	something that made me laugh at myself
_____	_____	_____
_____	_____	_____

- Plan to write a paragraph or a cartoon about a mistake you once made. First, brainstorm some ideas for your writing. The categories in the chart shown may help you think of ideas.

- Choose a mistake from your chart to write about. Write a paragraph or draw a cartoon describing your mistake.

Sequencing

❖ When reading a story or an article, it's helpful to think about the order of events.

  • As you read, ask yourself: **"What happened first? What happened after that?"**

  • Look for dates or signal words such as *first, then, next,* and *finally* for clues to the **sequence** of events.

  • If there are no signal words, look for story and picture clues.

❖ Read this paragraph. Look for the answers to these **sequence** questions:

  • Which event happened first?

  • What events happened next?

  • What was the last thing that happened

This date
1977 is a clue to the first thing that happened.

These dates
1979 and 1980 are clues to the next events that happened.

This date
1998 tells the last thing that happened.

Voyager Sets Distance Record

    Voyager, a U.S. spacecraft carrying Earth's message to the universe, is now the most distant human-made object. In February 1998, *Voyager* surpassed the distance reached by the older *Pioneer 10* spacecraft. Launched in 1977, *Voyager* has traveled more than 6.5 billion miles from home. It passed by Jupiter in 1979 and Saturn in 1980. *Voyager* should continue sending back signals from the edge of the solar system until 2020.

❖ You could **sequence** this paragraph like this:

| Voyager launched in 1977. | → | Voyager passes Jupiter in 1979 and Saturn in 1980. | → | Voyager sets distance record in February 1998. |

Your Turn

❖ Read this selection. Look for the **sequence** of events in the building of the International Space Station. Make a chart like the one above.

Space Station Comes Together

A new space era began on December 3, 1998, when the space shuttle *Endeavour* lifted off. Its crew's mission was to place the first two sections of the International Space Station in orbit.

The astronauts' first task was to capture the Russian-built command module, *Zarya*, which had been launched November 20. That task accomplished, the astronauts connected *Zarya* to the American-made module, *Unity*. Together, *Zarya* and *Unity* formed a 77-foot, 35-ton tower. Once the two modules were docked, two spacewalking astronauts hooked up electrical connections between them.

Then it was lights on! On December 11, six astronauts swung open the doors to the new space station and flipped on the lights. Entering the station, they became the first guests aboard the 250-mile-high outpost in space.

Triathlon
The Sport That Does It All
by John James

Set Your Purpose

In what sport do athletes need a swimsuit, a bike, and sneakers? Read this article to find out about a very hard sport called the triathlon.

You're talking sports with your friends. Someone asks a question. "What's the world's most **demanding** sport?" Kim replies, "I think football is the hardest sport." "Soccer is the toughest sport," Miguel says.

You're not sure what to say. Well, the next time you hear that question, try this. Say, "The triathlon." More and more people believe it is the hardest sport. What is a triathlon?

The word *triathlon* comes from the Greek language. *Tri* means "three"; *athlon* means "sporting event." There are three different races in one triathlon. There is a swimming race, a bike race, and a footrace. Triathletes must be good at all three. And they must finish all three races the same day. There is no time to **pause** between events.

Every triathlon is difficult, but some are shorter than others. The sprint is the shortest triathlon. "The Ironman" is the longest and hardest; it takes more than eight hours from start to finish. In the Ironman, the swimming

Think About It

Do you agree that the triathlon is the most demanding sport? Why or why not?

race comes first. The athletes start out at the same time. They each swim about two-and-one-half-miles. The bike race comes next. All the athletes start to bike immediately after they finish the swim. The bike race covers 112 miles. It goes uphill and down. The athletes must **pedal** extra hard going uphill. The footrace is the last event in the Ironman. The footrace covers about 26 miles. By this point, the athletes are very tired. Their wish to **succeed** keeps them going.

The athlete who finishes the three events in the fastest time wins. But no triathlete is a loser. Just crossing the **final** finish line makes each one a winner.

Name _____ Date _____

Check Your Understanding

Fill in the letter with the best answer for each question.

1. Which race in the Ironman comes first?
- Ⓐ the bike race
- Ⓑ the footrace
- Ⓒ the swimming race
- Ⓓ the sprint

2. Athletes are usually most tired at the beginning of the Ironman
- Ⓐ bike race.
- Ⓑ footrace.
- Ⓒ swimming race.
- Ⓓ sprint.

3. Which words help us understand the sequence, or order, of events in the Ironman?
- Ⓐ swim, bike, foot
- Ⓑ bike, foot, swim
- Ⓒ sprint, Ironman, triathlon
- Ⓓ next, last, first

4. Which sentence is <u>not</u> true?
- Ⓐ All triathlons have three races.
- Ⓑ All triathlons are the same length.
- Ⓒ All triathlons have a swimming race.
- Ⓓ All triathlons are completed in one day.

5. Why do some people think the triathlon is the hardest sport?
- Ⓐ because they like to argue
- Ⓑ because triathlon athletes are stronger than wrestlers
- Ⓒ because triathlon athletes need to be experts in three sports
- Ⓓ because triathlons last longer than any other sports event

Vocabulary

Find each vocabulary word in the selection. The words and sentences around it will help you figure out its meaning.

Fill in the letter with the best definition of the underlined word.

1. Triathlon is probably the world's most <u>demanding</u> sport.
- Ⓐ easy
- Ⓑ hard
- Ⓒ short
- Ⓓ tiny

2. There is no time to <u>pause</u> between events.
- Ⓐ move faster
- Ⓑ keep going
- Ⓒ stop for a short time
- Ⓓ turn in a circle

3. The athletes <u>pedal</u> up a steep hill.
- Ⓐ ride a bike
- Ⓑ swim
- Ⓒ slide
- Ⓓ march

4. Their wish to <u>succeed</u> keeps them going.
- Ⓐ stop
- Ⓑ quit
- Ⓒ fail
- Ⓓ do well

5. Just crossing the <u>final</u> finish line makes each one a winner.
- Ⓐ first
- Ⓑ second
- Ⓒ last
- Ⓓ start

Name_____ Date_____

Word Work

> The letters **ar** stand for the sound you hear in *car*. The letters **or** stand for the sound you hear in *horn*. The letters **ir** stand for the sound you hear in *bird*.
>
> <u>car</u>   h<u>or</u>n   b<u>ir</u>d

Read the definitions. Complete the word by adding the letters *ar*, *or*, or *ir*.

1. part of a rose   th____n

2. part of a body   ____m

3. not south   n____th

4. large fish   sh____k

5. number after 29   th____ty

Each sentence below has an incomplete word. Add *ar*, *or*, or *ir* to complete the word.

6. The triathlon is my favorite **sp____t**.

7. A **sh____t** triathlon is called a sprint.

8. The athletes must pedal **h____d** when biking uphill.

9. The swimming race comes **f____st** in the Ironman triathlon.

10. **St____t** running as soon as you finish the bike race.

Write Now

In this selection, you read about the events in an Ironman triathlon. Describe what happens during each one of the three events. Use a chart like the one below to help you organize your ideas.

Ironman Triathlon		
First Event	Second Event	Third Event
_____	_____	_____
_____	_____	_____
_____	_____	_____

- Plan to write a paragraph summarizing what happens in an Ironman Triathlon. Think of phrases that tell about each of the three events in an Ironman triathlon. Write these phrases in the different parts of the chart.
- Write your summary. Use the ideas from your chart to help you. Be certain that you tell about the different events of the Ironman Triathlon in the correct sequence or order. Add a conclusion that tells how you feel about this sports event.

Life in the COMICS

by Frances Storey

Set Your Purpose

Read this article to find out how a real cartoon artist creates his strip.

Cartooning can be a wonderful career for people who don't mind the hard work that comes with it. Robb Armstrong is one person who has chosen this career. He writes and draws a popular comic strip called *Jump Start*. *Jump Start* can be seen in more than 450 newspapers in eight countries. What's it like to draw a comic **strip** for a living? Let's find out!

"I began drawing comics when I was four years old," says Robb. "When I was 17, I sold some cartoons to a newspaper. I thought I'd found an easy career. I didn't **realize** how much work it takes to be a cartoon artist."

Robb's comic strip is a big hit. But he still has to work very hard. Robb has **deadlines** to meet every week.

When he sits down to **create** a new strip, he says, the ideas come first. Then comes the writing. Robb writes the words in the spots where they will be in the strip. Next it's time to draw. Robb draws first in pencil. At the end, he goes over the finished strip with a black marker. On Sundays, the cartoon page is in color. Robb uses a computer to apply color to the drawings for his Sunday strips.

When he's not working, Robb likes to talk to kids about drawing cartoons. What's his advice for kids who would like to do their own comic strips? It's important to keep on drawing. It's also important to continue your education. "Go to **college**!" Robb says.

Who knows? Maybe you'll be the next Robb Armstrong!

Think About It

What steps does Robb Armstrong follow as he creates his comic strip?

Name_____   Date_____

Check Your Understanding

Fill in the letter with the best answer for each question.

1. What is the first thing Robb Armstrong does when he's creating a cartoon?
   - Ⓐ He writes the words.
   - Ⓑ He draws the pictures.
   - Ⓒ He uses colored markers.
   - Ⓓ He comes up with ideas.

2. What is the last thing Armstrong does to his cartoons?
   - Ⓐ He thinks of the words.
   - Ⓑ He draws the pictures in pencil.
   - Ⓒ He writes the words in the frames.
   - Ⓓ He goes over the words and pictures in black marker.

3. Why did Armstrong want to become a cartoon artist when he was young?
   - Ⓐ He thought it would be easy and fun.
   - Ⓑ He liked the deadlines.
   - Ⓒ He wanted to go to college.
   - Ⓓ He enjoyed talking to kids.

4. What does Armstrong say is the most important thing he has learned about cartooning?
   - Ⓐ It takes a lot of work.
   - Ⓑ His strip is a big hit.
   - Ⓒ It is an easy job.
   - Ⓓ It is in color on Sundays.

5. In which book might you find this article?
   - Ⓐ Drawing With Markers
   - Ⓑ How to Be Funny
   - Ⓒ Conversations About Careers: What Can You Be?
   - Ⓓ Keeping Up With the News

Vocabulary

Find each vocabulary word in the selection. The words and sentences around it will help you figure out its meaning.

Fill in the letter with the best definition of the underlined word.

1. Robb Armstrong draws a comic <u>strip</u> for a living.
   - Ⓐ line of drawings
   - Ⓑ character on TV
   - Ⓒ image
   - Ⓓ poster

2. Most people don't <u>realize</u> how much work it takes to create comic strips.
   - Ⓐ make something bigger
   - Ⓑ pretend
   - Ⓒ forget about
   - Ⓓ understand

3. Armstrong must get the comic strips done in time for the <u>deadlines</u>.
   - Ⓐ dangerous places
   - Ⓑ dates when work must be finished
   - Ⓒ rear lines on a tennis court
   - Ⓓ times when things are not going well

4. Armstrong has to <u>create</u> a new comic strip every week.
   - Ⓐ read
   - Ⓑ sell
   - Ⓒ make
   - Ⓓ understand

5. Armstrong advises kids to go to <u>college</u> to continue their education.
   - Ⓐ place of higher learning after high school
   - Ⓑ where to find a job after high school
   - Ⓒ place to meet other artists
   - Ⓓ where to see more comic strips

Name _____ Date _____

Word Work

A **suffix** is a word part that comes at the end of a base word. Knowing the meaning of a suffix helps you figure out the meaning of the whole word. The suffix **-ful** means "full of." The suffix **-y** means "having."

care<u>ful</u>	full of care
bumpy	having bumps

If a base word ends in *e*, drop the *e* before adding the suffix -y.

ice → icy

Write a word that fits the definition by adding the suffix *-ful* or *-y* to the base word.

1. full of wonder   **wonder_____**

2. having snow   **snow_____**

3. full of respect   **respect_____**

4. full of color   **color_____**

5. having lace   **lace_____**

Read each sentence. Add the suffix *-ful* or *-y* to the word in dark type to complete the sentence. Write the new word.

6. dirt When drawing cartoons, do not use a _____ eraser.

7. care Be _____ with sharp tools.

8. ease It is not always _____ to come up with ideas for cartoons.

9. joy I like to listen to _____ music while I draw.

10. thought I give drawings to others when I'm in a _____ mood.

Write Now

In "Life in the Comics," you learned how Robb Armstrong draws cartoons. Think about a cartoon that you might like to draw.

- Plan to draw a two- or three-frame cartoon. Use a chart like the one below to help you plan the characters, the setting, and the plot for the cartoon.
- Draw your cartoon. Use speech bubbles to show what the characters are saying.

Characters	
Setting	
Plot	

Driving Through
TIME

adapted by Jocelyn Piro

Can machines have birthdays?

If machines can have birthdays, the car had one in 1996. That was when the car turned 100 years old.

It was 1896 when the brothers Frank and Charles Duryea started the first car company, the Duryea Motor Wagon Company. That year it built 13 cars.

Let's take an imaginary ride through time in the Duryea Motor Wagon and see what's happened to the car since then. Toot, toot! Off we go!

It's 1899. A New York taxi driver gets the first speeding ticket. He was going far too fast—12 miles an hour!

Now it's 1919. The First World War is just ending. This year, Detroit, Michigan, puts up the first traffic light.

It's 1922. Hold on, we're going faster. In this year, the Ford Motor Company introduces the "assembly line." That means each worker puts one or two parts on a car body as it moves past. This allows Ford to build more than a million cars a year.

It's 1935. The number of cars made in the United States has risen to more than 3 million.

It's 1942. We're in the Second World War. U.S. car companies stop building cars and turn out tanks, jeeps, and other war **vehicles**.

Set Your Purpose

Cruise through time as you read this article to learn about the history of the car.

It's 1968. The U.S. government requires front-seat shoulder belts in all new American cars. Thousands of lives are saved. By now, the car is an **essential** part of American life.

Now it's 1971. American astronauts on the moon go off-road with a car called the *Lunar Rover*. They drive it across the **surface** of the moon. They leave the *Rover* behind on the moon. That makes the moon the largest known parking lot!

But that's nothing. Guess what might be in your **driveway** someday? Cars of the future may obey your voice commands. Magnets may make your car hover over local **country** roads, replacing rubber tires. Whoo-ee! Let's go!

Think About It

What do you think were the most important events in car history? Why?

Name _____ Date _____

Check Your Understanding

Fill in the letter with the best answer for each question.

1. Which came first?

    Ⓐ the assembly line   Ⓒ the traffic light

    Ⓑ the Duryea   Ⓓ front-seat shoulder
       Motor Wagon   belts

2. From all the changes we saw in cars from 1896 to the present, we can predict that cars of the future will be

    Ⓐ without drivers.   Ⓒ different.

    Ⓑ about the same.   Ⓓ without wheels.

3. Which came after tanks, jeeps, and other war vehicles?

    Ⓐ front-seat shoulder belts

    Ⓑ the first car company

    Ⓒ the Second World War

    Ⓓ the first speeding ticket

4. The United States could never have built millions of cars a year without

    Ⓐ the First World War.

    Ⓑ the Duryea Motor Wagon Company.

    Ⓒ the Second World War.

    Ⓓ the assembly line.

5. Which came before the first traffic light?

    Ⓐ tanks and jeeps for the war

    Ⓑ electric cars

    Ⓒ a cab being ticketed for going 12 miles per hour

    Ⓓ cars with voice commands

Vocabulary

> Find each vocabulary word in the selection. The words and sentences around it will help you figure out its meaning.

Fill in the letter with the best definition of the underlined word.

1. There are millions of <u>vehicles</u> on the road today.

    Ⓐ motors

    Ⓑ moving parts in a machine

    Ⓒ means of carrying people or things

    Ⓓ pieces of equipment

2. It is <u>essential</u> for most people to own cars these days.

    Ⓐ very hard to find   Ⓒ not necessary

    Ⓑ excellent   Ⓓ very much needed

3. The car they left is sitting somewhere on the <u>surface</u> of the moon.

    Ⓐ something that is very hot

    Ⓑ outside layer of something

    Ⓒ the breaking of waves on a beach

    Ⓓ rough, rocky ground

4. A different car might be in your <u>driveway</u> someday.

    Ⓐ sidewalk   Ⓒ street

    Ⓑ private road   Ⓓ garage
       connected to a house

5. <u>Country</u> roads are not meant for big cars.

    Ⓐ land away from towns or cities

    Ⓑ place with many people

    Ⓒ hilly

    Ⓓ along the ocean

Name _____ Date _____

Word Work

> Adding the suffix **-ed** to the end of a base word that is a verb usually turns it into a **past-tense verb**.
>
> report → reported
>
> Sometimes the final e is dropped before adding the suffix -ed.
>
> compare → compared

Add the suffix -ed to each verb. Write the new word.

1. park _____

2. happen _____

3. rake _____

4. turn _____

5. care _____

Read each sentence. Add the suffix -ed to the base word in dark type to complete the sentence.

6. A small crowd **assemble**_____ to look at the new car.

7. The company **start**_____ to put better safety belts in their cars.

8. These well-built cars have **save**_____ many lives.

9. Recently, many states have **require**_____ the use of safety belts.

10. This new vehicle is **call**_____ an "off-road car."

Write Now

In "Driving Through Time," you read about the history of the automobile. Cars have come a long way in their first 100 years, and they will go further still!

| 1896 | 1996 | Future

- Plan to make a timeline showing the history of cars in the United States. A timeline is a way of showing what happened when.

- Make your timeline. Mark the dates mentioned in this article on the line. Then label each date with the historic event that goes with it. Feel free to add any other important events you know and their dates. You can also add pictures to go with the events on the timeline.

Marie Curie:
A Woman Ahead of Her Time

by Frank Bear

Set Your Purpose

At one time, the idea of a woman scientist was considered ridiculous. Read this article to find out about one woman who was serious about science.

A story is told of Marie Curie. It is said that her sisters once built a pyramid of chairs around her. Marie was busy reading. She did not even notice until she stood up and knocked them all over!

It would not be surprising if this story were true. As a child, Marie loved books and experiments. Nothing could distract her from her studies. She did not lose this love of learning as she got older. In the 1880s, very few women went to college, and even fewer women became scientists. Marie did both.

After she met and married another scientist, Pierre Curie, the two of them began working together. Their studies **focused** on the element radium. They had discovered it during their research. An element is one of about 100 basic substances that make up everything in the world. Radium is found in some rocks. It is a white **metallic** element with a blue glow. The glow lasts for a thousand years.

The Curies spent their life savings on eight tons of rock called ore.

The radium glows because it emits energy. That is one reason the Curies were so intrigued by it. But studying radium is not like opening a book. Radium must be **isolated** from the rock around it. That is like trying to take just the chocolate out of chocolate milk.

The couple spent their life savings on eight tons of rock called ore. An old **shack** became their workplace. They heated the rock to remove the bits of radium from it. Days of work turned into months. Ultimately, they spent four years in that shack studying the mysterious element with the blue glow.

During their research, the Curies found that radium could help treat cancer. That is when Marie and her husband became big news. They were written about often. This got the **public** interested in radium. Soon, the Curies' work earned them the Nobel Prize in Physics. This award is one of the highest honors in the world. Marie had come a long way from the days of chair pyramids.

Name _____ Date _____

Check Your **Understanding**

Fill in the letter with the best answer for each question.

1. Marie Curie's love of learning
- (A) began as a child.
- (B) began in college.
- (C) ended after she met Pierre.
- (D) ended before she met Pierre.

2. The Curies began working in the shack
- (A) before they discovered radium.
- (B) before they bought their ore.
- (C) while attending college.
- (D) after their discovery of radium.

3. Newspapers began writing about the Curies
- (A) shortly after the two met and married.
- (B) when they bought eight tons of rock.
- (C) when it was discovered that radium might treat cancer.
- (D) after they died.

4. Which sentence supports the idea that Marie Curie was different from most women in the 1880s?
- (A) She met and married a scientist.
- (B) She went to college and became a scientist.
- (C) She loved books and experiments.
- (D) Nothing could distract her from her studies.

5. Which sentence states a fact about the Curies?
- (A) Their work earned them the Nobel Prize in Physics.
- (B) They were foolish to spend their life savings on eight tons of rock.
- (C) It took them too long to find a cure for cancer.
- (D) They deserved to get the highest honor in the world.

Vocabulary

Find each vocabulary word in the selection. The words and sentences around it will help you figure out its meaning.

Fill in the letter with the best definition of the underlined word.

1. The Curies' work <u>focused</u> on the element radium.
- (A) concentrated upon
- (B) made believe
- (C) ignored
- (D) wished for

2. Radium must be <u>isolated</u> from the rock around it.
- (A) slept
- (B) kept apart
- (C) painted
- (D) drank

3. Radium is a white <u>metallic</u> element with a blue glow.
- (A) many colors
- (B) made of something hard and shiny
- (C) diamond ring
- (D) mindful manner

4. Marie and Pierre Curie worked in an old <u>shack</u>.
- (A) car
- (B) place where food is served
- (C) poorly built cabin
- (D) village

5. The <u>public</u> became interested in radium.
- (A) radio stations
- (B) doctors and nurses
- (C) newspapers and magazines
- (D) people of the community

Name _____ Date _____

Word Work

A **suffix** is an ending that changes the meaning of a base word. Knowing the meaning of a suffix helps you figure out the meaning of the whole word. The suffix **-ist** means "a person who." The suffix **-able** means "capable of" or "able to."

geolog<u>ist</u>: a person who studies geology

correct<u>able</u>: able to be corrected

Each word on the left contains a base word and a suffix. Complete the definition by writing the correct form of the base word.

1. scientist someone who studies _____

2. treatable capable of being _____

3. honorable capable of being _____

4. pianist someone who plays the _____

5. hypnotist someone who _____

Synonyms are words that have similar meanings. For example, *little* and *small* are synonyms.

Read the sentences and the words below. Write the word that means almost the same as the word in dark type.

notice   interests   often   emits   basic

6. Radium still **fascinates** scientists today.

_____

7. The fact that it **gives off** energy makes it glow. _____

8. Frequently, this energy can be dangerous if humans aren't careful. _____

9. The precautions people should take are pretty **simple**, but very necessary.

_____

10. It's important to **be aware of** the dangers when working with any kind of material.

_____

Write Now

The selection you just read discussed Marie Curie and the work she and her husband did with radium. Their research was difficult and took a long time, but in the end, it all came together. A flowchart like the one below could help show how their research developed.

| Marie meets and marries Pierre Curie. | → | The Curies begin working together. | → | The Curies discover and study radium. | → | They discover that radium helps treat cancer. | → | The Curies are awarded the Nobel Prize in Physics. |

- Plan to write a short speech about a new element you have discovered. Use a chart like the one above to help you organize the process you used to discover it.

- Write a short speech talking about a new element you have just discovered. Use details from your flowchart to help you.

LOST & FOUND
THE FIRST FORT

|||||||||||||||||||||||||||||||||||||||||||||||||||||||||||||||

adapted by Jack Wittier

Set Your Purpose

Bill Kelso is an archaeologist. Read this article to find out what he dug up.

Jamestown Island is full of buried treasures!
At least, it is if you are a scientist.

Jamestown was the first **permanent** English colony in the Americas. It existed for many years. In September of 1994, archaeologists uncovered the remains of a long-lost fort there. It was the first fort built in Jamestown to protect the colony from enemy attack. The diggers also discovered old English coins, jewelry, and swords. They even found the skeleton of one of the first settlers. No bones about it—they had found a lost colony in Jamestown.

What Was Jamestown?

On May 13, 1607, colonists from England landed their boats on an island that is now part of Virginia. They built a **settlement** there. They called it Fort James—and later Jamestown—in honor of the king of England. But life in Jamestown was difficult. The settlers suffered from disease and hunger. The winters were very cold. **Disputes** with the Native Americans made life in Jamestown dangerous. Many people died. But the **survivors** did not give up. When their fort burned down, they rebuilt it and made it larger. The colonists stayed in Jamestown for almost 100 years. Today, there is a city nearby called Jamestown.

Uncovering Buried Treasures

Most people thought the James River had washed away the old Jamestown fort. But archaeologist Bill Kelso wanted to uncover the truth. "Some people thought I was wasting my time," Kelso said. "But there was one small area left that hadn't been explored in depth. I thought it would be worth a look."

Kelso showed that it was indeed worth a look. Thanks to his discovery, scientists will be able to learn more about how the first settlers in America lived. Archaeologists are still at work **uncovering** the old Jamestown fort. They hope to be done in the year 2007, the 400th anniversary of the establishment of Jamestown. Until then, visitors can watch the archaeologists at work. "We're having a thrill every day here," says Bill Kelso.

Think About It

What did Bill Kelso find?

Name _____   Date _____

Check Your Understanding

Fill in the letter with the best answer for each question.

1. What happened first?

Ⓐ The colonists built Fort James.

Ⓑ The colonists died from disease and hunger.

Ⓒ The colonists set sail for America.

Ⓓ The colonists landed on Jamestown Island.

2. What happened after the colonists' fort burned down?

Ⓐ They honored the king of England.

Ⓑ They named it Fort James.

Ⓒ They sailed to America.

Ⓓ They rebuilt it and made it larger.

3. Which word does not describe Bill Kelso?

Ⓐ curious

Ⓑ unrealistic

Ⓒ optimistic

Ⓓ motivated

4. Which statement is not true?

Ⓐ Visitors watch while archaeologists uncover the old Jamestown fort.

Ⓑ At the same time that colonists were dying from disease and hunger, they were having disputes with the Native Americans.

Ⓒ When the colonists landed on Jamestown Island, they built a settlement there.

Ⓓ King James was the king of England when archaeologists first discovered the fort.

5. What is the main idea of the section called "What Was Jamestown?"

Ⓐ Life in Jamestown was difficult.

Ⓑ The colonists rebuilt the fort that burned down.

Ⓒ Winters in Jamestown were very cold.

Ⓓ The settlers died from disease and hunger.

Vocabulary

Find each vocabulary word in the selection. The words and sentences around it will help you figure out its meaning.

Fill in the letter with the best definition of the underlined word.

1. Jamestown was the first underline permanent English colony in the Americas.

Ⓐ brave

Ⓑ temporary

Ⓒ English-speaking

Ⓓ lasting for a long time

2. Colonists built a settlement on an island.

Ⓐ shopping center

Ⓑ city housing project

Ⓒ small village

Ⓓ church

3. Disputes with the Native Americans made life in Jamestown dangerous.

Ⓐ ceremonies

Ⓑ fights

Ⓒ illnesses

Ⓓ discussions

4. Many people died, but the survivors did not give up.

Ⓐ people who live through an event

Ⓑ people who die

Ⓒ people who settle an area

Ⓓ soldiers

5. Archaeologists are still at work uncovering the old fort.

Ⓐ exposing

Ⓑ removing the lid of

Ⓒ changing

Ⓓ talking about

Name _____ Date _____

Word Work

The **long-o** sound can be spelled several different ways. Look at these examples:
h<u>o</u>pe   b<u>oa</u>t   fl<u>ow</u>

Circle the word in each group that has the long-o sound.

1. hot   throw   soil   doll
2. phone   shock   shout   knock
3. front   prong   slope   oil
4. lock   frolic   soup   groan
5. elbow   strong   dog   moon

Circle all the words in each sentence that have the long-o sound. Then underline the letters that spell the long-o sound in each word.

6. The scientists closed off the roads to begin digging.

7. They dug deep holes and moved heavy stones.

8. They uncovered broken pots, bowls, and even some bones.

9. They took pictures and jotted down notes.

10. They hoped the items would be shown in museums.

Write Now

Congratulations on your new job as an on-site newspaper reporter for the *Virginia Times*! Your first assignment is to write a short article about the discovery of the lost colony of Jamestown.

- Plan to write your article. First, brainstorm catchy headlines for your article. Then gather the information for your article by completing a chart similar to the one shown.

- Write your article. Choose the headline you think will grab the reader's interest. Use the information you have gathered in your chart. Remember to begin with a strong lead sentence. Include quotations from archaeologists on the site to make your article more believable.

Who?	
What?	
Where?	
When?	
Why?	

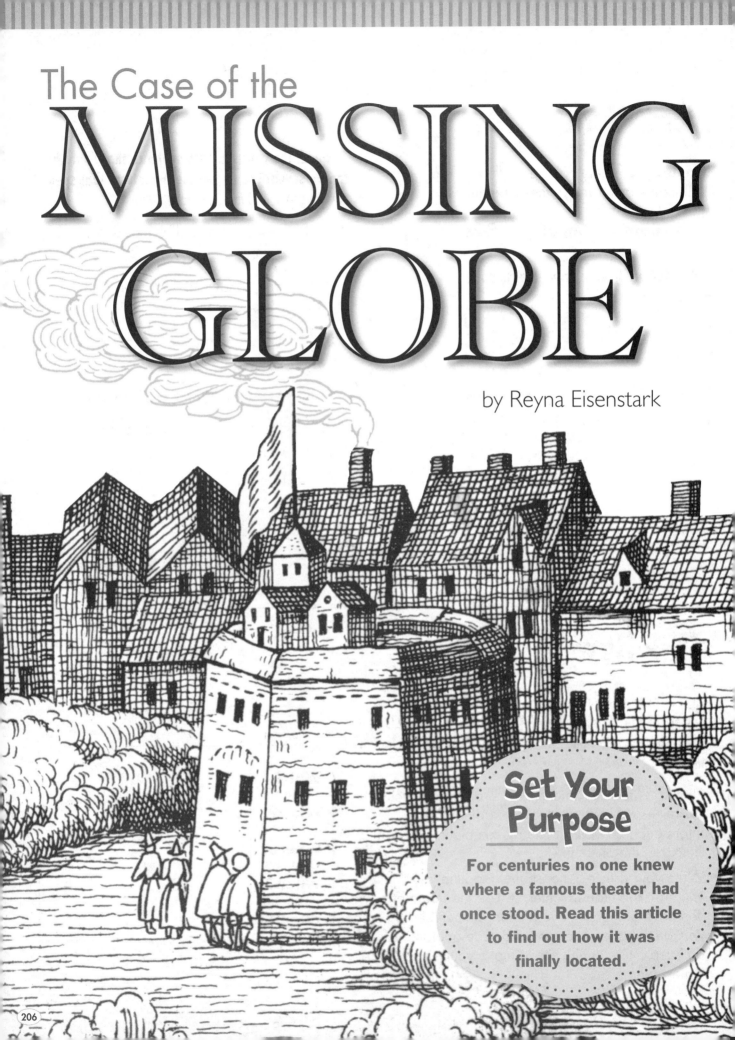

The Case of the
MISSING
GLOBE

by Reyna Eisenstark

Set Your Purpose

For centuries no one knew where a famous theater had once stood. Read this article to find out how it was finally located.

The Globe Theater may be the most famous theater in the world. Where is it? That was a great mystery for nearly 400 years.

The theater was built in London, England, in 1599. The **revered** writer William Shakespeare staged some of his most famous plays at the Globe. In 1613, a cannon was fired during a play. The cannon set fire to the theater's straw roof. An hour later, the building had burned down. It was rebuilt the next year. This time, the roof was made of tiles.

The Globe was closed in 1642 when the Puritans, a religious group, shut all of London's theaters. Two years later, the Globe was torn down to build **tenements**. Its foundations were buried under the apartment buildings. Until recently, no one knew anything else about the Globe's location or design.

Over the years, people have tried to **reconstruct** the Globe. No one had any luck rebuilding it. In 1970, however, American actor Sam Wanamaker started the Shakespeare Globe Playhouse Trust. He raised money to build a new Globe. The ground was cleared for the new building in 1987. Then, in 1989, something **incredible** happened.

Workers from the Museum of London were digging just 200 yards away from the new site and discovered part of the old Globe! Most of the Globe is still buried under a nineteenth-century building. Only a small section of the old building could be studied. Even so, builders were able to complete the new Globe. They based their designs on what they saw. They also used what they already knew about buildings from that time.

In 1994, the new Globe opened to the public. It doesn't look exactly like the old theater. However, the building **approximates** how the Globe looked and felt 400 years ago. Visitors truly feel that they have stepped back in time!

Think About It

What happened after the old Globe Theater was discovered underground?

Name _____ Date _____

Check Your Understanding

Fill in the letter with the best answer for each question.

1. Which event happened first?

Ⓐ The Globe got a new tile roof.

Ⓑ The Globe's roof caught fire during a play.

Ⓒ Workers discovered part of the old Globe.

Ⓓ The new Globe was completed.

2. What happened before the Globe was torn down in order to build tenements?

Ⓐ Sam Wanamaker started the Shakespeare Globe Playhouse Trust.

Ⓑ The Puritans closed down all of the theaters in London.

Ⓒ The new Globe was opened to the public.

Ⓓ Ground for the new Globe was cleared.

3. The new Globe opened _____ after the construction of the original theater.

Ⓐ nearly 50 years

Ⓑ about 75 years

Ⓒ almost 100 years

Ⓓ almost 400 years

4. What statement is an opinion?

Ⓐ The new Globe is better than the old Globe.

Ⓑ Sam Wanamaker raised money to build a new Globe.

Ⓒ The old Globe's foundations are buried under a nineteenth-century building.

Ⓓ The roof of the original Globe theater was made of straw.

5. The location of the Globe Theater was a mystery for nearly 400 years because

Ⓐ it was kept a secret.

Ⓑ no one knew what city it had been built in.

Ⓒ it was buried under new buildings.

Ⓓ no one knew when it was torn down.

Vocabulary

Find each vocabulary word in the selection. The words and sentences around it will help you figure out its meaning.

Fill in the letter with the best definition of the underlined word.

1. The <u>revered</u> writer William Shakespeare staged some of his most famous plays at the Globe.

Ⓐ respected

Ⓑ stubborn

Ⓒ angry

Ⓓ excitable

2. Two years later, the Globe was torn down to build <u>tenements</u>.

Ⓐ theaters

Ⓑ roofs

Ⓒ cannons

Ⓓ apartments

3. Over the years, people have tried to <u>reconstruct</u> the Globe.

Ⓐ destroy

Ⓑ burn

Ⓒ rebuild

Ⓓ bury

4. Then, in 1989, something <u>incredible</u> happened.

Ⓐ unbelievable

Ⓑ ridiculous

Ⓒ disappointing

Ⓓ impossible

5. The new theater <u>approximates</u> how the Globe looked and felt 400 years ago.

Ⓐ is nothing like

Ⓑ is close to

Ⓒ is identical to

Ⓓ is better than

Name _____ Date _____

Word Work

> Every **syllable**, or word part, has just one vowel sound. By using what you know about sounds and letters, you can figure out how to read a word that has more than one syllable.
>
> | tenements | = | 3 syllables |
> |-----------|---|-------------|
> | incredible | = | 4 syllables |

> When a word ends in **-le** or **-al** following a consonant, those three letters usually form the final syllable of the word.
>
> | historical | his/tor/i/cal |
> |------------|---------------|
> | unbelievable | un/be/lie/va/ble |

Write the number of syllables that the underlined word contains.

1. Firefighters rushed to the Globe Theater, but it had <u>already</u> burned to the ground. _____

2. The <u>foundations</u> of the old Globe were buried for hundreds of years. _____

3. People searched through Shakespeare's notes for <u>information</u> about the Globe. _____

4. Today, people can see <u>performances</u> in the new Globe. _____

5. It was noon when workers from the Museum of London started <u>digging</u>. _____

Circle the words that contain either a consonant + -le or a consonant + -al. Draw lines between the syllables in each word.

6. Many people longed to find the location of the old Globe.

7. Digging up the foundations was not a simple task.

8. It would not have been practical to tear down the nineteenth-century building on top of the old Globe.

9. The location of the old Globe remained a famous puzzle until 1989.

10. The original Globe Theater had a star roof.

Write Now

In the article "The Case of the Missing Globe," you read about a famous theater that was discovered after being buried for hundreds of years.

What is the object?	How did it get lost?	How was it discovered?
The Globe Theater	It was torn down to make tenements and its foundations were buried.	Workers from the Museum of London discovered it while they were digging.

- Write a story about the discovery of a famous missing object. First, decide what the missing object is. Then, decide how it got lost and how it came to be discovered.
- Make a chart like this one to list the important details of your story. Use your chart to help you explain what happened.

JIM CARREY

Class Clown Makes Good

adapted by Julie Brand

Today, Jim Carrey is a comedy superstar, but his younger years weren't always a laughing matter.

Jim was born and raised in Toronto, Canada. He grew up in a home with music and laughter. At first, Jim didn't know how to make friends, so he started "acting goofy." Soon everyone wanted to hang out with him. "Acting goofy became an entire **motivation** for living," he says. Jim was the class clown but also a straight-A student.

Set Your Purpose

The road to success wasn't smooth for actor Jim Carrey. Read to find out how Jim overcame obstacles to become a highly paid actor.

Then Jim's dad lost his job. The Carreys lost their home and had to live in a van for a while. Eventually, Jim, his mom, and his dad found work in a factory as caretakers.

By tenth grade, Jim no longer felt like clowning around and had little interest in school. He finally dropped out of school. There was little joy in his life. He found he really missed the laughter. So he created a comedy act and tried it out at a local club. The crowd booed him right off the stage!

Jim didn't quit, but instead continued to work the comedy **circuit** for the next 15 years. He took acting lessons, appeared in several movies, and starred in a short-lived TV sitcom called *The Duck Factory*. Jim wasn't "discovered" until he brought his wacky characters to life on the TV comedy series *In Living Color*.

Jim Carrey is now one of the highest-paid actors in Hollywood. In 1998, he earned $20 million for his **role** in *The Truman Show*, a movie with a serious side.

Carrey continues to display his **formidable** talents in both comedies and serious movies. He even played a cartoon character. In 2000, Carrey starred in the live-action **version** of Dr. Seuss's *How the Grinch Stole Christmas*.

Of all his roles, Carrey says he most resembles Truman Burbank, his character in *The Truman Show*. "I want to be the guy who won't be caged, but still has hope and faith in people, and in life," he says.

Think About It

How did Jim Carrey's ability to overcome obstacles help him become successful?

Name _____ Date _____

Check Your Understanding

Fill in the letter with the best answer for each question.

1. Which one of these events happened first in Jim Carrey's life?

Ⓐ His father lost his job.

Ⓑ He dropped out of school.

Ⓒ His family lived in a van.

Ⓓ He earned $20 million for *The Truman Show*.

2. Which one of these events happened most recently?

Ⓐ He acted in the TV series *In Living Color*.

Ⓑ He starred in *How the Grinch Stole Christmas*.

Ⓒ He earned $20 million for *The Truman Show*.

Ⓓ He worked the comedy circuit.

3. Before Jim Carrey first tried out his comedy act in a club, he

Ⓐ played a cartoon character on film.

Ⓑ took acting lessons.

Ⓒ starred in a TV sitcom.

Ⓓ worked in a factory.

4. In the 15 years before he was "discovered," Jim Carrey did not

Ⓐ take acting lessons.

Ⓑ star in a TV sitcom.

Ⓒ appear in several movies.

Ⓓ star in a Broadway show.

5. Which statement best summarizes Jim Carrey's road to success?

Ⓐ Sometimes he needed help on the way up.

Ⓑ Some problems aren't really that bad.

Ⓒ He always got what he deserved.

Ⓓ He didn't let obstacles stand in his way.

Vocabulary

> Find each vocabulary word in the selection. The words and sentences around it will help you figure out its meaning.

Fill in the letter with the best definition of the underlined word.

1. Acting goofy became Jim Carrey's <u>motivation</u> for living.

Ⓐ style   Ⓒ reason

Ⓑ method   Ⓓ daily habit

2. Jim Carrey worked the comedy <u>circuit</u> for 15 years.

Ⓐ tour   Ⓒ practice sessions

Ⓑ stage lights   Ⓓ television series

3. Jim Carrey was paid $20 million for his <u>role</u> in *The Truman Show*.

Ⓐ piece of bread   Ⓒ acting part

Ⓑ help   Ⓓ list of names

4. Jim continues to display his <u>formidable</u> talents in both comedies and serious movies.

Ⓐ amusing   Ⓒ serious

Ⓑ powerful   Ⓓ average

5. Jim Carrey starred in the live-action <u>version</u> of Dr. Seuss's *How the Grinch Stole Christmas*.

Ⓐ form   Ⓒ book

Ⓑ mistake   Ⓓ computer software

Name _____   Date _____

Word Work

> A **compound word** is made up of two or more shorter base words. The meaning of a compound word can often be found by combining the meaning of the two base words.
>
> **superstar** = a **star** who is **superior** to other stars

Read the compound words below. Write the word that best completes each sentence. Then draw a line between the two base words.

homeowners   classroom   worldwide

nightclubs   moviegoers

1. Jim Carrey started his comedy career in the _____.

2. Later, he lived in a van because his parents were no longer _____.

3. He performed in _____ for many years.

4. Many _____ appreciate his comic talents.

5. Carrey overcame many obstacles and now enjoys _____ fame.

> Most **past-tense verbs** are formed by adding *-ed*. **Irregular verbs** change their spelling to form the past tense.
>
> Present: Jim Carrey **makes** people laugh.
> Past: Jim Carrey **made** people laugh.

Write the past tense of the verb in dark type.

6. Jim Carrey **grows** up in a home filled with music and laughter. _____

7. He **finds** that comedy helped him in school. _____

8. Do you know how Carrey **overcomes** obstacles? _____

9. Comedy **brings** out the best of his talents. _____

10. Carrey **says** he most resembles the character Truman Burbank. _____

Write Now

In the article, you read how Jim Carrey went from living in a van to becoming a famous actor.

As a child, Jim Carrey loved to make people laugh.	→	He was also a straight–A student.	→	At age 13, Jim was homeless.
				↓
	←		←	Jim worked in a factory.
↓				
	→		→	

- Plan to write a summary describing Jim Carrey's rise to fame. Complete a sequence chain like the one shown to organize your ideas.

- Write your summary, using the sequence chain to help you.

Making Stories Come Alive

adapted by Beth Bonet

Set Your Purpose

Where does author Ashley Bryan get his story ideas? Read this article to find out.

Ashley Bryan is a treasure hunter. He seeks treasures from the ancient days of Africa and brings them back for modern-day children to enjoy. But his treasures aren't gold coins or rare jewels. They are the folk stories the African people once told.

"African tales are a beautiful means of **linking** the living Africa, past and present, to our own present," says Ashley Bryan. Folktales **reveal** valuable information, like how did the ancient African people see the world? How did they feel? What did they imagine?

Ashley believes that answers to these questions can be found in the tales. "Stories are always a **treasury** of the history of a people," Ashley explains.

Ashley Bryan spends long hours in the library, searching for ancient African folktales in **scholarly** books. Often all he finds is a short description of a story. "I look at those words and say, 'Nobody would tell a story like that!'" Ashley's job, as he sees it, is to **recapture** the spirit of the original story. He tries to imagine how the story might have sounded when it was first told by an African storyteller surrounded by a circle of listeners. What words would the storyteller choose? What would the words sound like? What type of voice would the storyteller use to say the words?

Ashley Bryan begins to rewrite the story, using his own words. He reads his first version aloud, listening to how it sounds. Ashley believes that the sound of words is like a song. He always tries to make that song as beautiful as possible. He adds and changes words as he writes his second version of the story. He reads this new version aloud, too, again testing it with his ear. Ashley continues this process of writing, speaking, listening, and revising. "By the time I reach a fifth version, [the story] begins to have its own voice," he says. "Finally, the story reaches the point where I can say to it, 'You are alive!'"

Think About It

What steps does Ashley Bryan follow when he writes a story?

Name _____   Date _____

Check Your Understanding

Fill in the letter with the best answer for each question.

1. What is the first step Ashley Bryan takes when writing his own telling of a folktale?
   (A) He writes an outline and brainstorm ideas.
   (B) He searches through books to find an ancient folktale.
   (C) He tells the story.
   (D) He listens to the story.

2. After Ashley Bryan writes his first version, he
   (A) silently reads over it.
   (B) immediately writes a second version.
   (C) reads the version aloud.
   (D) searches for another folktale.

3. Why does Ashley Bryan read his writing aloud?
   (A) He wants to hear the words of the story.
   (B) He wants to hear his own voice.
   (C) He doesn't like to read silently.
   (D) He wants everyone to hear his story.

4. What is Ashley Bryan's goal as an author?
   (A) to write as many stories as he can
   (B) to write his stories so they come alive for the reader
   (C) to write about treasure hunting in Africa
   (D) to write stories he remembers from his childhood

5. Which of the following best describes how Ashley Bryan feels about ancient African folktales?
   (A) They are more valuable than gold or jewels.
   (B) They are not a good way to get information about the history of a people.
   (C) They are not interesting.
   (D) They are easy to locate in the library.

Vocabulary

Find each vocabulary word in the selection. The words and sentences around it will help you figure out its meaning.

Fill in the letter with the best definition of the underlined word.

1. Folktales are a means of <u>linking</u> the past with the present.
   (A) tearing apart   (C) hiding
   (B) connecting   (D) imagining

2. Folktales <u>reveal</u> valuable information.
   (A) make known   (C) close
   (B) hide away   (D) listen

3. According to Ashley, "Stories are always a <u>treasury</u> of the history of a people."
   (A) pirate's loot
   (B) person who keeps the money
   (C) storehouse of valuables
   (D) tank

4. Ashley looks for ancient African folktales in <u>scholarly</u> books.
   (A) new and up-to-date   (C) older, out-of-date
   (B) written for children   (D) written by an expert

5. Ashley's job is to <u>recapture</u> the spirit of the original story.
   (A) arrest   (C) put on a cap
   (B) regain   (D) remove

Name_____   Date_____

Word Work

A **prefix** comes at the beginning of a word and changes the meaning of the word. Knowing the meaning of a prefix helps you figure out the meaning of the whole word. The prefix **inter-** means "between." The prefix **trans-** means "across." The prefix **en-** means "to make; to put." The prefix **sub-** means "under; below."

international	between two nations
transcontinental	across the continent
enslave	to make a slave
submerge	to place under water

Add the prefix *inter-*, *trans-*, *en-*, or *sub-* to each base word to form a new word.

1. _____ lock

2. _____ close

3. _____ plant

4. _____ marine

5. _____ form

Read the definition below. Add the prefix *inter-*, *en-*, or *sub-* to the base word to make a new word that fits the definition. Write the entire word.

6. action between people   _____ **action**

7. across ports   _____ **port**

8. to put in a case   _____ **case**

9. below standards   _____ **standard**

10. to put inside a circle   _____ **circle**

Write Now

In "Making Stories Come Alive," you read about Ashley Bryan, an author who loves to tell and retell stories. What are some of the stories that your family or friends like to tell and retell?

• Plan to write a story that you have often heard told. It could be a true story about something that happened or a made-up story that you know well. List at least three ideas, then choose the one you like best.

• Write the first version of your story. Then use Ashley Bryan's technique for making your story come alive. Read the story aloud, listening to the sound of the words. Change and add words to make your story sound even better.

Comparing & Contrasting

❖ When reading a story or an article, it's helpful to think about how things are similar and how they are different.

- As you read, ask yourself: **"What is similar about these things?"** and **"How are they different?"**
- When you think about how things are similar, you **compare** them.
- When you think about how things are different, you **contrast** them.

❖ Read this paragraph. Look for the answers to these **compare/contrast** questions:

- How are frogs and toads similar?
- How are they different?

Compare

These sentences tell how frogs and toads are **alike**.

Contrast

These sentences tell how frogs and toads are **different**.

Frogs and Toads—Alike, Then Different

Frogs and toads start out life a lot alike. They are both amphibians, so they lay their eggs in water. After the eggs hatch, both frogs and toads spend part of their lives—the tadpole stage—in water breathing with gills. The difference comes after the tadpoles lose their tails, grow legs, and develop lungs. Frogs have a smooth, moist skin and spend the rest of their lives in and near water. Toads have a rough, dry skin and live on land.

❖ You could make a chart like this to **compare** and **contrast** frogs and toads.

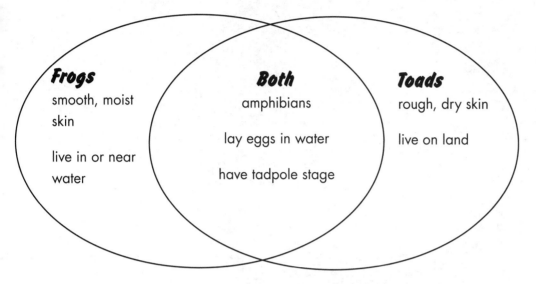

Frogs
smooth, moist skin

live in or near water

Both
amphibians

lay eggs in water

have tadpole stage

Toads
rough, dry skin

live on land

Your Turn

❖ Read this passage. **Compare** and **contrast** the black bear and the polar bear. Make a chart like the one above.

The Bear Facts

Although black bears and polar bears are different in many ways, they also have a lot in common. Their body shape is similar, and they both have thick coats of fur. Newborn bear cubs of all kinds are very tiny and stay with their mother for a year or more.

A major difference between black bears and polar bears is their size. A full-grown black bear can be 4 to 5 feet long and weigh 150 to 400 pounds. The huge polar bear, at 6 to 8 feet long, can weigh up to 1,500 pounds! Black bears eat mostly green plants, berries, nuts, ants, and small animals such as mice. The chief food of polar bears is seals, although they also eat birds' eggs and berries.

Black bears have black or dark brown fur. Polar bears have fur that is yellowish-white.

YO-YOs ARE FOREVER

by Jim McCloskey

I t's lunchtime. The schoolyard buzzes with activity. Jesse is rocking the cradle. Maria is walking the dog. Billy is going around the world. Are we kidding? No, we're not. Jesse, Maria, and Billy are playing with yo-yos. "Rock the cradle," "walk the dog," and "around the world" are yo-yo tricks.

People have always loved yo-yos. Why do people find yo-yos so **appealing**? For one thing, they are fun. Another reason is that toy makers keep trying to make better yo-yos.

Years ago, all yo-yo parts were made of wood. Wooden parts can wear out quickly. Toy makers tried new ideas. Some began using plastic instead of wood. Plastic parts do not wear out the way wood does.

Set Your Purpose

People never seem to tire of yo-yos. Read this article to find out why people of all ages like this toy.

DID YOU KNOW?
The people of the Philippines gave the yo-yo its name.
The Philippines is in Southeast Asia.

Believe it or not, the string is important. The string has to let the yo-yo glide up and down easily. It needs to be thin. Yet, it must be **durable**. It cannot break easily. Toy makers try to find string that is just right for a yo-yo.

Toy makers also make yo-yos that look different. Once, all yo-yos looked the same. Today you can find many **unusual** ones. Some have colored shapes painted on the outside. Some look like butterflies as they spin. One kind lights up and plays music. It looks and sounds like a merry-go-round. Some yo-yos have cloth **coverings** that make them look like round, furry animals. You can use these yo-yos for a trick such as walking a sheep or a bear or another animal.

We cannot predict what kind of new, **improved** yo-yo will appear next. But we know one thing. People will love playing with it.

Think About It

What do you look for in a yo-yo? Do you like unusual ones? Why?

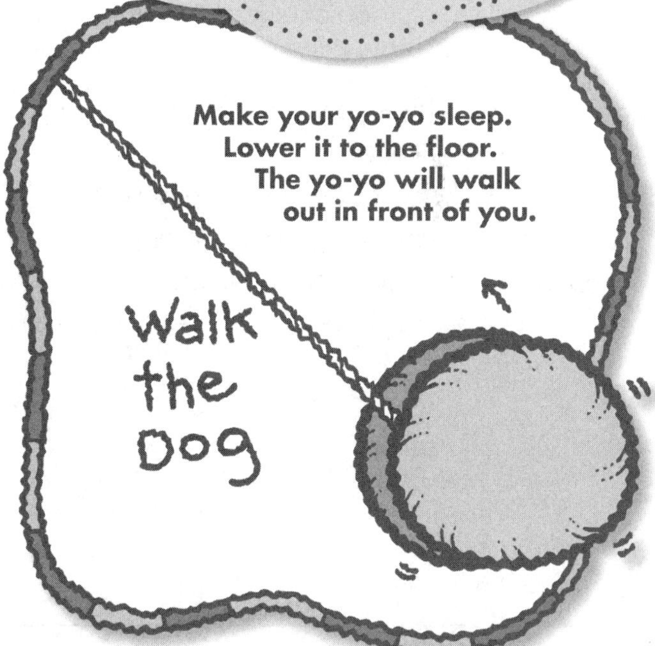

Walk the Dog

Make your yo-yo sleep. Lower it to the floor. The yo-yo will walk out in front of you.

Creeper/Land Rover/Call the Dog

As you "walk the dog," lower your hand to the floor. Whistle and tug the string. The yo-yo will walk back along the floor, into your hand.

The Speed Boat

Stand over a bathtub or puddle. Lower the sleeping yo-yo to the surface. Prepare to get wet!

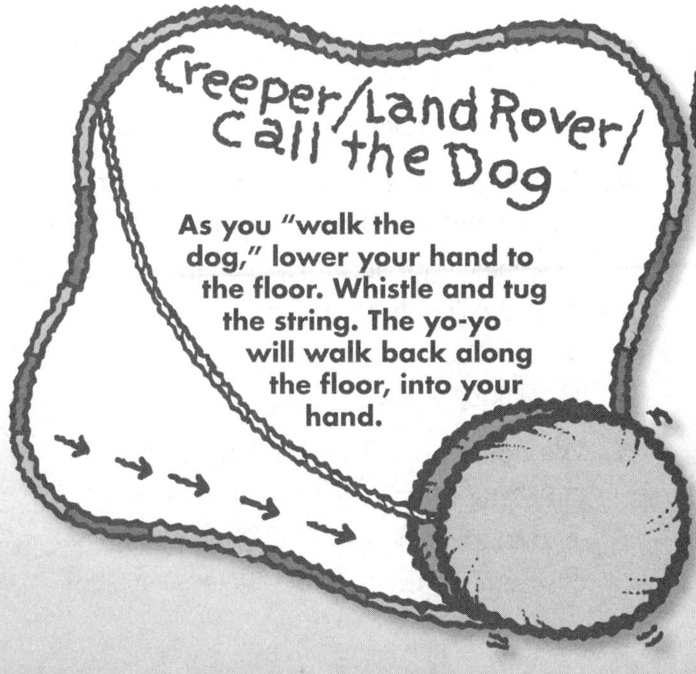

Name _____   Date _____

Check Your Understanding

Fill in the letter with the best answer for each question.

1. How are today's yo-yos like yo-yos made years ago?

Ⓐ Many of today's yo-yos are made of wood.

Ⓑ Many of today's yo-yos are made of plastic.

Ⓒ They are enjoyed by children.

Ⓓ Most people do not like to play with today's yo-yos.

2. How are today's yo-yos different from yo-yos made years ago?

Ⓐ Many yo-yos today are made of wood.

Ⓑ Many yo-yos today are made of plastic.

Ⓒ Yo-yos today do not use strings.

Ⓓ Yo-yos do not have colored designs painted on them.

3. Which statement shows the difference between yo-yos today and yo-yos years ago?

Ⓐ Yo-yos today all look the same.

Ⓑ Yo-yos years ago played music.

Ⓒ Today there are many different yo-yos.

Ⓓ There were more different yo-yos years ago.

4. What should a yo-yo string be like?

Ⓐ thin, rough, and lasting

Ⓑ short, thick, and smooth

Ⓒ thick, breakable, and rough

Ⓓ thin, lasting, and smooth

5. Why did toy makers use plastic for some yo-yos?

Ⓐ Plastic is more colorful and attractive.

Ⓑ Plastic parts don't wear out the way wood does.

Ⓒ Plastic yo-yos sell better.

Ⓓ Wooden yo-yos are old.

Vocabulary

Find each vocabulary word in the selection. The words and sentences around it will help you figure out its meaning.

Fill in the letter with the best definition of the underlined word.

1. People find yo-yos <u>appealing</u>.

Ⓐ annoying   Ⓒ dull

Ⓑ hateful   Ⓓ pleasing

2. The string must be <u>durable</u>; it cannot break easily.

Ⓐ very soft   Ⓒ very long

Ⓑ easily broken   Ⓓ long-lasting

3. Today, you can find many <u>unusual</u> yo-yos.

Ⓐ seen all the time   Ⓒ hardly ever seen

Ⓑ very common   Ⓓ worn out

4. Some yo-yos have cloth <u>coverings</u> that make them look like round, furry animals.

Ⓐ something that covers

Ⓑ something that lights up

Ⓒ new rings

Ⓓ without covers

5. We cannot predict what kind of new, <u>improved</u> yo-yo will appear next.

Ⓐ disappointing   Ⓒ larger

Ⓑ better than before   Ⓓ experimental

Name _____ Date _____

Word Work

> **Synonyms** are words with similar meanings. For example, *light* and *heavy* are synonyms.

Fill in the letter of the word that means the same as the word in dark type.

1. Another word for **kidding** is
Ⓐ ringing. Ⓒ singing.
Ⓑ joking. Ⓓ spinning.

2. Another word for **usual** is
Ⓐ rare. Ⓒ unfair.
Ⓑ ordinary. Ⓓ old.

3. Another word for **easy** is
Ⓐ weak. Ⓒ simple.
Ⓑ silly. Ⓓ tired.

4. Another word for **same** is
Ⓐ different. Ⓒ few.
Ⓑ alike. Ⓓ short.

5. Another word for **quickly** is
Ⓐ rapidly. Ⓒ slowly.
Ⓑ loudly. Ⓓ softly.

Write the word that means the same as the underlined word.

appealing unusual durable similar quickly

6. Yo-yos today do not all look <u>alike</u>.
_____

7. The butterfly yo-yo is very <u>rare</u>-looking.
_____

8. The musical yo-yo has a very <u>pleasing</u> sound. _____

9. You learned how to walk the dog very <u>fast</u>.
_____

10. I have owned this <u>long-lasting</u> yo-yo for three years. _____

Write Now

Many yo-yos today are colorful. Some have attractive pictures painted on the sides. They come in packages. Words on the package tell why the yo-yo inside is special. Look at the list to the right. It shows the special features of one new yo-yo.

- Plan to create a new yo-yo package. Draw a picture of a yo-yo that you would like to own. Make it colorful and give it a name. Print the name above the drawing. Think of things that would make your yo-yo special. Write three phrases that describe these special things. See the example shown for some ideas.

- Create a yo-yo package. How can your package make people want to buy this yo-yo?

> ### The Songbird Yo-yo
> - sings while it spins
> - spins longer
> - made of durable plastic

GIVING TV THE BOOT!

adapted by Adrienne Hathoway

A re you an average American kid? If so, you watch TV about three hours and 17 minutes a day. That means you spend more than one-and-one-half months a year glued to the tube. Imagine all the things you could do if you didn't watch TV at all!

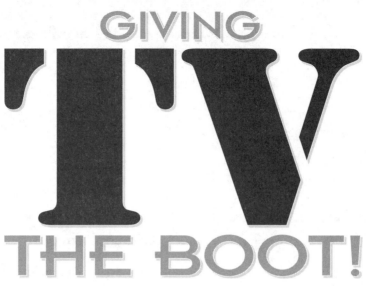

Set Your Purpose

What happens to kids who decide to give up TV? Read this article to find out.

The Weiskopfs

Saying "no" to TV isn't new for Ethan and Matthew Weiskopf. Every year, they have a TV-Turnoff week.

"Sometimes I get bored and I miss TV," says Ethan, age 8. "But most of the time, I think it's fun."

Ethan's brother Matthew, age 10, agrees with him. He **discovered** a new hobby, building models, during his first week without TV. "When kids turn off the TV, they get to use other **abilities**," says Matthew.

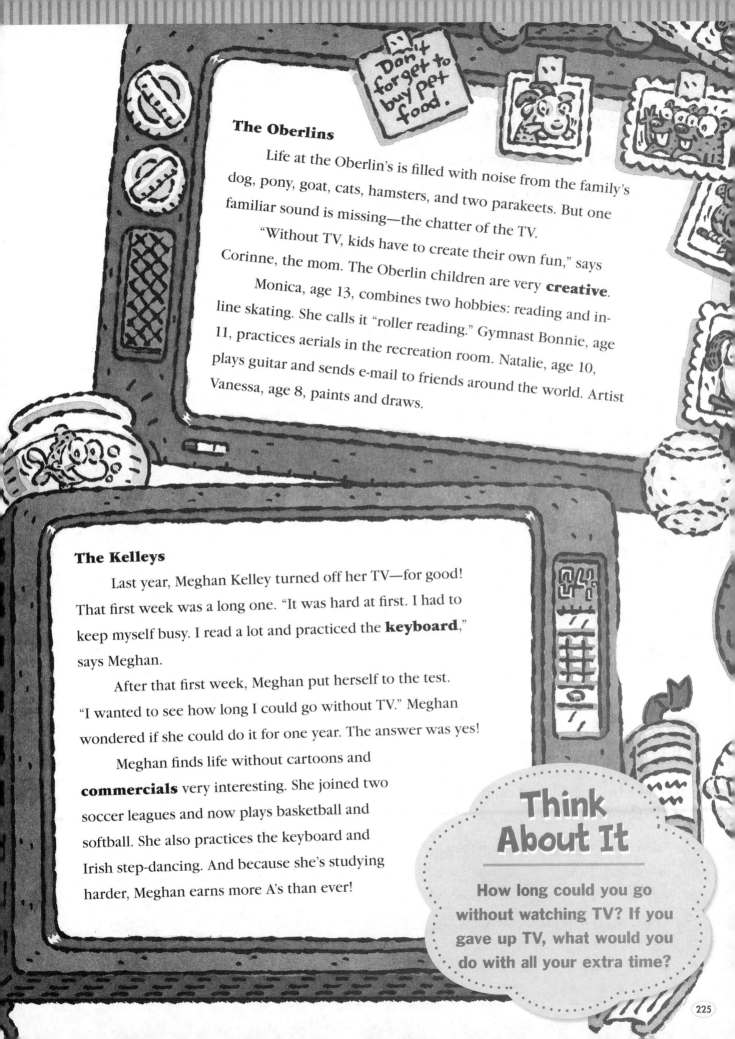

The Oberlins

Life at the Oberlin's is filled with noise from the family's dog, pony, goat, cats, hamsters, and two parakeets. But one familiar sound is missing—the chatter of the TV.

"Without TV, kids have to create their own fun," says Corinne, the mom. The Oberlin children are very **creative**. Monica, age 13, combines two hobbies: reading and in-line skating. She calls it "roller reading." Gymnast Bonnie, age 11, practices aerials in the recreation room. Natalie, age 10, plays guitar and sends e-mail to friends around the world. Artist Vanessa, age 8, paints and draws.

The Kelleys

Last year, Meghan Kelley turned off her TV—for good! That first week was a long one. "It was hard at first. I had to keep myself busy. I read a lot and practiced the **keyboard**," says Meghan.

After that first week, Meghan put herself to the test. "I wanted to see how long I could go without TV." Meghan wondered if she could do it for one year. The answer was yes!

Meghan finds life without cartoons and **commercials** very interesting. She joined two soccer leagues and now plays basketball and softball. She also practices the keyboard and Irish step-dancing. And because she's studying harder, Meghan earns more A's than ever!

Think About It

How long could you go without watching TV? If you gave up TV, what would you do with all your extra time?

Don't forget to buy pet food.

Name _____ Date _____

Check Your Understanding

Fill in the letter with the best answer for each question.

1. Now that the Oberlins have turned off their TV, how have their lives changed?

Ⓐ They are cranky and bored all the time.

Ⓑ They are far more creative and active.

Ⓒ They are mean and unkind to each other.

Ⓓ They have become lazy and stupid.

2. During Matthew Weiskopf's first week without TV, he discovered

Ⓐ that he missed TV a lot.

Ⓑ a new hobby, building models.

Ⓒ an old friend named Ethan.

Ⓓ that he wasn't good at anything but watching TV.

3. How have Meghan Kelley's grades changed since she gave up TV?

Ⓐ They have improved.

Ⓑ They have declined.

Ⓒ They have stayed the same.

Ⓓ They have gone up and down.

4. Most American kids watch TV for

Ⓐ less than two hours a day.

Ⓑ more than four hours a day.

Ⓒ more than three hours a day.

Ⓓ two weeks every year.

5. How hard was it for Meghan Kelley to give up TV?

Ⓐ easy as can be

Ⓑ very hard

Ⓒ easy at first, but then it was harder

Ⓓ hard at first, but then it was easier

Vocabulary

Find each vocabulary word in the selection. The words and sentences around it will help you figure out its meaning.

Fill in the letter with the best definition of the underlined word.

1. Matthew <u>discovered</u> a new hobby.

Ⓐ learned about   Ⓒ pretended

Ⓑ fought   Ⓓ jumped up

2. Without TV, kids get to use other <u>abilities</u>.

Ⓐ important objects   Ⓒ friends

Ⓑ skills or talents   Ⓓ decisions

3. The Oberlin children are very <u>creative</u>.

Ⓐ able to make things

Ⓑ difficult to understand

Ⓒ wild and crazy

Ⓓ noisy and loud

4. Meghan read a lot and practiced the <u>keyboard</u>.

Ⓐ math problem

Ⓑ set of scientific experiments

Ⓒ electric piano

Ⓓ set of keys on a computer

5. Meghan likes life without <u>commercials</u>.

Ⓐ store sales   Ⓒ TV shows

Ⓑ TV ads   Ⓓ contents

Name _____ Date _____

Word Work

> **Antonyms** are words that have opposite meanings. For example, *hot* and *cold* are antonyms.

Read each sentence. Fill in the letter of the antonym of the word in dark type.

1. Turn down the TV. It's too **loud!**

    Ⓐ funny   © difficult

    Ⓑ quiet   Ⓓ bright

2. This is a **familiar** poem.

    Ⓐ worried   © unknown

    Ⓑ small   Ⓓ pretty

3. We like to do things **together**.

    Ⓐ apart   © straight

    Ⓑ simple   Ⓓ formal

4. These suitcases are **heavy**.

    Ⓐ little   © frightening

    Ⓑ smart   Ⓓ light

5. Don't do anything **dangerous!**

    Ⓐ safe   © intelligent

    Ⓑ strong   Ⓓ understanding

> A **past-tense verb** is a verb that tells about something that has already happened. Most past-tense verbs are formed by adding **-ed**. If the verb ends in *e*, drop the *e* before adding the suffix *-ed*.

Read the sentences and the verbs below. Write the past tense of the verb that best completes each sentence.

    laugh   plant   jump   decide   play

6. On Sunday, the children _____ to turn off the TV for a week.

7. On Monday, the family told jokes and _____ out loud.

8. On Tuesday, the kids _____ basketball and soccer.

9. On Wednesday, the family _____ a small garden.

10. On Thursday, the kids _____ rope.

Write Now

In "Giving TV the Boot!" you read about kids who turned off the TV. What would happen if you gave up TV? Imagine the possibilities.

My Afternoon Without TV
3:00 p.m. _____
4:00 p.m. _____
6:00 p.m. _____
8:00 p.m. _____

- Plan to write a schedule for an afternoon without TV. Think of all the things you would like to do with your free time. First, copy the chart and jot down some ideas.

- Write out the schedule of your afternoon without TV. Use your chart to help you.

SPORT$: For Fun or Money?

adapted by Patricia Levitt

It's a do-or-die situation. Bases are loaded, there are two outs, and it's the bottom of the ninth. Your team trails by a run. The fans roar as the star hitter strides to the plate. "Come on!" screams a fan. "Show them why you get the big money!"

Moments later, it's all over. The superstar has struck out and is walking off the field. A fan quickly mocks the player. "You lousy bum!" the fan taunts. "When will you start earning the megabucks they're paying you?"

Set Your Purpose

Are high salaries for players ruining professional sports? Read this article to find facts and opinions on the subject.

228

From Poor Heroes to Rich Bums

In most professional sports today, players earn millions of dollars. Fans swing from **adoring** to angry and back again. Americans' love affair with sports has turned into a love-hate relationship. In the past, athletes didn't earn very much money, but we idolized them. Today, athletes get high salaries, but often we're not happy with how they play.

Who has changed, the athletes or the fans? The answer is both. Dollar signs and shifting **expectations** lie at the root of these changes.

The Money Game

In 1976, the average salary for a professional baseball player was $51,500. That average zoomed to more than $2.9 million in 2006! Professional athletes are earning more money than ever before. Does that mean that professional sports are better? Fans say, "No way."

Many sports fans say that team owners and players are ruining the simple pleasure of sports. Owners run teams as businesses. They look only at the bottom line as they buy and sell players and make deals with TV networks. Players are accused of having no **loyalty**. They grasp the biggest offer as soon as they become free agents, which means they are not bound to a team by **contract**.

When it comes to inferior performances, some fans blame new contracts. In the past, most players' contracts ran for one year. If a player wanted to be sure that his contract would be **renewed**, he hustled all season to prove his worth. Today, though, contracts fix salaries for years at a time. Why should a player go all out game after game if he is assured of big money for years?

Great Expectations

Do fans expect too much of players? Some say, "If they're raking in all that cash, they should be working harder and winning more games." Unfortunately, in most sports there has to be both a winner and a loser.

Think About It

What are some facts about salaries in professional sports? What are some opinions?

Name _____ Date _____

Check Your Understanding

Fill in the letter with the best answer for each question.

1. Compared with player salaries 30 years ago, salaries today are

   Ⓐ about the same.   Ⓒ somewhat higher.

   Ⓑ much higher.   Ⓓ somewhat lower.

2. How have fans' attitudes toward players changed?

   Ⓐ Fans swing between admiring players and being angry with them.

   Ⓑ Fans don't expect much from players.

   Ⓒ Fans idolize players.

   Ⓓ Fans think players should earn more money.

3. According to this selection, an important difference between player contracts in the past and today is

   Ⓐ the amount of players' salaries.

   Ⓑ the number of games players must play.

   Ⓒ the number of years salaries are guaranteed for.

   Ⓓ the popularity of a player.

4. Which of the following statements reflects an opinion about team owners?

   Ⓐ Owners sign players to multimillion-dollar contracts.

   Ⓑ Owners make huge deals with TV networks.

   Ⓒ Owners are ruining the pleasure of sports.

   Ⓓ Owners buy and sell players.

5. Fans accuse players of not being faithful to their teams because players

   Ⓐ are all lazy.

   Ⓑ are winning fewer games.

   Ⓒ have guaranteed salaries.

   Ⓓ go to the team that offers the most money.

Vocabulary

Find each vocabulary word in the selection. The words and sentences around it will help you figure out its meaning.

Fill in the letter with the best definition of the underlined word.

1. Fans will swing from <u>adoring</u> to angry.

   Ⓐ disliking strongly   Ⓒ liking very much

   Ⓑ angering   Ⓓ rejecting

2. Maybe the fans' <u>expectations</u> for the players are too high these days.

   Ⓐ interest   Ⓒ love

   Ⓑ feelings   Ⓓ hopes

3. Players are accused of having no <u>loyalty</u>.

   Ⓐ faithfulness to a team

   Ⓑ lottery

   Ⓒ love for money

   Ⓓ patience for losing

4. The player's <u>contract</u> ran for one year.

   Ⓐ popularity

   Ⓑ legal agreement to work for someone

   Ⓒ illness

   Ⓓ good behavior

5. To be sure that his contract is <u>renewed</u>, a player hustled all season.

   Ⓐ moved to another team   Ⓒ torn apart

   Ⓑ signed again   Ⓓ canceled

Name _____ Date _____

Word Work

Many English words have Greek or Latin **roots**. Understanding the meaning of the roots can help us understand the meaning of the English word. Here are two common roots:

spect	to look or watch
tract	to draw, to pull

Read each word. Write the letter of the matching definition.

___ **1.** spectator

___ **2.** contract

___ **3.** attract

___ **4.** respect

___ **5.** spectacular

A. to look at with high regard

B. someone who watches an event

C. remarkable or dramatic to look at

D. a work agreement drawn up between a worker and an employer

E. to draw or pull toward itself

Read each definition. Add the root word *spect* or *tract* to complete the word.

6. to look at something carefully   in_____

7. a vehicle used to pull things   _____or

8. a remarkable and dramatic sight   _____acle

9. to draw the mind away from something   dis_____

10. to look at with mistrust   su_____

Write Now

This chart shows facts and opinions about professional athletes from "Sports: For Fun or Money?"

Facts	Opinions
have million-dollar salaries	should work harder and win more games
have contracts for many years	have no loyalty to teams or fans

- Plan to write a brief letter to an editor of a newspaper expressing your opinion of the state of professional sports today. First, brainstorm some ideas by making a chart like the one shown.

- Write your letter. Begin by stating your position. Support your opinions with facts. Conclude your letter by restating your position.

The Water Festival

by Paul Mores

Up go 50 oars! Down come 50 oars! Fifty rowers give a powerful **thrust**. The boat **surges** forward as the race begins! Thousands of people cheer their favorite boats.

It is early November. More than 1,000 competitors from all over Cambodia have gathered at the nation's capital, Phnom Penh (puh-NOM-pen). Today is the first day of the annual Water Festival! For three days, hundreds of colorful boats will race along the Tonle Sap River.

Backward-Flowing River

The Water Festival celebrates an amazing natural event. Normally, the Tonle Sap River flows from Tonle Sap Lake into the Mekong River. Each summer, though, the monsoon rains come. For months, rain pours down each day. The Mekong River fills with raging waters. The Mekong's powerful floodwaters push the Tonle Sap River backward! Instead of flowing into the Mekong, it flows into the lake! Then,

Set Your Purpose

What unusual event do people celebrate in Cambodia? Read this newspaper article to find out.

this lake—the largest in Southeast Asia— becomes even larger. The floodwaters **expand** the lake to many times its normal size.

In the fall, the rains lessen. The dry season begins. The water level goes down. Then the Tonle Sap River reverses its direction. Once again, it flows from the lake into the Mekong River. Tonle Sap Lake shrinks to its normal size.

Time to Celebrate

The Water Festival celebrates the reversal of the river's life-giving waters.

Exciting boat races are the main events of this unusual festival. The boats are named after different farming groups and temples. On the last night, fireworks light up the skies over Phnom Penh. This signals the festival's end. Then boats hung with lighted lanterns float down the river. To watchers on the shore, the river looks like a moving stream of light.

Life-Giving Waters

Each fall, the **receding** floodwaters leave behind mineral-rich soil. Farmers depend on this soil to **nourish** their crops. Where the flooded lake's waters once spread, rice and vegetables will grow. This is also the time when the fishing season begins.

Every year, the entire cycle repeats. In the summer, the rains fall and the Tonle Sap Lake floods. In the fall, the water recedes and the Tonle Sap River reverses its direction. And once again, the Water Festival celebrates the event with boat races.

Why do Cambodians celebrate the reversal of the Tonle Sap River?

Name _____ Date _____

Check Your Understanding

Fill in the letter with the best answer for each question.

1. How is the Tonle Sap River different during the rainy season?
   - Ⓐ It flows directly into the ocean.
   - Ⓑ It flows backward into the Tonle Sap Lake.
   - Ⓒ It flows into the Mekong River.
   - Ⓓ It flows much more slowly.

2. How is Tonle Sap Lake the same during both the rainy and the dry seasons?
   - Ⓐ It increases in size many times.
   - Ⓑ It is the largest lake in Southeast Asia.
   - Ⓒ It shrinks in size.
   - Ⓓ It provides mineral-rich soil.

3. How is the Tonle Sap River like other rivers?
   - Ⓐ It flows in different directions in different seasons.
   - Ⓑ Boat races are held on it in the fall.
   - Ⓒ It flows into another body of water, such as an ocean, lake, or another river.
   - Ⓓ It is the longest river in Southeast Asia.

4. The river's backward flow during summer is caused by the
   - Ⓐ need for water at the Mekong River.
   - Ⓑ increased size of Tonle Sap Lake.
   - Ⓒ start of the dry season.
   - Ⓓ change in the amount of rainfall.

5. What does the Water Festival celebrate?
   - Ⓐ the growing of rice and vegetables
   - Ⓑ the beginning of the tourist season
   - Ⓒ the Tonle Sap River's change of direction
   - Ⓓ boat races and fireworks

Vocabulary

> Find each vocabulary word in the selection. The words and sentences around it will help you figure out its meaning.

Fill in the letter with the best definition of the underlined word.

1. Fifty rowers give a powerful <u>thrust</u> to move the boats forward.
   - Ⓐ loud shout
   - Ⓑ splash
   - Ⓒ sudden, hard push
   - Ⓓ blow with a heavy object

2. Each boat <u>surges</u> forward as the race begins.
   - Ⓐ rushes with force
   - Ⓑ sings
   - Ⓒ celebrates
   - Ⓓ sinks

3. The floodwaters <u>expand</u> the lake to many times its normal size.
   - Ⓐ blow apart
   - Ⓑ make larger
   - Ⓒ make smaller
   - Ⓓ upset

4. The <u>receding</u> floodwaters leave behind mineral-rich soil.
   - Ⓐ powerful
   - Ⓑ gradually moving back
   - Ⓒ deep
   - Ⓓ unusual

5. The soil is rich enough to <u>nourish</u> their crops.
   - Ⓐ feed
   - Ⓑ destroy
   - Ⓒ water
   - Ⓓ dry out

Name _____   Date _____

Word Work

A **prefix** comes at the beginning of a word and changes the meaning of the word. Knowing the meaning of a prefix helps you figure out the meaning of the whole word. The prefix **re-** means "again." The prefix **un-** means "not."

reopen	to open again
unlike	not like

Fill in the letter of the best definition of the word in dark type.

1. rewrite
- Ⓐ to write first
- Ⓑ to write again
- Ⓒ to write back
- Ⓓ to write before

2. unusual
- Ⓐ as usual
- Ⓑ very usual
- Ⓒ not usual
- Ⓓ fairly usual

3. unaware
- Ⓐ highly aware
- Ⓑ aware again
- Ⓒ becoming aware
- Ⓓ not aware

4. reassign
- Ⓐ to make a sign
- Ⓑ to assign
- Ⓒ to assign again
- Ⓓ not to turn

5. unbeaten
- Ⓐ badly beaten
- Ⓑ beaten again
- Ⓒ not beaten
- Ⓓ beaten back

A **suffix** is an ending that changes the meaning of a base word. Knowing the meaning of a suffix helps you figure out the meaning of the whole word. The suffix **-al** means "having to do with." The suffix **-en** means "to cause to be."

magic**al**	having to do with magic
deep**en**	to cause to be deep

Each word on the left contains a base word and a suffix. Complete the definition by writing the correct form of the base word.

6. musical   having to do with _____

7. brighten   to cause to be _____

8. lessen   to cause to be _____

9. regional   having to do with a _____

10. frighten   to cause _____

Write Now

In "The Water Festival," you learned about a special seasonal celebration in Cambodia. Some information about the festival is recorded on the chart.

- Plan to write a news story about the Cambodian Water Festival. First, copy the chart at right. Fill in the missing information.

- Write a headline for your news story and the lead paragraph of the story. The headline should grab your reader's attention. The beginning paragraph should answer *Who? What? Where? When? Why?*

Who?	_____
What?	_____
Where?	Cambodia
When?	in November
Why?	celebrates reversal of Tonle Sap River

Cartoons Come to Life

by Adrienne Hathoway

Set Your Purpose

How have cartoons changed? Read the article to find out about traditional and new cartooning techniques.

In the movie *Toy Story*, a group of toys comes to life. In a TV commercial, a car races down the highway. The car is going so fast that it flies into the air. Suddenly, the car has stripes and claws. It has turned into a tiger! How do all these things happen? The answer is in the fascinating world of computer animation.

Animation has been around for a long time. You may remember Mickey Mouse and Bugs Bunny. These cartoon characters were created in a procedure called cel animation.

Cel-animation cartoons are drawn on clear sheets of plastic. To make them move, the artist draws a **series** of pictures. The artist makes each picture slightly different from the one before. Then, the artist shows the pictures at an **accelerated** pace. This process makes the cartoons seem to move. To make longer films, like *Bambi* or *Snow White*, artists need to draw thousands of cels. It is very tedious work.

A newer technique uses computers to make cartoons seem alive. It is different from cel animation in many ways. One of the most **significant** changes is very simple. If you look closely, you'll notice that cel animation cartoons look flat. You can see them move, but they don't look real. The images are two-dimensional—they have height and width, but they have no depth.

Computers enable animators to create lifelike, three-dimensional, or 3-D, images. First, the animator or artist records the shape of an object, animal, or person from all sides. Once recorded in the computer, the 3-D image can be **rotated**, moved, and twisted. The artist can add and change details. The image is transformed into a cartoon character with its own personality and flair. Cartoon artists have discovered a **sensational** new tool. Cartooning will never be the same.

Think About It

How have computers changed cartooning techniques?

Name _____   Date _____

Check Your Understanding

Fill in the letter with the best answer for each question.

1. What is one main difference between the two kinds of animation?

   Ⓐ Cel animation is more interesting to watch.

   Ⓑ Cel-animation images are two-dimensional, while computer-animation images are three-dimensional.

   Ⓒ Movies with cel animation are longer.

   Ⓓ Both forms of animation are difficult to create.

2. Computer and cel animation are alike because

   Ⓐ both are used only in movies.

   Ⓑ both are done on a computer.

   Ⓒ both make images that move and seem to come to life.

   Ⓓ both are easy to do.

3. Which of the following statements is true?

   Ⓐ Cel-animation images are big, but computer-animation images are small.

   Ⓑ Computer animators record the shape of objects from all sides.

   Ⓒ Cel animation is only in black and white, but computer animation is in color.

   Ⓓ Cel animation is new, and computer animation is old.

4. Which of the sentences below states a fact?

   Ⓐ Computer animation is great art.

   Ⓑ Cartoons are only for kids.

   Ⓒ Animation has been around for a long time.

   Ⓓ New cartoons are terrific pictures of real people.

5. Which sentence is the best description of computer animation?

   Ⓐ Cel-animation cartoons look flat.

   Ⓑ Cartoon artists have discovered a terrific new tool.

   Ⓒ With computer animation, an artist can draw two-dimensional images.

   Ⓓ Computer animation makes it possible to create lifelike images.

Vocabulary

> Find each vocabulary word in the selection. The words and sentences around it will help you figure out its meaning.

Fill in the letter with the best definition of the underlined word.

1. The artist draws a <u>series</u> of pictures.

   Ⓐ related group   Ⓒ unrelated group

   Ⓑ baseball field   Ⓓ water tank

2. Pictures are shown at an <u>accelerated</u> pace.

   Ⓐ difficult   Ⓒ slow

   Ⓑ easy   Ⓓ speeded-up

3. One <u>significant</u> change is the use of computers.

   Ⓐ small   Ⓒ important

   Ⓑ simple   Ⓓ enjoyable

4. The 3-D image can be <u>rotated</u>, moved, and twisted.

   Ⓐ sold   Ⓒ bought

   Ⓑ turned   Ⓓ hidden

5. Cartoon artists have discovered a <u>sensational</u> new tool.

   Ⓐ terrific   Ⓒ expensive

   Ⓑ soft   Ⓓ dangerous

Name _____ Date _____

Word Work

> The letter combinations **sh**, **ch**, and **th** each stand for a special sound that is different from the sounds of the two letters pronounced separately.
>
> <u>fi**sh**</u>   <u>**ch**ee**s**e</u>   <u>ma**th**</u>

Read the definitions. Complete the word by adding the letters sh, ch, or th.

1. a board game with red and black pieces   ____eckers

2. how wide something is   wid____

3. the outline of something   ____ape

4. ground to walk on   pa____

5. how deep something is   dep____

> A **suffix** is a word part that comes at the end of a base word. Adding the suffix **-ion** to the end of a base word usually turns a verb into a noun.
>
> **direct**   **direction**
>
> Sometimes the final *e* is dropped before adding the suffix *-ion*.
>
> **participate**   **participation**

Add the suffix *-ion* to the base word in dark type to complete each sentence.

6. Computers are a significant **invent**____.

7. A computer can be an expensive **possess**____.

8. Your computer drawings are an **express**____ of how you see things.

9. Your drawings can come alive with computer **animate**____.

10. A computer can be your **connect**____ to people around the world.

Write Now

Look at the Venn diagram. It shows some of the ways computer animation and cel animation are alike and different.

- Plan to write a conversation between two different kinds of cartoonists. First, go back to the selection and add details to the Venn diagram at right.

- Write the conversation. Use your Venn diagram to help you figure out what each cartoonist would say.

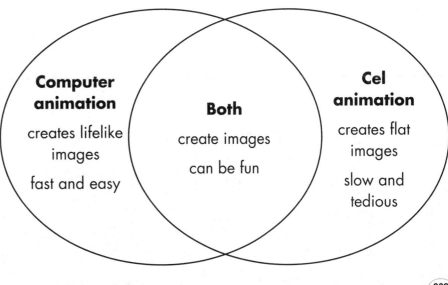

Computer animation
creates lifelike images
fast and easy

Both
create images
can be fun

Cel animation
creates flat images
slow and tedious

Foods With a Difference

by Shelley Francis

Sugar-free beets that still taste sweet, tastier tomatoes, and brighter-colored fruits and vegetables that stay ripe longer are all foods that are being grown now. How can they carry **traits**, such as being tastier, brighter, and riper? They are genetically engineered.

Genetic engineering is like making a change in a recipe. For example, when you make brownies, you mix together all of the usual **ingredients**. If you add an

Set Your Purpose

What happens to your food before it reaches your table? Read this article to find out what's new in the farming business.

extra ingredient, like salt, the brownies will taste differently.

Genes are ingredients in the recipe for life. They carry the traits of living things. Your genes dictate what color hair and eyes you'll have, how tall you'll be, as well as many other traits. Genes carry traits for plants, too. By adding genes to a plant, you can sometimes create new traits. For example, adding a certain gene to a potato plant can make the potato plant **distasteful** to bugs. This makes some farmers happy because they don't have to use chemicals to keep bugs away from their plants.

It sounds great, but some people are **opposed** to the idea of food that is genetically engineered. Ronnie Cummins, from the Campaign for Food Safety, is against it. He says that one of the major **concerns** is allergies. Supermarkets don't always label foods that are genetically engineered. A customer could unknowingly buy food that has an added gene from another plant that he or she is allergic to. It could be dangerous.

Gary Burton from Monsanto, a seed company that engineers food, disagrees. He says his company tests for allergies. Burton believes that genetic engineering is a valuable tool for making better food. The technology can help farmers use less insecticide and grow healthier crops. Burton thinks there are many advantages.

But Cummins says that we just don't know what will happen in the future if we keep adding genes to foods. We could mistakenly create a monster.

People have different opinions about genetic engineering. One side supports it and thinks it will only help us. The other side is opposed to playing with nature and fears unknown danger. Which side do you think is right?

Think About It

How do you feel about food that is genetically engineered? Do you think the possibilities are exciting or scary?

Name _____ Date _____

Check Your **Understanding**

Fill in the letter with the best answer for each question.

1. In what ways could food that is genetically engineered be a good thing?

Ⓐ It is not labeled in the supermarket.

Ⓑ It could taste different.

Ⓒ It is more expensive.

Ⓓ It requires fewer insecticides.

2. In what ways could food that is genetically engineered be a bad thing?

Ⓐ We don't know what future dangers this new food could create.

Ⓑ Genetic foods will taste bad.

Ⓒ You could end up creating new fruits.

Ⓓ Tomatoes could be too red to eat.

3. In general, who does not support food that is genetically engineered?

Ⓐ people from seed companies

Ⓑ farmers who use engineered seeds to grow healthy crops

Ⓒ people from the Campaign for Food Safety

Ⓓ scientists who create foods that are genetically engineered

4. What do some people believe is a danger of food that is genetically engineered?

Ⓐ People will like eating sugar-free beets.

Ⓑ People may eat food that contains genes from another food that they are allergic to.

Ⓒ Some fruits will stay ripe forever.

Ⓓ Farmers will grow better crops.

5. Which sentence best describes how people feel about genetically engineered food?

Ⓐ Most shoppers don't care about it.

Ⓑ Most farmers oppose it.

Ⓒ Most scientists fully support it.

Ⓓ People have different opinions about it.

Vocabulary

> Find each vocabulary word in the selection. The words and sentences around it will help you figure out its meaning.

Fill in the letter with the best definition of the underlined word.

1. Some foods carry <u>traits</u> such as being tastier, brighter, and riper.

Ⓐ features of something   Ⓒ writing utensils

Ⓑ bumps on a surface   Ⓓ long sticks

2. Genes are the <u>ingredients</u> in the recipe for life.

Ⓐ liquid things   Ⓒ recipes

Ⓑ questions   Ⓓ parts that make up the whole

3. A certain gene can make a potato plant <u>distasteful</u> to bugs.

Ⓐ not appealing   Ⓒ inviting

Ⓑ attractive   Ⓓ look like

4. Some people are <u>opposed</u> to the idea of genetic engineering.

Ⓐ in favor of   Ⓒ against

Ⓑ acted positively   Ⓓ misbehaved

5. Allergies are one of the major <u>concerns</u>.

Ⓐ things that one cares about   Ⓒ things that one can't see

Ⓑ things that aren't good   Ⓓ things that one is against

Name _____   Date _____

Word Work

A **suffix** is a word part that comes at the end of a base word. Knowing the meaning of a suffix helps you figure out the meaning of the whole word. The suffix **-er** means "more." The suffix **-est** means "most."

lighter   more light
lightest   most light

Write a word that fits the definition by adding the suffix -er or -est to the base word.

1. more loud   **loud____**

2. most old   **old____**

3. most great   **great____**

4. more fast   **fast____**

5. most sharp   **sharp____**

Add the suffix -er or -est to the base word in dark type to complete the sentence. Write the new word.

6. Her tomato vines grew **high____** than mine.

7. It is the **red____** tomato I have ever seen.

8. These tomatoes stay ripe the **long____**.

9. Is this tomato **small____** than that one?

10. This is the **bright____** tomato ever.

Write Now

"Foods With a Difference" describes a debate that is going on in the food world. Some people are in favor of food that is genetically engineered, and some people are against it. Both sides have arguments that support their point of view. Look at the chart below.

For	Against
better nutrition	allergies
better crops	unknown dangers
not dangerous	lack of labels in supermarkets

- Plan to write a speech defending one side of an issue. First, think of an issue at school or in your community that has two sides to it. For example, should the school day be one hour longer? Or, should all students wear school uniforms? Make a chart like the one shown. List good arguments for both sides of the issue.

- Choose one point of view and write a speech explaining your opinion. Try to persuade others to agree with you. Use your chart to help you write. Think about how you can answer opposing arguments.

Summarizing

❖ When you read, it's good idea to stop now and then to summarize the important points.

- As you read, ask yourself: **"What is the selection about?"**
- The answer tells you the **topic**. This can be a word, a phrase, or a sentence.
- Ask yourself: **"What are the most important points?"** Restate these in your own words.
- Keep the summary short. Include only a topic sentence and a few important points.

❖ Read this paragraph. Think about the topic and the main points the author is making about the topic. How can you **summarize** the paragraph?

Topic

The first sentence states the **topic**: *huge drawings on Peru's Nazca plain.*

Main Points

These sentences make **important points** about the topic.

Mystery in the Desert

Huge drawings of spiders, birds, fish, and reptiles spread for miles across Peru's remote Nazca plain. Some of the figures are so large they can be recognized only from the air. To make the drawings, surface pebbles were removed to expose the lighter rocks and soil underneath them. The surface material was then piled along both sides of the line. Because it almost never rains in the desert, these mysterious drawings have survived for more than 1,500 years.

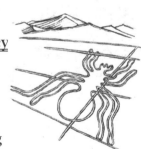

❖ You could **summarize** this paragraph like this:

The Nazca plain in Peru is covered with huge drawings of animals and other figures made more than 1,500 years ago.

Your Turn

❖ Read this selection. Look for the most important points to **summarize**. Make a chart to record the important points, then write your summary.

Easter Island

There are more mysteries per square mile on this barren dot of land than anywhere else on Earth. Nearly 800 statues—called *moai* (mo-AY) by the people who live there—are scattered around the island. Some weigh as much as 80 tons and stand 65 feet high. All have a powerful, forbidding appearance. At some point in the 18th century, nearly all the statues were knocked off their pedestals.

The walls of a volcanic crater in the middle of the island contain about 400 statues in various stages of completion. They are embedded in the stone where they were carved.

Who made these statues thousands of years ago? What became of these people? Why did they make them, and why did they stop? Why were the statues overturned? These questions about the mystery of Easter Island will probably never be answered.

PRESIDENTIAL PETS & KIDS

adapted by Frank Bean

Set Your Purpose

The White House is a stately place, but it has been home to many pets and children. Read this article to learn more!

The White House is usually a serious place. Leaders of other countries bring important business to the President. Senators give and receive advice. **Formal** tour guides lead visitors through rooms and hallways.

However, some presidential pets have turned the White House into a wild and crazy place! President George W. Bush's dogs, Barney and Miss Beazly, and his cat, India, are fairly ordinary pets. But President Rutherford B. Hayes had a goat and a canary among his 15 animals. Martin Van Buren owned tigers. James Buchanan kept elephants and eagles.

Children have also made the President's home a lively place. Tad Lincoln once drove goats through the East Room while his mother was giving a tour. Another time, he forced visitors to shop at a **refreshment** stand he had set up. One Thanksgiving, he convinced his dad to save the life of the turkey they were planning to **devour**.

President Theodore Roosevelt loved animals, and so did his six children. They moved into the White House in 1901. Soon they were joined by 11 kinds of animals, including a badger, a bear, raccoons, and a rat. The Roosevelt kids were also known for bicycling, skating, walking on stilts, and playing hide-and-seek in the White House halls and closets.

Compared to Theodore Roosevelt's White House, the first presidential home was quiet! George Washington had only five dogs. John Quincy Adams was more **daring**; he had an alligator. Calvin Coolidge had the most unusual pet of all: a two-headed rattlesnake. The two-headed snake could keep an eye on the other White House pets. One head could watch President Coolidge's antelope, while the other could spy on his pet emu.

Think About It

During the time of which president would you have wanted to visit the White House? Why?

Name _____ **Date** _____

Check Your Understanding

Fill in the letter with the best answer for each question.

1. Choose the best summary of the selection.

  Ⓐ Senators meet with the President.

  Ⓑ The White House has been a home for some wild pets and children.

  Ⓒ Children liven up the White House.

  Ⓓ Lincoln's White House was noisy.

2. Which statement best summarizes the description of Theodore Roosevelt's White House?

  Ⓐ It was full of animals and wild kids.

  Ⓑ It was a formal place where senators met.

  Ⓒ It had no animals.

  Ⓓ It was quiet.

3. Which detail supports the idea that children have made the White House a lively place?

  Ⓐ Martin Van Buren owned tigers.

  Ⓑ Theodore Roosevelt had six children.

  Ⓒ Calvin Coolidge had a very unusual pet.

  Ⓓ Lincoln's son once drove goats through the East Room.

4. Which sentence is an opinion?

  Ⓐ George Washington had dogs for pets.

  Ⓑ The strangest pet was a two-headed snake.

  Ⓒ Theodore Roosevelt had six children.

  Ⓓ Tad Lincoln once saved a turkey.

5. In which book might you find this selection?

  Ⓐ Families in the White House

  Ⓑ George Washington: First President

  Ⓒ Unusual Pets

  Ⓓ Bringing Up Polite Children

Vocabulary

> Find each vocabulary word in the selection. The words and sentences around it will help you figure out its meaning.

Fill in the letter with the best definition of the underlined word.

1. <u>Formal</u> tour guides lead visitors through rooms and hallways.

  Ⓐ proper and official   Ⓒ silly and funny

  Ⓑ old and well-paid   Ⓓ informal and casual

2. Tad Lincoln didn't want to <u>devour</u> the turkey.

  Ⓐ sell   Ⓒ eat

  Ⓑ play with   Ⓓ make angry

3. Tad Lincoln once set up a <u>refreshment</u> stand for White House visitors.

  Ⓐ place for putting hats

  Ⓑ food or drink

  Ⓒ place for playing games

  Ⓓ plants and flowers

4. <u>Compared</u> to Roosevelt's White House, Washington's home was quiet!

  Ⓐ according to   Ⓒ because of

  Ⓑ judged against   Ⓓ instead of

5. Adams was <u>daring</u>. He had an alligator!

  Ⓐ forgetful   Ⓒ adventurous

  Ⓑ careful   Ⓓ quiet

Name _____ Date _____

Word Work

> **Antonyms** are words that have opposite meanings. For example, *lively* and *dull* are antonyms.

Read each sentence. Fill in the letter of the antonym of the word in dark type.

1. Tour guides try to keep visitors **happy**.
- Ⓐ helpful
- Ⓒ sad
- Ⓑ busy
- Ⓓ awake

2. A two-headed snake is an **interesting** pet.
- Ⓐ fun
- Ⓒ beautiful
- Ⓑ boring
- Ⓓ silly

3. Theodore Roosevelt had **many** pets.
- Ⓐ wild
- Ⓒ large
- Ⓑ several
- Ⓓ few

4. Young Tad Lincoln **hated** eating turkey.
- Ⓐ loved
- Ⓒ forgot
- Ⓑ disliked
- Ⓓ mentioned

5. The first presidential home was **quiet**.
- Ⓐ noisy
- Ⓒ dull
- Ⓑ funny
- Ⓓ small

> A **noun** names a person, place, or thing. A **plural noun** names more than one person, place, or thing. To make the plural of most nouns, add **-s**. Add **-es** if the noun ends with s, ss, x, sh, ch, or tch.
>
> **pet** → **pets**   **leash** → **leashes**
>
> If a noun ends in *y*, we usually change the *y* to *i* and add *-es*.
>
> **bunny** → **bunnies**

Read each sentence. Write the correct plural form of the word in dark type.

6. country The leaders of other _____ went to the White House.

7. fox Maybe our next president will have several _____!

8. tiger It would be strange to see _____ in the White House.

9. guide The White House tour _____ have a great job.

10. business The heads of several _____ visited the president.

Write Now

Read this list that describes the different animals that have lived in the President's home. If your father or mother were elected president, what pet would you like to bring to the White House?

- Plan to write a letter to your parents telling them what pet you would like to bring to the White House. First, make a list of all the animals you would like to add to the "Presidential Zoo." Then choose one pet that you would like best.

- Write your letter. Explain to your parents why you would like that special pet.

Some of the Animals That Have Lived in the White House	
cats	dogs
goat	canary
tigers	elephants
eagles	alligator
rattlesnake	antelope
emu	

History of MARBLES

by Pat Cusick

Set Your Purpose

Read this article to learn about a common, everyday game that has a long history.

Let's play a game of marbles! Get a bag of those little colored balls. They come in an **assortment** of sizes and colors. They may be striped or speckled, cloudy or clear. They are made of clay, glass, or plastic. A bag of marbles can glitter like a bag of **jewels**!

You can play marbles almost anywhere. Set up a game in a driveway. Play a game in your backyard. All you need is your marbles and maybe a friend.

The object of the game is to "shoot" your marble at another marble. To shoot, place a marble between your index finger and your

Think About It

Why do you think the game of marbles has been played for so many years?

thumbnail. A flick of your thumb will **propel** the marble forward. If you hit another marble, you will send it flying!

Here's how to play a game called Ringer. Set up a large circle on smooth ground. Inside the circle, make an "X" shape with 13 marbles. This is your **target**. Each player "knuckles down" at the circle's edge and shoots a marble at the target. To knuckle down, place one knuckle of your shooting hand on the ground as you shoot your marble. The first player to knock seven target marbles out of the circle wins the game.

People have enjoyed playing marbles for centuries. Marbles made of stone and clay have been found in the tombs of the Egyptian pharaohs. The game spread from Egypt to Rome. Artworks from ancient Rome show children playing marbles. The Romans brought the game to England. The English brought it to America. George Washington and Thomas Jefferson played marbles. Abraham Lincoln was an **expert** player.

Think about the game of marbles. It goes back to the earliest times. It has been played in most parts of the world. A game with such an impressive history deserves to be kept alive! So keep those marbles rolling. Play a game of marbles today!

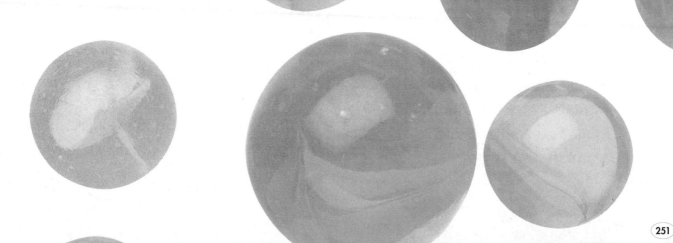

Name _____   Date _____

Check Your Understanding

Fill in the letter with the best answer for each question.

1. Which sentence best summarizes the history of marbles?
   - Ⓐ Playing marbles is a fun and easy game that's been around for a long time.
   - Ⓑ Marbles have been found buried in the tombs of the Egyptian pharaohs.
   - Ⓒ In colonial America, George Washington played marbles.
   - Ⓓ Marbles have been played in Egypt, ancient Rome, and England.

2. Which sentence best summarizes the way to play Ringer?
   - Ⓐ Place a group of marbles in a big circle.
   - Ⓑ Shoot at the marbles in the center and try to knock them outside the circle.
   - Ⓒ "Knuckle down" on the edge of the circle to shoot.
   - Ⓓ Play this game of marbles against one or more persons.

3. How do you shoot a marble?
   - Ⓐ You use a stick.
   - Ⓑ You use your thumb.
   - Ⓒ You throw your marble toward the center.
   - Ⓓ You kick your marble with your foot.

4. You can play marbles almost anywhere because
   - Ⓐ you only need a smooth surface and a bag of marbles.
   - Ⓑ marbles are free.
   - Ⓒ everyone knows how to play marbles.
   - Ⓓ you don't need to keep score.

5. Where was the earliest evidence of marble playing found?
   - Ⓐ in George Washington's journal
   - Ⓑ in ancient Roman artwork
   - Ⓒ among treasures buried in Egyptian pyramids
   - Ⓓ in photos of Abraham Lincoln

Vocabulary

Find each vocabulary word in the selection. The words and sentences around it will help you figure out its meaning.

Fill in the letter with the best definition of the underlined word.

1. Marbles come in an <u>assortment</u> of sizes and colors.
   - Ⓐ large variety
   - Ⓑ small bag
   - Ⓒ box
   - Ⓓ group

2. A bag of marbles can glitter like a bag of <u>jewels</u>.
   - Ⓐ trash
   - Ⓑ gems
   - Ⓒ toys
   - Ⓓ rocks

3. A flick of your thumb will <u>propel</u> the marble forward.
   - Ⓐ move
   - Ⓑ stop
   - Ⓒ blow
   - Ⓓ connect

4. The marbles in the center of the circle are the <u>target</u>.
   - Ⓐ teammates
   - Ⓑ enemies
   - Ⓒ something to avoid
   - Ⓓ something to aim at

5. Abraham Lincoln was an <u>expert</u> player.
   - Ⓐ poor
   - Ⓑ ordinary
   - Ⓒ excellent
   - Ⓓ confused

Name_____ **Date**_____

Word Work

A **suffix** is word part that comes at the end of a base word. Knowing the meaning of a suffix helps you figure out the meaning of the whole word. The suffix **-ment** means "the state of being" or "something that." The suffix **-ive** means "doing or tending to do."

arrang<u>ement</u> something that is arranged

instinct<u>ive</u> doing something by instinct

Write a word that fits the definition by adding the suffix -ment or -ive to the base word.

1. something that amuses **amuse**_____

2. tending to impress **impress**_____

3. something that governs **govern**_____

4. tending to keep secrets **secret**_____

5. the state of being improved **improve**_____

A **noun** names a person, place, or thing. A **plural noun** names more than one person, place, or thing. To make the plural of most nouns, add **-s**. Add **-es** if the noun ends with s, x, sh, or ch.

glass	→	glasses
box	→	boxes
dish	→	dishes
patch	→	patches

Read each sentence. Write the correct plural form of the word in dark type.

6. grass Many different _____ grow on the prairie.

7. wish Kim made three _____ and blew out the candles.

8. fox The red _____ slept in their den in the forest.

9. latch Both _____ on the trunk are broken.

10. bunch I need two _____ of carrots for the salad.

Write Now

You have just read about the long history of the game of marbles. Imagine that you are playing a game of marbles long ago in Egypt, in Rome, or in colonial America.

Where am I?	Who am I playing with?	What happens to make the game exciting?
in ancient Egypt	a group of royal children	a poisonous snake slithers out of the grass

• Plan to write an imaginary diary entry. Pretend that you are playing a marble game in the past. Write a diary entry describing the game. Make it exciting by describing something unusual that happens during the game. Use a chart to plan the details of your story.

• Write your diary entry. Use the chart to help you. Include the place and the date at the top of the entry.

Flying Friends of the
AIR FORCE

by Frank Bear

A falcon soars over the heads of people at an Air Force Academy football game. It climbs high into the sky, and then it dives. During a dive, falcons can reach speeds of 220 mph (354 kph).

Trained falcons are Air Force Academy **mascots**. Their job is to warm up the crowd at games. When fans see the falcons fly into the **stadium**, they cheer.

Set Your Purpose

What kinds of things can trained falcons do? Read this article to find out about this fast and fearless bird.

Falcons in Training

The Air Force Academy trains future members of the Air Force. Academy cadets chose the falcon for their mascot because of its speed and fearlessness. Academy sports teams are called the Falcons to honor their swift, fearless mascot. The cadets who train the birds belong to the academy's Falconry Club. Some of the falcons are hatched and raised at the academy. Even so, falcons are wild birds that follow their **instincts**. Without training, they can be **unruly**. Other birds distract them easily. During games, falcons have been known to chase pigeons in the stands.

It's not easy to train falcons. They are nervous birds. The cadets keep a falcon calm by putting a leather hood on the bird's head. The hood covers the falcon's eyes. It keeps the bird from seeing things that might scare it.

Helping the Air Force

Air Force cadets and their high-flying mascots form a **bond**. They spend a lot of time training together. Cadets and their birds also travel together to Air Force sports events.

Falcons have other talents. When they retire, they are sent to airfields. Their job is to scare other birds away. This keeps those other birds from getting stuck in plane engines.

Think About It

What kinds of things do falcons do for the Air Force?

Name _____ Date _____

Check Your Understanding

Fill in the letter with the best answer for each question.

1. Which statement best summarizes the role of falcons at Air Force Academy games?
   - Ⓐ Falcons fly over the crowd to excite them.
   - Ⓑ Falcons soar high and then dive.
   - Ⓒ Falcons chase other birds away.
   - Ⓓ Falcons chase pigeons in the stands.

2. Which statement best summarizes the role of cadets in training falcons?
   - Ⓐ Cadets put leather hoods on the birds.
   - Ⓑ Cadets form a bond with their birds by spending time with them.
   - Ⓒ Cadets and birds travel together to games.
   - Ⓓ Cadets keep their falcons in a cage.

3. When falcons chase other birds, they show
   - Ⓐ their training as mascots for the Air Force.
   - Ⓑ that they don't like other birds.
   - Ⓒ that they get bored easily.
   - Ⓓ their natural instincts as wild birds.

4. Which of these events happens last?
   - Ⓐ Some of the falcons are hatched and raised at the academy.
   - Ⓑ The falcons are trained by the cadets.
   - Ⓒ Fans cheer as they see the falcons fly into the stadium.
   - Ⓓ A cadet puts a hood on the falcon's head.

5. Which statement is the best summary of the selection?
   - Ⓐ Falcons are fearless and fly at high speeds.
   - Ⓑ Falcons entertain crowds at Air Force Academy sports games.
   - Ⓒ The Air Force Academy trains future members of the Air Force.
   - Ⓓ Academy sports teams are called the Falcons.

Vocabulary

> Find each vocabulary word in the selection. The words and sentences around it will help you figure out its meaning.

Fill in the letter with the best definition of the underlined word.

1. Trained falcons are Air Force Academy team <u>mascots</u>.
   - Ⓐ members of the Air Force
   - Ⓑ animals kept by a sports team
   - Ⓒ officials
   - Ⓓ cadets

2. Air Force cadets and their falcons form a <u>bond</u>.
   - Ⓐ close friendship
   - Ⓑ organization
   - Ⓒ problem
   - Ⓓ parade

3. Wild birds follow their <u>instincts</u>.
   - Ⓐ source of food
   - Ⓑ best friends
   - Ⓒ examples
   - Ⓓ natural ways of doing things

4. Without training, the birds can be <u>unruly</u>.
   - Ⓐ entertaining
   - Ⓑ hard to control
   - Ⓒ very intelligent
   - Ⓓ hungry

5. When the falcons fly into the <u>stadium</u>, fans cheer.
   - Ⓐ room in a ship
   - Ⓑ building where horses are kept
   - Ⓒ place where sports events are held
   - Ⓓ table where people sit

Name _____ Date _____

Word Work

> The **long-*i*** sound can be spelled several different ways. Look at these examples:
>
> ## d**i**v**e** w**i**ld h**igh** fl**y**

Circle the word in each group that has the long-*i* sound.

1. air   will   find   bird
2. wait   sits   flight   stadium
3. sky   train   their   easy
4. first   time   weight   join
5. soil   third   speedy   right

Circle all the words in each sentence that have the long-*i* sound. Then underline the letters that spell the long-*i* sound in each word.

6. A falcon will fly high in the sky.

7. This fine bird will mind its trainer.

8. When it dives, a falcon may frighten you.

9. Bright sunlight may blind a bird for a while.

10. Falcons never tire of their swift flight.

Write Now

This chart shows information from "Flying Friends of the Air Force." What other animals might make good mascots? Brainstorm some ideas by making a chart like the one shown.

Mascot	School	Reason for Choosing
falcon	Air Force Academy	flies at high speeds; fearless

- Plan to write a paragraph suggesting an animal mascot for your school. Choose one animal from your chart.
- Write your paragraph. Present the reasons for your choice of mascot.

FLY ING

MACHINE

adapted by T. Rodriguez

What kind of machine can fly through windows? A tiny one can. To create a **miniature** flying machine, one inventor has turned to the experts—insects! Robert Michelson is **designing** a "micro-flyer" that flies like an insect.

How fast can you flap your arms up and down? If you were a bee, you could do it more than 100 times per second! Quick flapping pushes air down, which pushes the bee up. To move forward, the bee rotates its wings. This pushes the air backward and enables the bee to move forward very rapidly.

Why does Michelson want his micro-flyer to fly like an insect? Why doesn't he make a machine that **soars** like an eagle or a plane? The answer is that in nature, small flying animals work differently than larger flying animals. So Michelson is following nature's lead. In its final version, Michelson's micro-flyer invention will be only six inches wide! Its moving parts will **imitate** the movements of insects. The small wings will flap more than 25 times per second and rotate to move air in different directions. A tiny computer on board will control the micro-flyer's moves.

How could a micro-flyer help people? "The flyer could do jobs that are too dangerous or dull for humans to do," says Michelson. Like what? Well, a micro-flyer might fly indoor spy missions, snapping pictures with a tiny camera. Or it could use an **artificial** nose to sniff out dangerous chemical leaks around factories. Maybe students could come up with some interesting uses of their own, like programming a micro-flyer to visit the school cafeteria to see what's for lunch.

Set Your Purpose

Read this article to find out about a tiny new invention that may have important uses.

Think About It

Name three things that you learned about micro-flyers.

Name _____ **Date** _____

Check Your Understanding

Fill in the letter with the best answer for each question.

1. Which sentence best summarizes the selection?

Ⓐ Small insects flap their wings rapidly so that they can move through the air like an eagle or an airplane.

Ⓑ Robert Michelson believes that flying like a bee is better than walking.

Ⓒ Michelson is designing a micro-flyer that flies like an insect so that it can do tasks that are too dull or too dangerous for humans.

Ⓓ Equipped with a computer on board, a micro-flyer can be made to do dangerous tasks.

2. Which sentence best summarizes the first paragraph?

Ⓐ Keep your windows closed, or something might fly in.

Ⓑ Robert Michelson likes insects better than birds or bats.

Ⓒ Insects fly in a different way than eagles and planes do.

Ⓓ Michelson is building a machine that flies like an insect.

3. Which sentence best summarizes the last paragraph?

Ⓐ Micro-flyers can work at factories.

Ⓑ Micro-flyers can do useful tasks that would be dull or dangerous.

Ⓒ Micro-flyers could help students at school.

Ⓓ Micro-flyers can have cameras.

4. To detect chemical leaks around a factory, a micro-flyer would need to

Ⓐ gather samples for tests.

Ⓑ carry a camera.

Ⓒ be equipped with an artificial nose.

Ⓓ fly backwards.

5. What can a big bird do that a micro-flyer is **not** designed to do?

Ⓐ glide through the air

Ⓑ see small objects

Ⓒ rotate its wings

Ⓓ flap it wings more than 25 times per second

Vocabulary

Find each vocabulary word in the selection. The words and sentences around it will help you figure out its meaning.

Fill in the letter with the best definition of the underlined word.

1. An insect is like a <u>miniature</u> flying machine.

Ⓐ very slow Ⓒ very small
Ⓑ very skilled Ⓓ very large

2. Robert Michelson is <u>designing</u> a micro-flyer that flies like an insect.

Ⓐ watching Ⓒ creating
Ⓑ studying Ⓓ writing

3. Why doesn't he make a machine that <u>soars</u> like an eagle or a plane?

Ⓐ glides through the air Ⓒ looks big
Ⓑ makes a landing Ⓓ flaps rapidly

4. Its moving parts will <u>imitate</u> the movements of insects.

Ⓐ make fun of Ⓒ do better than
Ⓑ copy Ⓓ practice

5. Its <u>artificial</u> nose can sniff out dangerous chemical leaks around factories.

Ⓐ not sharp Ⓒ not difficult
Ⓑ not interesting Ⓓ not real

Name _____ Date _____

Word Work

> **Synonyms** are words that have similar meanings. For example, *big* and *large* are synonyms.

Read the sentences and the words below. Write the word that means almost the same as the word in dark type.

    smell   tiny   dull   invent   photos

1. Michelson is a man who likes to **create** machines. _____

2. Right now he is working on a very **small** machine. _____

3. The machine may do jobs too **uninteresting** for people. _____

4. It may also use an artificial nose to **sniff** out leaks. _____

5. It might even be able to take **pictures** with a tiny camera! _____

> A **suffix** is an ending that changes the meaning of a base word. Knowing the meaning of a suffix helps you figure out the meaning of the whole word. The suffix *-ist* means "a person who." The suffix *-ly* means "in a way."
>
> **art<u>ist</u>**   a person who does art
> **slow<u>ly</u>**   in a slow way

Write a word that fits the definition by adding the suffix *-ist* or *-ly* to the base word.

6. in a rapid way   **rapid____**

7. a person who is in the finals   **final____**

8. a person who plays the guitar   **guitar____**

9. in a different way   **different____**

10. a person who makes cartoons   **cartoon____**

Write Now

"Flying Machine" is about inventing a micro-flyer. It's your turn to be an inventor. What sort of tiny flying machine can you invent? What will it look like? What will it do?

- Plan to design and describe an original micro-flyer. Use a web like the one shown to help you organize your thoughts.

- Describe your new micro-flyer. Tell what it looks like, what it can do, and what it is called. Use your web to help you write. If you wish, add a drawing of your invention and label the parts.

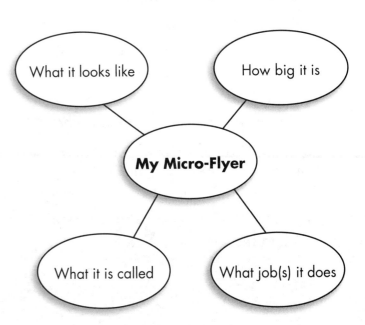

FIGHTING FOR THEIR LIVES

adapted by Nora Samuels

A male Yanomami places white cotton on another Yanomami during preparation for a dance.

Amazon Basin, Brazil — The Yanomami Indians in northern Brazil think it is the end of the world. And for the remaining 9,000 tribe members, it could be. Recently, fires raging in the rain forests endangered the Yanomami's homes, food supply, and health. But the fires are not the only threat to the Yanomami and other tribal people still living in the Amazon rain forest.

Set Your Purpose

People of the Brazilian rain forest are fighting for their lives. Read this article to find out why.

Lumber companies are cutting down trees. **Mining** companies are digging up the land for gold. Gold was discovered on the Yanomami reserve in the 1980s. About 20,000 miners descended on the area. The miners brought diseases that killed many of the native people.

The Yanomami live in the **secluded** rain forests and scattered grasslands along the Brazil-Venezuela border. Their culture is very old; it dates back 3,000 years. The life of the tribe has not changed much in all that time. Some Yanomami had no direct contact with the outside world until last decade.

The Juma people also live in the Amazon rain forests. Less than 100 years ago, there were thousands of Juma living in the forests. Now only six Juma remain. The Juma still eat traditional foods and hunt with bows and arrows. Since they have contact with the outside world, it is common for them to wear modern clothing. Recently, the last young Juma warrior was killed by a jaguar.

"The Yanomami are heading for where the Juma are now," says Pam Kraft, who educates the public about native people. There are 250 million indigenous, or native, people who belong to endangered tribes around the world.

The basic human rights of these people are recognized, but their rights to their land, their **resources**, and their culture are not.

Firefighters from all over the world flew to Brazil in **response** to the fire threatening the homes of the Yanomami. In the jungle, the tribal people held ceremonies, praying for rain to come and quench the fire. The rains came and began to **extinguish** the flames. The threat of the fire is over, but the Yanomami still face many urgent problems. They are still in danger.

"The future of these people is related to our behavior," says Sydney Posseulo, of the Federal Indian Bureau in Brazil. "We have to show more support for their way of life."

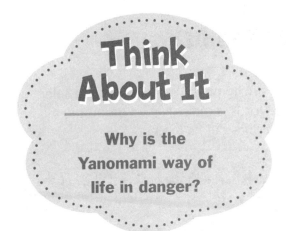

Think About It

Why is the Yanomami way of life in danger?

Name _____   Date _____

Check Your Understanding

Fill in the letter with the best answer for each question.

1. Which is the best summary of this selection?
   - Ⓐ Fires are burning thousands of acres of rain forests.
   - Ⓑ Diseases are killing native people.
   - Ⓒ Native people of the rain forest are being wiped out for several reasons.
   - Ⓓ Valuable rain forests are being destroyed.

2. Why have the Yanomami remained mostly unchanged for 3,000 years?
   - Ⓐ They've had no reason to leave their lands.
   - Ⓑ They live without outside influences.
   - Ⓒ They weren't allowed to leave the forests.
   - Ⓓ They didn't know about modern tools and conveniences.

3. How did the discovery of gold cause the deaths of many Yanomami?
   - Ⓐ They caught diseases from the miners.
   - Ⓑ The miners killed the Yanomami to get the gold.
   - Ⓒ The Yanomami moved off their land.
   - Ⓓ The Yanomami died of starvation.

4. What does "The Yanomami are heading for where the Juma are now" mean?
   - Ⓐ The Yanomami will live near the Juma.
   - Ⓑ The Yanomami tribe will soon be as close to extinction as the Juma tribe is now.
   - Ⓒ The Yanomami tribe is going the wrong way.
   - Ⓓ The Yanomami and Juma travel together.

5. How were the fires in the rain forests finally extinguished?
   - Ⓐ Firefighters flew to Brazil.
   - Ⓑ Tribal people prayed.
   - Ⓒ People held ceremonies.
   - Ⓓ The rains came.

Vocabulary

> Find each vocabulary word in the selection. The words and sentences around it will help you figure out its meaning.

Fill in the letter with the best definition of the underlined word.

1. The Yanomami live in <u>secluded</u> rain forests.
   - Ⓐ hot and humid
   - Ⓑ friendly
   - Ⓒ scenic
   - Ⓓ hidden

2. Many people don't recognize the tribes' rights to the <u>resources</u> of their land.
   - Ⓐ things available to use
   - Ⓑ traditional clothing
   - Ⓒ culture
   - Ⓓ music

3. <u>Mining</u> companies arrived when they heard there was gold in the rain forest.
   - Ⓐ having to do with fires
   - Ⓑ having to do with extinction
   - Ⓒ having to do with digging for minerals or metals
   - Ⓓ having to do with rain forests

4. Firefighters from all over the world flew to Brazil in <u>response</u> to the fire.
   - Ⓐ refusal
   - Ⓑ fear
   - Ⓒ quiet manner
   - Ⓓ reaction or reply

5. The rains came and began to <u>extinguish</u> the fires.
   - Ⓐ spread
   - Ⓑ put out
   - Ⓒ increase
   - Ⓓ avoid

Nonfiction Passages for Struggling Readers: Grades 6–8 • Scholastic Inc.

Name _____ Date _____

Word Work

> **Antonyms** are words that have the opposite meanings. For example, *hot* and *cold* are antonyms.

Read the sentences and the words below. Write the word that means the opposite of the word in dark type.

endangered   ancient   wet   create   future

1. dry   The climate in rain forests is _____ and humid.

2. destroy   It is important to _____ laws to help the tribes.

3. modern   The Yanomami are people of an _____ tribe.

4. past   No one knows what the _____ will hold for the tribe.

5. protected   Many native cultures are _____ and might disappear.

Read the sentences and the words below. Write the word that means the opposite of the word in dark type.

vital   arriving   recognize   scarce   young

6. The miners were not **leaving**. They were _____.

7. We cannot **ignore** the needs of native people. We must _____ them.

8. This is **unnecessary**. It is _____ that we do something.

9. The warrior who was killed was not **old**. He was _____.

10. Gold is not a **common** mineral. It is _____.

Write Now

The slogans below are designed to convince people to help the native tribes you read about in "Fighting for Their Lives."

> **Save the Yanomami from extinction.**
> **The Yanomami people need your help.**
> **Protect our native peoples.**

- Plan to write a poster recommending ways to help save the Yanomami from extinction. Give the poster a catchy slogan.
- Write your poster. For a poster to provide a strong message it should be easy to read, with brief ideas and vivid words. It might help to think of actual posters that you've seen recently.

CRUNCHY CRITTERS

adapted by Jocelyn Piro

It's time for lunch in Tokyo, Japan. Your friend Hiroshi is eating weird-smelling grilled octopus. "Want a bite?" he asks. "No way!" you reply. You watch the squiggly octopus legs disappear into Hiroshi's mouth. Gross!

But is it really? Octopus is good for you and very **nutritious**. Why not eat it?

On the other hand, Hiroshi is like people in many parts of the world. He grew up drinking very little milk or eating cheese. To him, cheese is just spoiled cow's milk, and that's disgusting! Hiroshi would rather eat a bug than your grilled-cheese sandwich.

Bugs on the Menu

Speaking of bugs, did you know there are millions of people who think insects are **delectable**? In parts of South America, fried grasshoppers are a snack food.

Set Your Purpose

Which foods do you think are delicious or disgusting? Read this article to find out how people around the world may agree or disagree.

In Madagascar, an island off Africa, people eat fried crickets. In Asia, they like their crickets grilled. People in the U.S. used to eat crickets, too. Food fashions change.

If you don't want your bugs plain, how about **candied**? Children in South Africa were recently served chocolate-covered termites (bugs that eat wood). It was part of a program about insects at the zoo. Chocolate-covered ants have been around for years. You can find them in some fancy food stores.

Good Grub!

The word "grub" is slang for "food," but most of your friends would probably run for home if you served them grubs or worms. Yet in Australia, the aborigines, who lived there before European people came, think highly of witchety grubs. Witchety grubs are an Australian moth larva. When cooked in ashes, they have an almond **flavor**.

Then there are the mammals. Dogs have been eaten in Asia and in Mexico. The Aztec Indians even had a special **breed** of edible dog. In Peru, South America, guinea pigs can turn up on your dinner plate. And in Thailand, people smack their lips over roasted rat.

What you want to eat depends on where you live. You like the foods you grew up with. So do kids in other countries. And that's food for thought!

Think About It

Do you think there are any foods that everyone would agree are delicious?

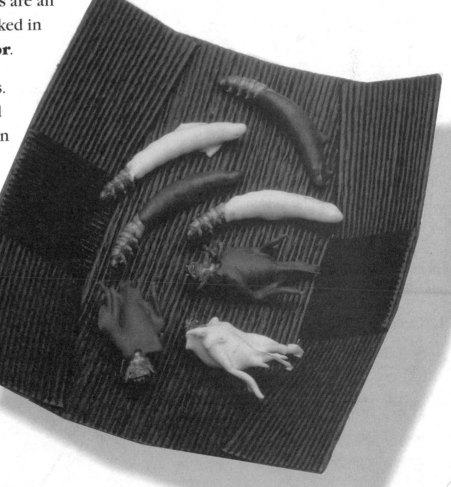

Name _____   Date _____

Check Your Understanding

Fill in the letter with the best answer for each question.

1. What is the best summary of the selection?
   Ⓐ People from other parts of the world have weird taste in food.
   Ⓑ People from different parts of the world enjoy different kinds of food.
   Ⓒ Asians have better taste in food than Americans.
   Ⓓ Eating insects will make you sick.

2. What is the best summary of the section "Bugs on the Menu"?
   Ⓐ If you try a different food, you may like it.
   Ⓑ Some people eat roasted rats.
   Ⓒ Chocolate-covered ants are treats.
   Ⓓ People in many parts of the world eat insects.

3. What is the best summary of the section "Good Grub!"?
   Ⓐ "Grub" is a slang term for food.
   Ⓑ What you like to eat depends on where you live.

   Ⓒ People in Peru eat guinea pigs.
   Ⓓ People in the United States eat cows.

4. What is a witchety grub?
   Ⓐ a slang term for a great meal
   Ⓑ a moth larva that is sometimes eaten in Australia
   Ⓒ a worm that is sometimes eaten in Asia
   Ⓓ a type of toasted almond

5. What is one probable reason why the Japanese like to eat octopus?
   Ⓐ Japan is an island, and it is easy to get seafood.
   Ⓑ Japan is a place where they can't get hamburgers.
   Ⓒ In Japan, they serve octopus at restaurants.
   Ⓓ The Japanese enjoy watching the faces of the Americans when someone eats octopus.

Vocabulary

> Find each vocabulary word in the selection. The words and sentences around it will help you figure out its meaning.

Fill in the letter with the best definition of the underlined word.

1. Octopus is very <u>nutritious</u>.
   Ⓐ sharp tasting   Ⓒ neutral
   Ⓑ hard to find   Ⓓ healthful to eat

2. A zoo recently served <u>candied</u> bugs for children to taste.
   Ⓐ coated in sugar   Ⓒ bad tasting
   Ⓑ lit by candles   Ⓓ canned

3. Millions of people think insects are <u>delectable</u>.
   Ⓐ very tasty   Ⓒ easily annoyed
   Ⓑ weak or feeble person Ⓓ supermarket food

4. When cooked in ashes, witchety grubs have an almond <u>flavor</u>.
   Ⓐ flame   Ⓒ taste
   Ⓑ color   Ⓓ feeling

5. The Aztec Indians had a special breed of <u>edible</u> dog.
   Ⓐ incredible   Ⓒ able to be eaten
   Ⓑ peculiar   Ⓓ gross

Name _____ Date _____

Word Work

> **Antonyms** are words that have opposite meanings. For example, *good* and *bad* are antonyms.

Read the sentences and the words in the box. Write the word that means the opposite of the word in dark type.

ask   disgusting   cooked   fancy   before

1. delicious For some kids, cheese is just spoiled cow's milk, and that's _____.

2. plain You can find chocolate-covered ants in _____ food stores.

3. after You can eat fried grasshoppers for a snack _____ lunch.

4. raw In some parts of Asia, they like their crickets _____.

5. answer If you want to know more about edible bugs, _____ your local zoo.

> A **contraction** is two words joined to make one. One or more letters have been left out. The apostrophe shows where the letters were left out.

Fill in the letter of the contraction that is formed by the underlined words.

6. Hiroshi <u>does not</u> want pizza for lunch.
Ⓐ don't   Ⓒ won't
Ⓑ can't   Ⓓ doesn't

7. <u>He will</u> be happier with a plate of raw fish.
Ⓐ He'll   Ⓒ He's
Ⓑ He'd   Ⓓ Here

8. <u>Who is</u> hungry? It's time for fried crickets.
Ⓐ Whose   Ⓒ Who's
Ⓑ Who'd   Ⓓ Who'll

9. <u>They are</u> going to serve us witchety grubs.
Ⓐ There   Ⓒ Their
Ⓑ They're   Ⓓ They've

10. <u>It has</u> been a long time since I had such delicious boiled worms.
Ⓐ It'd   Ⓒ It's
Ⓑ It'll   Ⓓ Isn't

Write Now

There are lots of unusual foods described in "Crunchy Critters." People in different countries follow some very different recipes when it's time to prepare a meal. Why not write a recipe of your own?

- Plan to write a recipe. It doesn't have to be serious, and it doesn't have to be edible! First, list the ingredients—the things that will go in your recipe. Be sure to tell how much of each ingredient you need. Then, write step-by-step instructions for putting the recipe together. Don't forget to give your recipe a name!

- Write your recipe. Remember it can be edible or inedible, silly or serious. Have fun!

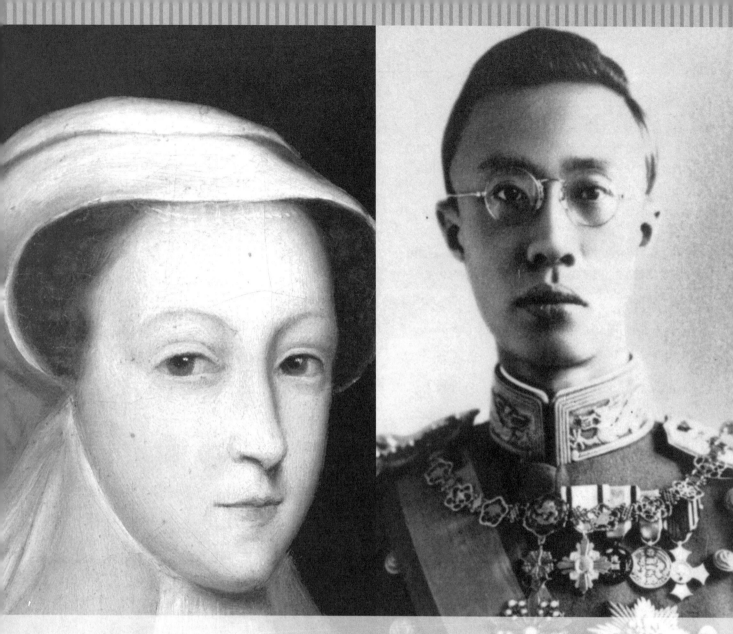

Children Who Ruled

by C. Lee Micklow

Throughout history, there have been many child monarchs. Tutankhamen (too than KAH men) was one of them. He was only 9 years old when he became King of Egypt, in the year 1347 B.C.

The reign of "King Tut," as he is called, wasn't very important. It lasted only nine years because Tut died when he was 18. However, the boy king became a **celebrity** almost 3,300 years after his death.

In 1922, **archaeologist** Howard Carter discovered Tut's tomb. The world gasped at the treasures Carter found. Everything was covered in gold, silver, and jewels. The treasures included Tut's throne, several golden chariots, and a solid gold coffin.

In A.D. 1542, an infant named Mary became Queen of Scotland. She was only six days old! Of course, Mary couldn't actually rule. A series of **surrogates** ran the country for her. At 15, Mary married a French prince. This made her a princess of France as well as Queen of Scotland. Mary's husband died three years later. When Mary returned to Scotland, she was still a teenager.

Mary, Queen of Scots, was not well prepared to rule, and the Scots never accepted her as their queen. In 1586, when she was 44, Mary was imprisoned in a tower and later **decapitated**.

Pu-Yi was born in 1905. He became the last emperor of China when he was 3 years old. Even though he was so young, all the adults had to bow down to him. During his

brief reign, Pu-Yi never once left the royal palace, known as the Forbidden City. In 1912, a revolution **dethroned** Pu-Yi. The boy who once ruled all of China began a hard life.

When he was old enough, he took a job as a gardener. He also spent a short time as a singer. He became known as Henry Pu Yi. From time to time, the new rulers of China imprisoned Henry. He never saw the Forbidden City again. He died at age 62.

The lives of King Tut, Mary, Queen of Scots, and Pu-Yi prove that being a child king, queen, or emperor is not fun and games.

Set Your Purpose

Have you ever dreamed of being a king or queen? Read this article to find out about three children who were heads of state before their tenth birthday.

Think About It

Did Tutankhamen, Mary, and Pu-Yi have the kinds of lives you imagined? What surprised you?

Name _____ Date _____

Check Your **Understanding**

Fill in the letter with the best answer for each question.

1. Which statement best summarizes the article?

Ⓐ Three child rulers died young.

Ⓑ Mary, Queen of Scots, was the youngest person ever to rule.

Ⓒ Three child rulers had short and unimpressive reigns.

Ⓓ King Tut was the most famous child ruler.

2. How would you summarize Pu-Yi's life?

Ⓐ He went from rags to riches.

Ⓑ He went from riches to rags.

Ⓒ He steadily increased in power.

Ⓓ He steadily decreased in power.

3. Another good title for the selection would be

Ⓐ Dreaming of Kings and Queens.

Ⓑ King Tut's Tomb Discovered.

Ⓒ Three Young Monarchs from the Past.

Ⓓ The Last Emperor of China.

4. Why did King Tut become famous in 1922?

Ⓐ Howard Carter wrote a book about him.

Ⓑ Egyptians became interested in their history.

Ⓒ His tomb was discovered.

Ⓓ He was beheaded.

5. The child who became a monarch at the youngest age was

Ⓐ Prince William.

Ⓑ King Tut.

Ⓒ Emperor Pu-Yi.

Ⓓ Mary, Queen of Scots.

Vocabulary

Find each vocabulary word in the selection. The words and sentences around it will help you figure out its meaning.

Fill in the letter with the best definition of the underlined word.

1. The boy king became a <u>celebrity</u> almost 3,300 years after his death.

Ⓐ winner in battle   Ⓒ unknown person

Ⓑ child monarch   Ⓓ famous person

2. A series of <u>surrogates</u> ran the country for Mary.

Ⓐ relatives   Ⓒ soldiers

Ⓑ substitutes   Ⓓ elders

3. In 1922, <u>archaeologist</u> Howard Carter dug up Tut's tomb.

Ⓐ a scientist who studies plants

Ⓑ a scientist who studies child behavior

Ⓒ a scientist who studies ancient objects

Ⓓ a person who reads about kings and queens

4. Mary was imprisoned in a tower and later <u>decapitated</u>.

Ⓐ allowed to pass laws   Ⓒ crowned as queen

Ⓑ beheaded   Ⓓ released

5. In 1912, a revolution <u>dethroned</u> Pu-Yi.

Ⓐ took away his royal chair

Ⓑ allowed him to leave his palace

Ⓒ crowned him emperor

Ⓓ took away his royal powers

Name _____ Date _____

Word Work

> The sound /**ow**/ can be spelled in two ways:
> **ow** as in **t<u>ow</u>er**   **ou** as in **f<u>ou</u>nd**

> **Synonyms** are words that have similar meanings. For example, *last* and *final* are synonyms.

Each sentence below has an incomplete word. Add *ou* or *ow* to complete the word.

1. Many children have ruled **through___t** history.

2. Pu-Yi worked as a gardener and may have pushed a **pl___**.

3. Most child rulers didn't wear their **cr___ns** for long.

4. Queen Mary had a French prince for a **sp___se**.

5. Buried with King Tut were treasures, too many to **c___nt**.

Read the sentences and the words below. Write the word that means almost the same as the word in dark type.

king nation grave jailed gems

6. Carter found many treasures in King Tut's **tomb**. _____

7. Everything was covered in gold, silver, and **jewels**. _____

8. Tutankhamen was a child **monarch**.
_____

9. The new rulers of China **imprisoned** Henry Pu-Yi. _____

10. Several people ran the **country** for the infant Mary, Queen of Scots. _____

Write Now

In the article "Children Who Ruled," you read about three people who became rulers at an early age. How were they different from one another?

Pu-Yi
ruled China
reign began in 1908 at the age of 3

Both
child rulers

Mary, Queen of Scots or King Tut
ruled _____
reign began in _____ at the age of _____

- Plan to write a paragraph comparing and contrasting two of the young rulers in this article. Use a Venn diagram like the one shown to help you organize your ideas.

- Write your paragraph. Use transition words such as *and*, *too*, *but*, and *however* to show how similarities and differences are related.

FRIENDLY ROOMS

by S.A. Beres

Imagine having a bedroom that **interacts** with you. If you're sad, it will **arrange** for some of your friends to come over to cheer you up. If you're happy, it might respond by playing your favorite game with you.

Does it sound like something out of a sci-fi movie? Well, it's really something out of the Georgia Institute of Technology. Irfan Essa works at the computer lab there. He has **developed** a computer

Set Your Purpose

Will a computerized bedroom of the future understand how you are feeling? Read this article to find out.

I am sorry you are sad. I will put on some music.

system that can look at you and recognize your mood. He calls it the "**expression** recognition system." Essa says, "We are trying to get computers to act like a human brain. But the human brain is not like one computer, it is like many working together."

In Essa's system, many computers work together. First, a camera in the bedroom takes a picture of your face. The camera feeds the image to a computer. In the computer's memory, there are pictures showing how the muscles of your face move when you are in different moods. For example, cheek muscles move in one way when you are happy and smiling and in another way when you are nervous and tense. The computer compares your picture to the face-muscle images stored in its memory. It tries to find the best match. That's how it figures out your mood! Then the computer sends messages to other computers in the system. If you look happy, a computer may put on lively music. If you look tired and **discouraged**, a different computer may turn on the TV for you.

How could the "expression recognition system" help us in important ways? Essa thinks that the system can help us create computers that are better teachers. Many people learn new skills through computer programs. "When I teach, I look at people's faces," Essa explains. "If my students look confused, I know they didn't understand. With this technology, a computer can also know if a student is learning."

Today, this new technology can be found only in labs, but Essa predicts we'll see it out of the lab in a few years. So get ready. One day, you might walk into a room that will soon become your best friend.

Think About It

Would you like to have a computerized room like the one described in this selection? Why or why not?

Name _____ Date _____

Check Your Understanding

Fill in the letter with the best answer for each question.

1. Which statement summarizes what is special about the bedroom of the future?

Ⓐ It has a computer and a TV.

Ⓑ It recognizes what mood you're in and tries to make you feel better.

Ⓒ Computers in the bedroom play music.

Ⓓ Computers can make you feel better.

2. Who is Irfan Essa?

Ⓐ a science-fiction character

Ⓑ a man who owns a high-tech bedroom

Ⓒ the inventor of the "expression recognition system"

Ⓓ the author of this selection

3. Can you buy an "expression recognition system" for your bedroom today?

Ⓐ Yes, at the Georgia Institute of Technology.

Ⓑ No, it's just a dream.

Ⓒ Yes, at special computer stores.

Ⓓ No, but you may be able to in a few years.

4. How does the computer know what mood you're in?

Ⓐ It matches a picture of you to some descriptions of moods.

Ⓑ It matches a picture of you to pictures of face muscles in its memory.

Ⓒ It matches a picture of you to pictures of other people in its memory.

Ⓓ It just knows when it looks at you.

5. In which book might you find this selection?

Ⓐ Our High-Tech Future

Ⓑ Building Bedrooms for Active Kids

Ⓒ Computers in the Classroom

Ⓓ Computers Are Not So Smart

Vocabulary

Find each vocabulary word in the selection. The words and sentences around it will help you figure out its meaning.

Fill in the letter with the best definition of the underlined word.

1. Imagine having a bedroom that <u>interacts</u> with you.

Ⓐ interrupts

Ⓑ exchanges messages

Ⓒ stops for an intermission

Ⓓ acts like you

2. If you're sad, it will <u>arrange</u> for your friends to come and cheer you up.

Ⓐ to make happen   Ⓒ to clean

Ⓑ to hang   Ⓓ to make a speech

3. Essa has <u>developed</u> a new computer system.

Ⓐ walked on

Ⓑ closed the lid of something

Ⓒ built on something to create something

Ⓓ taken a picture

4. Essa calls his invention the "<u>expression</u> recognition system."

Ⓐ a book that tells a story

Ⓑ a quick movement

Ⓒ a look on your face that tells a mood

Ⓓ a stack of boxes

5. If you look tired and <u>discouraged</u>, a computer may turn on the TV for you.

Ⓐ brave and strong   Ⓒ dreamy

Ⓑ distant   Ⓓ sad and troubled

Name _____ Date _____

Word Work

A **possessive noun** shows ownership.
To form the possessive of a singular noun,
add an apostrophe and -s to the noun (**'s**).
To form the possessive of a plural noun, just
add an apostrophe after the final s (**s'**).
Add 's to plural nouns that do not end in s.

system	→	system's
muscles	→	muscles'
children	→	children's

Match the word on the left with its correct possessive form on the right.

___**1.** computer   **A.** people's

___**2.** people   **B.** computers'

___**3.** person   **C.** computer's

___**4.** computers   **D.** person's

Read each pair of sentences. Write the correct possessive noun that completes the second sentence.

5. My computer has a memory. It is the _____ memory.

6. But the memory of a human is different. That is a _____ memory.

7. My friends have a printer that I borrow. It is my _____ printer.

8. I read the newspaper my family gets. It is my _____ paper.

9. I like the computer game my sisters have. They are my _____ games.

10. The neighbors loaned the computer to them. It is the _____ computer.

Write Now

How would you like to have a computerized bedroom like the one described in "Friendly Rooms"? Start dreaming and designing!

Special equipment	Work my computers will do for me	How my computers will make my life more fun

• Plan to design and describe your own high-tech bedroom. What special equipment will your bedroom have? What sort of work will your computers do for you? How will they help make your life more fun? Write notes on a chart like the one above.

• Write a description of your high-tech bedroom. If you wish, draw a picture to go with your description. Label details on your drawing.

PEDAL POWER

PEDAL POWER

Set Your Purpose

How are more and more people getting from place to place? Read this article to find out.

adapted by Patricia Levitt

On Monday mornings, city streets are jammed with cars and buses filled with **commuters**. Take a closer look, and you might see plenty of people pedaling their way to work or school. The number of bike commuters has more than tripled over the last two decades. Worldwide, three times more bikes are built than cars.

Why do so many Americans like to ride bikes? Biking is a fun way to get outdoors and to exercise. More people are discovering that on a bike, they can get in shape and get where they need to go at the same time. In fact, nearly five million Americans commute to work on bicycles.

Two major bike-to-work cities are Tucson, Arizona, and San Diego, California. In these areas, warm weather makes year-round biking possible. Surprisingly, rainy Seattle, Washington, has the second-highest rate of bicycle commuters in the country.

Cities are racing to make the ride easier. More bike commuters mean fewer cars. Fewer cars mean less of a need for new roads. Creating bike paths or "Bikes Only" lanes on streets is far less expensive than building roads.

Officials in Portland, Oregon, came up with a unique idea. They wanted to encourage people to bike around town instead of drive. So the city rounded up used bikes—ones that people would have just thrown away. They repaired them and painted them yellow. Then they put the yellow bikes around the city and spread the word that they were free for anyone to use. When borrowers reach their **destination**, they just leave the bike for someone else. People are pedaling the yellow bikes all over Portland. The public bike fleet is growing as more people **donate** old bikes. Will your town be next? About 50 cities have asked Portland how to start their own public pedal-power program!

All of these healthy bikers help create a healthier **environment**. When it comes to planet-friendly modes of **transportation**, you can't beat a bike. Unlike cars, bikes burn no fossil fuels and create no air pollution. In addition, computer-aided design and new technologies have helped create a new breed of bicycles that make riding safer, easier, and a lot more fun.

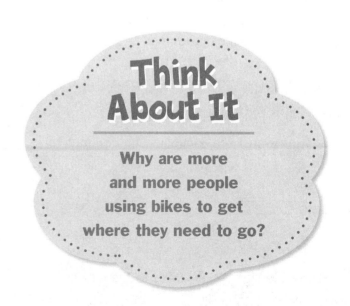

Think About It

Why are more and more people using bikes to get where they need to go?

Name _____   Date _____

Check Your Understanding

Fill in the letter with the best answer for each question.

1. Which statement best summarizes the second paragraph of the selection?
   - Ⓐ Americans have found that bikes are a great way to go places.
   - Ⓑ Nearly five million Americans commute.
   - Ⓒ Biking is a fun way to get outdoors.
   - Ⓓ People can get in shape by riding bikes.

2. Which statement best summarizes Portland's pedal-power program?
   - Ⓐ The city repairs bikes and paints them yellow.
   - Ⓑ People pedal the yellow bikes all over Portland.
   - Ⓒ The public bike fleet is growing.
   - Ⓓ The city repairs old bikes and offers them free for anyone to use.

3. Which statement summarizes the selection?
   - Ⓐ Cars create a lot of air pollution.
   - Ⓑ Biking is becoming popular in many areas.
   - Ⓒ Some cities encourage commuting by bike.
   - Ⓓ Biking is good for the environment.

4. Two effects of increased use of bikes are
   - Ⓐ people get more exercise and help reduce air pollution.
   - Ⓑ cities build fewer roads and more sidewalks.
   - Ⓒ people get exercise and gain weight.
   - Ⓓ new bikes are created and people are safer.

5. The authors of the selection want to
   - Ⓐ sell bikes to people.
   - Ⓑ persuade people that riding bikes is good.
   - Ⓒ build fewer cars and buses.
   - Ⓓ get people to stop walking.

Vocabulary

Find each vocabulary word in the selection. The words and sentences around it will help you figure out its meaning.

Fill in the letter with the best definition of the underlined word.

1. City streets are jammed with <u>commuters</u>.
   - Ⓐ persons with whom you spend time
   - Ⓑ persons involved in a contest
   - Ⓒ people who travel a distance to work or school each day
   - Ⓓ people who share information

2. People <u>donate</u> old bikes to the city.
   - Ⓐ sell for a profit   Ⓒ pay for
   - Ⓑ give as a gift   Ⓓ take off

3. Some people ride bikes to their <u>destination</u>.
   - Ⓐ dry, often sandy area
   - Ⓑ place to where a person is traveling
   - Ⓒ longer way to go
   - Ⓓ piece of equipment

4. Air pollution harms the <u>environment</u>.
   - Ⓐ natural world of the land, sea, and air
   - Ⓑ city with bike paths
   - Ⓒ way into a place
   - Ⓓ pleasure gotten from something

5. Bikes and cars are forms of <u>transportation</u>.
   - Ⓐ process by which plants give off moisture
   - Ⓑ act of giving something
   - Ⓒ means for moving things or people from one place to another
   - Ⓓ change from one place to another

Name _____ Date _____

Word Work

Some words have more than one meaning. You can often figure out the meaning of a word by looking at how the word is used in a sentence. For example, the word *row* can mean "a line" or "to paddle."

Decide if each underlined word has meaning A or B. Fill in the letter of the correct answer.

1. Portland has a public <u>fleet</u> of bikes.

 Ⓐ a number of vehicles that form a group

 Ⓑ fast

2. Cities are <u>racing</u> to make biking easier.

 Ⓐ running fast

 Ⓑ hurrying

3. The yellow bikes are <u>free</u> for anyone to use.

 Ⓐ not costing anything

 Ⓑ let a person or animal go from captivity

4. More bike commuters <u>mean</u> fewer cars.

 Ⓐ to show or indicate

 Ⓑ not kind or not nice

5. Many people in this <u>country</u> ride bikes.

 Ⓐ undeveloped land away from towns and cities

 Ⓑ a place with its own borders and government

6. The <u>program</u> encourages people to use bikes.

 Ⓐ a booklet that gives information about a performance

 Ⓑ a plan for doing something

Decide if each underlined word has meaning A or B. Fill in the letter with the correct answer.

7. People should use locks when they <u>park</u> their bikes in busy areas.

 Ⓐ an area of land used by the public

 Ⓑ to leave a car or other vehicle in a space

8. This bike path goes through a lovely <u>park</u>.

 Ⓐ an area of land used by the public

 Ⓑ to leave a car or other vehicle in a space

9. It is very easy to get in <u>shape</u> by riding a bike.

 Ⓐ the way a thing looks because of its outline

 Ⓑ condition

10. Do you think the <u>shape</u> of a bike's wheel is a circle or an oval?

 Ⓐ the way a thing looks because of its outline

 Ⓑ condition

Write Now

The web shows reasons for riding bikes presented in "Pedal Power."

• Plan to write a speech to persuade officials in your town or city to begin a pedal-power program like the one in Portland, Oregon. First, brainstorm some ideas by making a web like the one shown.

• Write your speech. Begin by stating your purpose. Support this idea with strong reasons from your web. Save your best argument for last.

The Story That Stretched

by Emily Martin

Anyone listening to explorer Louis Hennepin today would say that the fellow needed glasses. How else could he have thought Niagara Falls was 600 feet high when it's actually only about 200? Granted, in 1697 few people knew how to **accurately** measure a huge waterfall. But a 400-foot difference? That's more than bad math!

Hennepin was certainly one to **exaggerate**. He claimed he canoed across what is now Illinois to the Mississippi River. Then he traveled down the Mississippi all the way to the Gulf of Mexico and back again. In the middle of winter! In forty days. That would have been quite a trip done in an unbelievably short time. The Sioux Indians who later captured him probably found his stories pretty amusing.

The Sioux knew the truth, but few others did. That's why people were so eager to write about North America. Hennepin and others figured that if they wrote about what the public wanted to read

Set Your Purpose

Some explorers "stretched" stories about early North America. Read this article to find out what they said.

—strange, exotic, dangerous things and places—they would be able to sell a lot of books and make a lot of money. They were right. Fact or fiction, people back in Europe bought up Hennepin's two books almost before the ink was dry.

That's because for most Europeans, Hennepin's stories only **confirmed** what they already believed. To them, North America represented everything Europe was not. It was unexplored and untamed. Their imaginations ran wild just thinking about it.

The scary thing is, Hennepin's stories were tame compared to those of Baron de Lahontan. De Lahontan also traveled in North America and then **fabricated** outrageous stories. To hear him tell it, he paddled up a huge, straight river leading west to the mountains. Near that river was another one leading to six stone cities.

He supposedly met some interesting people in those cities. One group was ruled by a king so powerful he was carried everywhere. Another group wore beards just like the Spanish. The third group fought with copper weapons and wore pointed caps.

It's a nice story. Too bad it's not true. No one has ever found any such river or cities. And Native Americans of that time did not look or act like the ones de Lahontan described.

The truth didn't matter back in Europe. De Lahontan became famous. People believed everything he said. In one book, he even wrote that Hennepin had been dead wrong about Niagara Falls. It was really 700 to 800 feet high! This **inflated** height actually appeared in a 1747 geography textbook.

From the looks of it, Hennepin wasn't the only one who needed to get his eyes checked—or his facts straight.

Think About It

Why did Louis Hennepin and Baron de Lahontan stretch the truth about North America?

Name_____ Date_____

Check Your **Understanding**

Fill in the letter with the best answer for each question.

1. Which is the best summary of this selection?

Ⓐ Some early European explorers wrote reports about North America that were not true.

Ⓑ Baron de Lahontan was a liar.

Ⓒ Hennepin said that Niagara Falls was three times taller than it really is.

Ⓓ Hennepin was captured by Sioux Indians.

2. In which book might you find this selection?

Ⓐ Great Waterfalls of North America

Ⓑ Early River Travel

Ⓒ The North American Wilderness As It Was

Ⓓ False History and Untrue Tales

3. Why did Baron de Lahontan claim Niagara Falls was even taller than Hennepin had said it was?

Ⓐ He wanted to state its height correctly.

Ⓑ He wanted to impress Hennepin.

Ⓒ He wanted to outdo Hennepin.

Ⓓ He wanted a job as an explorer.

4. Which of the following best summarizes why people in Europe were so eager to read about North America?

Ⓐ It was like reading about everyday life in Europe.

Ⓑ They liked to read about strange, exciting, dangerous places.

Ⓒ They liked Hennepin and de Lahontan.

Ⓓ They all wanted to move there.

5. Which statement below best summarizes de Lahontan's supposed travels?

Ⓐ He crossed Niagara Falls and discovered six cities of stone on the other side of it.

Ⓑ He canoed down the Mississippi and discovered Niagara Falls.

Ⓒ He paddled up a huge river to the mountains where another river lead to six stone cities.

Ⓓ He was captured by Native Americans who took him to the mountains.

Vocabulary

Find each vocabulary word in the selection. The words and sentences around it will help you figure out its meaning.

Fill in the letter with the best definition of the underlined word.

1. In 1697 few people knew how to underline{accurately} measure a huge waterfall.

Ⓐ correctly   Ⓒ quickly

Ⓑ falsely   Ⓓ simply

2. To underline{exaggerate} is to say that Niagara Falls is 400 feet taller than it really is.

Ⓐ punish   Ⓒ travel far

Ⓑ write by hand   Ⓓ stretch the truth

3. Hennepin's stories underline{confirmed} what early Europeans already believed.

Ⓐ asked   Ⓒ questioned

Ⓑ proved   Ⓓ amused

4. Baron de Lahontan was worse. He underline{fabricated} outrageous stories.

Ⓐ sewed   Ⓒ made up

Ⓑ drew   Ⓓ listened to

5. An underline{inflated} height of Niagara Falls actually appeared in a 1747 geography textbook.

Ⓐ made smaller   Ⓒ made flat

Ⓑ filled with air   Ⓓ made bigger

Name _____ Date _____

Word Work

> Some words have more than one meaning. You can often figure out the meaning of a word by looking at how the word is used in a sentence. For example, the word *desert* can mean "a large dry area" or "to run away from."

Decide if each underlined word has meaning A or B. Fill in the letter with the correct answer.

1. I never got a chance to <u>seal</u> the envelope.
- (A) a sea mammal
- (B) to close or fasten tightly

2. I used my new baby harp <u>seal</u> stationery.
- (A) a sea mammal
- (B) to close or fasten tightly

3. That company <u>bills</u> me every month.
- (A) birds' beaks
- (B) sends a request for payment

4. This book shows exotic birds' <u>bills</u>.
- (A) birds' beaks
- (B) sends a request for payment

5. They're nice, but I think I'll <u>pass</u> on them.
- (A) a narrow path
- (B) to decide not to take

6. The disagreements were a <u>grate</u> on our nerves.
- (A) something with an annoying effect
- (B) a framework of parallel or crossed bars

7. We had wanted to do a <u>live</u> presentation.
- (A) seen while actually being performed
- (B) to exist

8. We had to <u>fuse</u> our report into one paragraph.
- (A) a long wick used to carry flame to an explosive
- (B) to bring together

9. Abby still wanted to bring in a <u>perch</u> to represent North American wildlife.
- (A) a freshwater fish
- (B) a place to sit

10. I joked that we could <u>row</u> out and catch one.
- (A) people or things arranged in a line
- (B) to use oars to move a boat

Write Now

In the selection "The Story That Stretched," you saw how Hennepin and de Lahontan stretched the facts to make better stories to sell to people in Europe.

What really happened	What I'm going to say happened

- Plan to write a description of your day. Stretch the truth! Make the sights and events even bigger, better, or scarier than they really were. Copy the chart above and complete it.

- Write your "stretching the truth" description. Use your chart to help you.

Drawing Conclusions

❖ When an author does not spell out everything you want to know about a character or an event, you can combine story clues with what you already know to draw a conclusion that makes sense.

- As you read, look for clues that can help you form an idea about what the author does not tell you.
- Ask yourself: "What do I already know about something like this?"
- Use the story clues to **draw a conclusion**.

❖ Read this paragraph. What **conclusion** can you draw about Sacajawea's role in the expedition?

Her Name Was Sacajawea

In 1803, President Jefferson sent two men to explore part of the West. Their names were Lewis and Clark. There were no maps and they needed a guide. They hired a fur trader and his wife. Her name was Sacajawea (sah cuh juh WEE uh).

Sacajawea grew up in the Shoshone (shoh SHOH nee) tribe. She knew how to hunt and fish. She knew every inch of the land. She found food when there was none. They walked through deep snow and paddled on rough waters. The journey was dangerous.

Clues
The things Sacajawea did are a clue as to how she helped in the expedition.

❖ You could chart the information you learned to **draw a conclusion** like this:

Clues	What I Already Know	Conclusion
Sacajawea knew how to hunt and fish, knew every inch of the land, and found food when there was none.	On an exploration trip like this, food and directions are difficult to come by.	Sacajawea was very helpful and played an important part in the expedition.

Your Turn

❖ Read this selection. **Draw conclusions** about a demolition event. Make a chart like the one above.

Combine Crunch

What do you do with a $200,000 harvester when it becomes old and worn out? If you're a farmer in Washington State, you might enter it in a demolition derby for harvesting combines. Weighing as much as 15,000 pounds and standing 15 feet high, combines make a mighty crunch when they smash together! Demolition derbies with cars just don't compare, observers say.

As part of the town of Lind's annual rodeo, the combine demolition derby has been a great success. Participants paint their combines in bright colors and give them names like Grim Reaper and Red Baron. One year, the only woman competitor painted her rig purple and named it Raisin Cain.

Groups of five to six combines compete in heats that last ten minutes. Any rig that isn't able to move is forced to drop out. The last combine moving at the end of the night wins. And the crowd always goes home happy.

Mary McLeod Bethune

by Emily Ranish

Set Your Purpose

How can learning to read make a difference in someone's life? Read this article to find out.

Mary McLeod Bethune stands with students in front of Bethune-Cookman College, the school she helped establish.

Mary's papa stood in line to sell their cotton. Picking cotton was hard work. But the McLeod family was proud of their crop. This was their own cotton. They were working for themselves, not a white master. The days of slavery were over. Mary watched as the cotton dealer weighed her father's cotton.

"You have 250 pounds, Sam," said the cotton dealer.

Her father looked surprised. "Seems like it should be more than that, Mr. Cooper."

The dealer **shrugged**. "See for yourself," he said. "The scales say 250 pounds."

Mary was furious. Mr. Cooper knew that her father couldn't read numbers. Nor could any of the other farmers standing in line. During slavery, it was against the law for African Americans to learn to read. Now, slavery was **abolished**. But still there were no schools for African-American children in South Carolina.

Mary turned to her mother. "I'm going to learn to read, Mama," she said with **determination**.

"Maybe someday you will, child," her mother replied.

A year later, a school opened in Mary's town. As soon as she learned to read, Mary began to teach others. At cotton-picking time, Mary went with her father to the cotton **market**. When their cotton was placed on the scale, Mary called out, "Look, Father! We have 500 pounds!"

The cotton dealer was startled. He realized he could no longer cheat the McLeods. "That's a smart little girl you have there, Sam," he said to Mary's father.

Mary McLeod Bethune taught for most of her life. She started a school for African-American girls in Florida. Eventually it became Bethune-Cookman College. Mrs. Bethune became well known for her hard work and her belief in education and fair treatment for all. President Franklin D. Roosevelt invited her to work with him at the White House.

Mary McLeod Bethune died in 1955. In her will, she wrote: "I leave you love. I leave you hope. I leave you **dignity**."

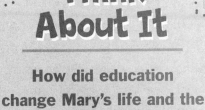

Think About It

How did education change Mary's life and the life of her family?

Name _____   Date _____

Check Your Understanding

Fill in the letter with the best answer for each question.

1. Which sentence best describes Mary McLeod Bethune?

Ⓐ She was rich and lucky.
Ⓑ She was clever and knew the right people.
Ⓒ She was angry and proud.
Ⓓ She was smart and determined.

2. The biggest problem Mary McLeod Bethune faced was

Ⓐ living on a farm.
Ⓑ unfair treatment because she was African American.
Ⓒ learning to read scales.
Ⓓ living during slavery.

3. Which did Mary McLeod Bethune value the most?

Ⓐ money
Ⓑ fame
Ⓒ government
Ⓓ education

4. Why was it a problem that the cotton farmers couldn't read numbers?

Ⓐ They couldn't tell time.
Ⓑ They couldn't read the date.
Ⓒ They couldn't tell if the cotton dealer was cheating them.
Ⓓ They couldn't tell how much they weighed.

5. Which of the following things happened last?

Ⓐ Mary McLeod Bethune became a teacher.
Ⓑ Mary McLeod Bethune worked for President Franklin D. Roosevelt.
Ⓒ Mary McLeod Bethune founded Bethune-Cookman College.
Ⓓ Mary McLeod Bethune decided she would learn to read.

Vocabulary

Find each vocabulary word in the selection. The words and sentences around it will help you figure out its meaning.

Fill in the letter with the best definition of the underlined word.

1. The dealer <u>shrugged</u>; he didn't care.

Ⓐ raised the shoulders
Ⓑ pushed with the elbows
Ⓒ shrunk because of being ashamed
Ⓓ took the farmers' crops without paying

2. After the Civil War, slavery was <u>abolished</u>.

Ⓐ became a law
Ⓑ adopted
Ⓒ made a practice
Ⓓ done away with

3. "I'm going to learn to read," said Mary with <u>determination</u>.

Ⓐ difference
Ⓑ hate
Ⓒ firmness
Ⓓ love

4. Farmers sold their cotton at the <u>market</u>.

Ⓐ place to park their cars and trucks
Ⓑ place to buy and sell crops and goods
Ⓒ meeting place
Ⓓ eating place

5. Mary McLeod Bethune had great <u>dignity</u>.

Ⓐ direction
Ⓑ quality worthy of respect
Ⓒ wealth and prestige
Ⓓ friends

Name _____ Date _____

Word Work

A **suffix** is a word part that comes at the end of a base word. Adding the suffix *-ion* to the end of a base word usually turns a verb into a noun.

subtract → **subtraction**

Sometimes the final *e* is dropped before adding the suffix *-ion*.

educate → **education**

Add the suffix *-ion* to each base word below to make a new noun. Write the new word.

1. invent   _____

2. act   _____

3. complete   _____

4. instruct   _____

5. concentrate   _____

Add the suffix *-ion* to the word in dark type to complete the sentence. Remember to drop the final *e* before adding *-ion*.

6. The cook was pleased with her **create**____.

7. That was a bad telephone **connect**____.

8. The beams are going up at the **construct**____ site.

9. We took up a **collect**____ for the people whose houses burned down.

10. The mayor won another **elect**____.

Write Now

Mary McLeod Bethune thought education was enormously important. Think of someone you know who values education. It could be someone in your family, a teacher, a friend, a sports star whom you have heard speak on TV, or even yourself.

- Plan to write a paragraph about that person explaining why he or she believes education is so important. First jot down a few notes. Can you think of some things that person has said to you while talking about education? Write down any quotes that you remember.

- Write a paragraph describing how the person you know feels about education and why.

Does Music Make You SMARTER?

adapted by Adrienne Hathoway

All across the country, babies are bouncing to an old beat. They are moving their **limbs** to the music of Mozart, Bach, and Beethoven. Why are they doing this? So they'll be smarter, of course! Let's find out how music can make a person smarter.

"Research proves it! Playing music for newborns is good for their brains," says Zell Miller, former governor of Georgia. Some babies may even hear their first CD on the day they are born. It could make them smarter.

Babies aren't the only ones who can be made smarter listening to music! Music can give you brain power, too.

"When you play music, you exercise your brain," says Norman M. Weinberger, a **professor** of brain science. "Everyone knows that exercise is good for the muscles. Making music is good for your brain."

Set Your Purpose

Can music make you smarter? Read this article to find out.

So, what kind of music is the best brain food? Is **classical** music better than rock, jazz, or rap? David Merrell, a teenager from Suffolk, Virginia, has his own **theories**. He decided to test them out. In his test, he used a pack of mice, a maze, and a little music.

First, Merrell divided 72 mice into three groups. One group listened to heavy-metal music. Another group listened to Mozart. The third group didn't listen to any music. Merrell ran the mice through the maze every day. He wanted to see if listening to music would make the mice smarter. Before they heard any music, the mice took about ten minutes to get through the maze. Then, after four weeks of jamming, they changed their tune.

The **results** were amazing. The mice who didn't listen to music cut their time in half, to five minutes. The mice who listened to heavy metal took almost an hour. The mice who listened to classical music beat the others by a huge margin—they zipped across the finish line in just one-and-one-half minutes!

What is Merrell's conclusion? He thinks classical music rocks!

Think About It

Why do some people think music can make us smarter?

Name_____ Date_____

Check Your Understanding

Fill in the letter with the best answer for each question.

1. How did Zell Miller conclude that music makes you smarter?

Ⓐ He likes music.

Ⓑ He says that research proves it.

Ⓒ Babies like to dance.

Ⓓ It just seems like a logical idea.

2. How did David Merrell conclude that music makes you smarter?

Ⓐ He asked babies what music they like.

Ⓑ He joined a band and went on tour.

Ⓒ He learned how to play the piano.

Ⓓ He conducted an experiment.

3. How did David Merrell try to test whether music makes you smarter?

Ⓐ He told people to listen to music.

Ⓑ He ran mice through a maze.

Ⓒ He listened to music while feeding mice.

Ⓓ He made babies listen to classical music.

4. Which of these is true of Merrell's experiment?

Ⓐ The mice that listened to classical music did the best.

Ⓑ The mice that listened to rock music did the best.

Ⓒ None of the music made the mice respond faster.

Ⓓ The mice preferred jazz.

5. Which of the sentences below is an opinion?

Ⓐ Music is exercise for your brain.

Ⓑ All across the country, babies are bouncing to an old beat.

Ⓒ Norman M. Weinberger is a professor of brain science.

Ⓓ Classical music is my favorite because it's the best brain food.

Vocabulary

Find each vocabulary word in the selection. The words and sentences around it will help you figure out its meaning.

Fill in the letter with the best definition of the underlined word.

1. Babies love to move their underlined limbs to music that makes them smart!

Ⓐ ears

Ⓒ bodies

Ⓑ cradles

Ⓓ arms and legs

2. Norman M. Weinberger is a underlined professor of brain science.

Ⓐ college teacher

Ⓒ brain surgeon

Ⓑ student

Ⓓ person who wants to learn

3. Is underlined classical music better than rock music?

Ⓐ modern or popular

Ⓑ time-honored and serious

Ⓒ loud and angry

Ⓓ with a strong and fast beat

4. There are many underlined theories on why some music is better than others.

Ⓐ humorous stories

Ⓒ explanations

Ⓑ directions

Ⓓ colleges that study music

5. The underlined results of the study are good.

Ⓐ questions and answers

Ⓑ people involved

Ⓒ printout

Ⓓ outcomes or effects

Name _____ Date _____

Word Work

Some words have more than one meaning. You can often figure out the meaning of a word by looking at how the word is used in a sentence.

1. row (*noun*) – a line
   We sat in the *row* behind our parents.

2. row (*verb*) – to paddle
   Let's *row* the boat to the island.

Decide if each underlined word has meaning A or B. Fill in the letter with the correct answer.

1. What <u>kind</u> of music is better brain food?

   Ⓐ a type; a sort
   Ⓑ friendly; nice

2. Hopefully, Merrell was <u>kind</u> to his mice.

   Ⓐ a type; a sort
   Ⓑ friendly; nice

3. Babies are bouncing to a different kind of <u>beat</u> these days.

   Ⓐ to defeat
   Ⓑ the unit of rhythm in music

4. The mice who listened to classical music <u>beat</u> all the others.

   Ⓐ to defeat
   Ⓑ the unit of rhythm in music

5. David Merrell used a <u>pack</u> of mice for his test.

   Ⓐ a group of animals
   Ⓑ to fill a space tightly

6. Crowds <u>pack</u> stadiums for concerts.

   Ⓐ a group of animals
   Ⓑ to fill a space tightly

Decide if each underlined word has meaning A or B. Fill in the letter with the correct answer.

7. Merrell <u>divided</u> 72 mice into three groups.

   Ⓐ caused to disagree
   Ⓑ separated into parts

8. The "no-music" mice <u>cut</u> their time.

   Ⓐ made less or reduced
   Ⓑ made an opening in with a sharp tool

9. The "heavy-metal" mice <u>took</u> an hour.

   Ⓐ used up, as in time
   Ⓑ grabbed hold of

10. All across the <u>country</u>, babies are bouncing to a different kind of beat.

   Ⓐ land outside of towns or cities
   Ⓑ nation with its own government

Write Now

In "Does Music Make You Smarter?" you learned how some types of music can be good for you. What types of music do you like?

- Plan to write a short article about your favorite kinds of music. Make a chart like the one shown. Name each type of music and describe it.

- Write your article. Use the information from your chart to help you convince your readers that your kind of music is the best.

Types of Music	Description
classical music	_____
	_____
	_____
	_____

GRANT HILL
Straight Shooter

Set Your Purpose

Grant Hill is a famous basketball player. Read this interview to find out what he has to say to young people.

adapted by Sharon Asta

Orlando Magic forward Grant Hill is one of professional basketball's best players. In this interview he talks about his career.

Interviewer: How would you describe yourself?

Grant Hill: I'm shy. Other than that, I'm no different from anyone else. Some people think I'm perfect, but I make mistakes every day.

Interviewer: Is there anything tough about being an NBA superstar?

Grant Hill: I'm happy, but it is a big **sacrifice**. It's hard to do things like shop in a mall or eat dinner in a restaurant because people recognize you and want your **autograph**. But I'm not complaining. I enjoy the fact that people want to meet me.

Interviewer: A lot of players are going to the NBA before graduating from college. You waited until you graduated. Was that a hard decision?

Grant Hill: No! Many young **athletes** skip school. They pin their whole future on making the pros. If they fail, which many do, they have no other **skill** to fall back on for a career.

Interviewer: What will you do when you finish your playing career?

Grant Hill: Well, in 1997 I wrote a book about myself called *Change the Game*. And I also play the piano. So maybe I'll be a writer or a musician.

Interviewer: How do you feel about being a role model for kids?

Grant Hill: I try to tell young people what my role models preached to me: Be **accountable** for your own actions!

Interviewer: What other advice do you have for young people?

Grant Hill: You have to stay in school and study! The key to life is a good education. Everyone can reach their potential if they apply themselves in school.

Think About It

Do you think Grant Hill has a good message for kids? Why or why not?

Name_____ Date_____

Check Your Understanding

Fill in the letter with the best answer for each question.

1. Because Grant Hill is an NBA superstar, he
Ⓐ is shy.
Ⓑ likes being famous.
Ⓒ is often recognized in public places.
Ⓓ does a lot of interviews.

2. What important decision did Grant make before playing professional basketball?
Ⓐ He decided to play the piano.
Ⓑ He decided to graduate from college.
Ⓒ He decided to sign autographs.
Ⓓ He decided to write a book.

3. Why does Grant Hill think an education is important?
Ⓐ It gives you more career choices.
Ⓑ You get to take interesting classes.
Ⓒ People will recognize you.
Ⓓ You can play sports.

4. Why do many young players skip school?
Ⓐ They fail in many subjects.
Ⓑ They don't like their teachers.
Ⓒ Players don't need an education.
Ⓓ They believe they can make it as professional players.

5. Which of these is a message Grant Hill gives to kids?
Ⓐ Don't sign autographs.
Ⓑ Play the piano.
Ⓒ Make big sacrifices.
Ⓓ Stay in school.

Vocabulary

Find each vocabulary word in the selection. The words and sentences around it will help you figure out its meaning.

Fill in the letter with the best definition of the underlined word.

1. Not being able to go out in public is a big <u>sacrifice</u>.
Ⓐ salary
Ⓒ surprise
Ⓑ statement
Ⓓ loss

2. People want the <u>autograph</u> of an NBA star.
Ⓐ signature
Ⓒ handshake
Ⓑ picture
Ⓓ title

3. Many young <u>athletes</u> skip school.
Ⓐ students
Ⓒ people skilled at sports
Ⓑ fans
Ⓓ children

4. You need a <u>skill</u> to get a good job.
Ⓐ star
Ⓑ ability
Ⓒ language
Ⓓ friend

5. Hill advises young people to be <u>accountable</u> for their own actions.
Ⓐ responsible
Ⓑ good at math
Ⓒ careless
Ⓓ type of table

Name _____   Date _____

Word Work

A **compound word** is made of two shorter words. To understand a compound word, separate it into the two shorter words and think about the meaning of those words.

Make compound words by combining each word on the left with a word on the right. Write the compound words.

1. dragon house _____

2. every port _____

3. bird fly _____

4. basket one _____

5. air ball _____

Read the definitions below. Join two words from each definition to make a compound word that fits the definition. Write the new word. Look at the sample.

SAMPLE definition: a **yard** in the **back**

compound word: **backyard**

Definitions

6. a ground where children play _____

7. a storm with thunder _____

8. a ball of snow _____

9. a time at night _____

10. a bell on a door _____

Write Now

Grant Hill has a very clear message to young people: Be accountable for your own actions!

• Plan to write a letter to Grant Hill telling him what you think of his message. First, make a chart of important actions you might do to show you understand the message. Then write possible results of those actions. Here is an example:

Actions	Results
Stay in school.	Learn the skills I can use in a job.
Say no to drugs.	Avoid trouble; stay healthy.

• Write your letter to Grant Hill. Tell him how strongly you feel about his message and what you are going to do with it. Use examples from your chart to support your opinion.

Surf's Up—
Way Up!

by Patricia Levitt

A small plane levels off at 7,000 feet (2,134 m) above the ground. One by one, sky divers jump through the open door. They spread their arms and soar off. But wait a minute. Something's different about that last sky diver. He has a surfboard strapped to his feet!

Set Your Purpose

Have you heard about the latest sport that's really taking off? Read this article to find out what makes sky surfing such a thrill.

High in the sky, the diver spins, swoops, and turns. He rolls upside down in a fast loop. Then he **straightens** up and surfs across the air as if on an invisible wave. What a wave it is! As he free-falls, his speed reaches 120 miles per hour (193 kph)! Then with a whoosh his parachute opens. Board and all, he floats safely down to earth.

Why sky-dive on a surfboard? It's the ride of a lifetime, sky surfers say. The board increases drag—the force that slows a **hurtling** body down. More drag means more time aloft. And that means more time to perform **stunts** in the sky.

Sky surfing started in France around 1980. It reached the United States about ten years later. The sport's gain in **popularity** has been rather slow. In a **poll** of its 33,000 members, the U.S. Parachuting Association found that fewer than 500 were interested in sky surfing. Part of the reason may be the sky-high price of equipment. Boards cost between $500 and $1,200. A parachute kit runs $2,300 to $5,000. A flight suit can be $170 to $200. Add a helmet, goggles, gloves, and altimeter, and the cost of the sport goes way up.

Still, the sport attracts people for whom jumping from a plane isn't enough of a thrill. And high in the sky, the surf is always up!

Think About It

Why are some people thrilled by sky surfing? And why are some not?

Name _____ Date _____

Check Your Understanding

Fill in the letter with the best answer for each question.

1. From this article you can tell that
- Ⓐ sky surfing will become very popular.
- Ⓑ sky surfers started as water surfers.
- Ⓒ sky surfers enjoy the thrill of the sport.
- Ⓓ sky surfing is not dangerous.

2. What conclusion might you draw about sky divers who use a surfboard?
- Ⓐ They don't need parachutes.
- Ⓑ They fall slower than regular sky divers.
- Ⓒ They reach speeds of 120 miles per hour.
- Ⓓ They fall faster than regular sky divers.

3. What conclusion might you draw about sky surfing's lack of popularity?
- Ⓐ It's an expensive sport.
- Ⓑ It's not dangerous enough.
- Ⓒ It doesn't offer enough of a thrill.
- Ⓓ It's no different from skydiving.

4. Sky surfers can perform more stunts in the sky because
- Ⓐ they make waves.
- Ⓑ they fall faster.
- Ⓒ they stay aloft longer.
- Ⓓ they jump from a higher plane.

5. Which of the following states an opinion about sky surfing?
- Ⓐ Sky surfing started in France around 1980.
- Ⓑ A sky surfer can reach speeds of 120 miles per hour.
- Ⓒ Fewer than 500 sky divers were interested in sky surfing.
- Ⓓ Sky surfing gives you the ride of a lifetime.

Vocabulary

Find each vocabulary word in the selection. The words and sentences around it will help you figure out its meaning.

Fill in the letter with the best definition of the underlined word.

1. The sky diver <u>straightens</u> up after rolling upside down.
- Ⓐ makes the body straight
- Ⓑ surfs straight up in the air
- Ⓒ makes a wave straight
- Ⓓ free falls straight to the ground

2. A surfboard can slow down a <u>hurtling</u> body.
- Ⓐ shining like a star
- Ⓑ sliding steadily
- Ⓒ hurting
- Ⓓ moving at great speed

3. Sky surfers often perform <u>stunts</u> in the sky.
- Ⓐ walks
- Ⓑ acts that show great skill or daring
- Ⓒ mistakes
- Ⓓ small things

4. The sport has been slow to gain in <u>popularity</u>.
- Ⓐ total number of people in a place
- Ⓑ enjoyment
- Ⓒ awareness
- Ⓓ condition of being liked by many people

5. The U.S. Parachuting Association took a <u>poll</u> of its members.
- Ⓐ collection of opinions
- Ⓑ picture
- Ⓒ bad opinion of
- Ⓓ list of names

Name _____   Date _____

Word Work

Some words have more than one meaning. You can often figure out the meaning of a word by looking at how the word is used in a sentence. For example, the word *row* has different meanings.

1. row (*noun*) – a line
We sat in the *row* behind our parents.

2. row (*verb*) – to paddle
Let's *row* the boat to the island.

Read the sentences below. Decide if each underlined word has meaning A or B. Fill in the letter with the correct answer.

1. A small plane <u>levels</u> off high above the ground.
Ⓐ gives an even surface to
Ⓑ flies straight after gaining height

2. He surfs as if on an invisible <u>wave</u>.
Ⓐ a moving ridge on the surface of water
Ⓑ a motion made by moving your hand back and forth

3. The board increases <u>drag</u> on the sky surfer.
Ⓐ pulling something along
Ⓑ the force that slows a moving body down

4. A parachute kit <u>runs</u> $2,300 to $5,000.
Ⓐ costs
Ⓑ moves quickly

5. Sky divers must follow certain safety <u>rules</u>.
Ⓐ instructions that tell the correct thing to do
Ⓑ has authority or control over

6. The sky surfer's stunts showed a <u>stroke</u> of genius.
Ⓐ an unexpected action that has a powerful effect
Ⓑ a line drawn by a pen, pencil, or brush

7. As sky surfers freefall, they might <u>reach</u> speeds of 120 miles per hour.
Ⓐ to touch by stretching out
Ⓑ get as fast as

8. Can you <u>reach</u> the rim of the basketball net by jumping?
Ⓐ to touch by stretching out
Ⓑ get as fast as

9. The small plane could <u>accommodate</u> ten sky divers.
Ⓐ do a favor for
Ⓑ hold comfortably

10. It was nice that they could <u>accommodate</u> me by finding an extra seat.
Ⓐ do a favor for
Ⓑ hold comfortably

Write Now

The web below shows information about sky surfing from "Surf's Up—Way Up!"

• Plan to write about an interview with a sky surfer. First, plan the questions you would like to ask the person about his or her sport.

• Write your interview. Try to avoid questions that can be answered with a simple "yes" or "no."

CORAL CRISIS

adapted by Paul Hart

If you want to see a lot of fish, then go to a coral reef. Thousands of species of ocean fish and animals, like lobsters and squid, stick close to coral reefs. These are stony structures full of dark hideaways where fish can lay their eggs and escape from predators. Without these underwater "apartment houses," there would be fewer fish in the ocean. Some species might even become endangered or disappear completely.

What some people don't realize is that reefs are living beings, too. They are made of thousands of tiny animals called polyps. These polyps soak seawater into their squishy bodies. They use the **nutrients** in the seawater to make stony tubes that fit around their bodies. These tubes protect the polyps and grow to make coral.

There are thousands of reefs in the world. Sadly, though, they are now in serious danger. More than one-third are in such bad shape that they could die within ten years. Many might not even last that long!

Scientists are working hard to find out how to help stop this **destruction**. There is a lot to learn, but there are some things we do know.

Set Your Purpose

Read this article to find out why the world's coral reefs are in danger.

Pollution

Pollution on land runs into rivers and streams, which carry the poisons into the ocean. Chemicals from pollution kill coral. They may also make polyps weak, so they have less **resistance** to diseases. Also, fertilizer from farms causes seaweed to grow wildly, choking polyps.

Global Warming

Global warming is an overall increase in Earth's temperature. High water temperatures kill the greenish-gold algae, or tiny water plants, that live on coral. Coral gets food from the algae. Without it, the coral loses its color and eventually dies. This process, known as "coral bleaching," is becoming more **frequent**. Many scientists believe global warming is to blame.

People

People sometimes ram into reefs with their boats or drop anchors on them, breaking off large chunks of coral. Divers who walk on reefs can also do major damage. Since coral is so colorful and pretty, some people even break it off to collect for **souvenirs**.

A Solution

How can we help the reefs? We can learn more about them! We need to find out what humans do that damages reefs so we can change those activities. We can work together to make sure that coral reefs will be healthy and beautiful in the future.

Think About It

What is a coral reef? Why are coral reefs in danger?

Name_____   Date_____

Check Your Understanding

Fill in the letter with the best answer for each question.

1. Which sentence does <u>not</u> support the conclusion that reefs are important to ocean life?

   Ⓐ Fish lay their eggs on reefs.

   Ⓑ Fish hide in the reefs to escape their predators.

   Ⓒ Coral reefs can be seen from the air in very clear water.

   Ⓓ Without coral reefs, there would be fewer fish in the ocean.

2. Based on the information in the article, which of the following conclusions can be drawn?

   Ⓐ Farms are the coral reefs' worst enemies.

   Ⓑ There is no solution to the coral-reef problem.

   Ⓒ Some people collect pieces of coral for souvenirs.

   Ⓓ People need to understand what endangers the coral reefs if they are to be saved.

3. Scientists believe the coral reefs are in danger from

   Ⓐ ocean animals like lobster and squid.

   Ⓑ greenish-gold algae.

   Ⓒ too many fish eggs hatching in them.

   Ⓓ higher water temperatures caused by global warming.

4. When a coral reef loses its color

   Ⓐ it eventually dies.

   Ⓑ it is thrown away.

   Ⓒ it is eaten by lobsters.

   Ⓓ it can't eat algae.

5. How does land pollution get into the ocean?

   Ⓐ Beach sand gets into the ocean.

   Ⓑ Seaweed grows wildly.

   Ⓒ Algae contains pollution from the land.

   Ⓓ Streams and rivers carry pollution from the land into the ocean.

Vocabulary

Find each vocabulary word in the selection. The words and sentences around it will help you figure out its meaning.

Fill in the letter with the best definition of the underlined word.

1. Living things need <u>nutrients</u> to stay healthy.

   Ⓐ stony tubes   Ⓒ pollution

   Ⓑ thieves   Ⓓ food

2. <u>Destruction</u> of reefs is a serious problem.

   Ⓐ extermination   Ⓒ pollution

   Ⓑ construction   Ⓓ exploration

3. Because of pollution, polyps have less <u>resistance</u> to disease.

   Ⓐ ability to swim

   Ⓑ ability to fight against

   Ⓒ ability to walk

   Ⓓ ability to drive

4. Coral bleaching is becoming more <u>frequent</u>.

   Ⓐ often   Ⓒ colorful

   Ⓑ hardly ever   Ⓓ tall and skinny

5. Some people break off pieces of coral to collect for <u>souvenirs</u>.

   Ⓐ barriers   Ⓒ things kept as reminders

   Ⓑ injuries   Ⓓ fees paid to swim

Name _____   Date _____

Word Work

Most nouns are made **plural** by adding *-s* or *-es*. If a noun ends in a consonant and *y*, change the *y* to *i* and add *-es*. If the word ends in a vowel and *y*, just add *-s*.

animal	→	**animals**
baby	→	**babies**

Read each sentence. Write the correct plural form of the word in dark type.

1. body   Polyps have stony tubes that fit around their _____.

2. nutrient   The _____ in seawater are used to make the tubes.

3. creature   Many _____ lay their eggs on coral reefs.

4. disease   Chemicals may weaken polyps, making them more likely to catch _____.

5. activity   Many different human _____ can be harmful to coral.

Read each sentence and the words below. Write the plural form of the word that best completes each sentence.

fin   ray   reef   tentacle   enemy

6. Pollution can kill coral _____.

7. _____ and skates are both relatives of sharks.

8. Most fish have _____ for swimming.

9. The sea nettle has long _____ that are armed with stinging cells.

10. Many fish travel in numbers to protect themselves from _____.

Write Now

In the selection "Coral Crisis," you read about some of the things that may be threatening coral reefs. This information could be organized in a chart like this.

Evidence from the selection	Conclusion
Coral reefs are an important part of the ocean environment.	If coral reefs are damaged, so is the whole ocean environment.
We need to find ways to prevent pollution from destroying the coral reefs.	Studying coral reefs and the effects of pollution will help us learn more.
People do things that can harm coral reefs.	Action needs to be taken to reduce or stop these activities.

- Plan to write an advertisement warning people about the harm being done to the ocean, land, or air. Use the chart to brainstorm ideas. Decide how to make a powerful beginning statement to get the reader's attention.

- Now write your advertisement. End your advertisement with a summary that will persuade the audience to take action.

A TRASH COLLECTOR'S WORK IS NEVER DONE

Brian Kane was a trash collector in Denver, Colorado. Eight hours a day, five days a week, fifty weeks a year, Brian rode on the back of a trash truck through the streets of this mile-high city.

At each stop, he'd jog quickly to the back of buildings. Then he'd drag heavy trash cans to the truck. Brian never complained—even when sweat stung his eyes or cold wind turned his fingers into sticks of ice.

by Amy Glaser Gage

Set Your Purpose

Read this article to find out where Brian Kane, a trash collector, goes to "get away from it all," and what he learns while he is away.

Brian saw these hardships as opportunities to become strong and **fit**. His job was a training ground for his **lifelong** dream. One day, he would climb Mount Everest, the highest mountain in the world. Every weekend, Brian climbed the peaks of Colorado to escape the crowds and trash of the city. On vacations, he climbed the highest peaks in the country—even Mount McKinley in Alaska. The peace and beauty of the mountains made his spirits soar.

On his thirtieth birthday, Brian decided to tackle his dream. He would stand on the "roof of the world." Brian took a three-month leave from his job and flew to Nepal. There he began the long, difficult journey up Mount Everest.

Brian first traveled to a base camp. He stayed there for several weeks to get used to the thinner air. Brian planned to bring three oxygen canisters with him to the **summit**. At 29,028 feet, it would be hard to survive without extra oxygen.

Over the next two months, Brian climbed to 26,000 feet. There he found Camp Four—the last place to rest below the summit. But when Brian saw this camp, he gasped and fell to his knees.

"Trash!" he cried. Nearly a thousand empty oxygen canisters **littered** the camp area. Humans had turned this beautiful, remote place into a giant trash heap.

Sad, but determined, Brian continued to follow his dream. Two days later he stood proudly on the peak of Mt. Everest. He had reached the "roof of the world!"

Two days after this great **achievement**, Brian stuffed a dozen empty oxygen canisters in his pack and headed down the mountain. He smiled to himself as he realized that the work of a trash collector is never done.

Think About It

Do you think one person can make a difference in the fight against pollution and trash? Why or why not?

Name _____ Date _____

Check Your Understanding

Fill in the letter with the best answer for each question.

1. How does Brian feel about his job as a trash collector?

Ⓐ He does not like his job.

Ⓑ He hates the smell of garbage.

Ⓒ He likes to work outside and to be in shape.

Ⓓ He always complains about the hard work.

2. Why did Brian drop to his knees when he saw the pile of trash on Mount Everest?

Ⓐ He missed his job as a trash collector.

Ⓑ He was so tired he could not stand.

Ⓒ He realized that pollution and trash are everywhere.

Ⓓ He wanted to see how many oxygen canisters there were.

3. Which word best describes Brian?

Ⓐ lazy   Ⓒ funny

Ⓑ positive   Ⓓ careless

4. What did Brian do after he saw the trash on the mountain?

Ⓐ Brian visited the base camp.

Ⓑ Brian flew to Nepal.

Ⓒ Brian climbed to the top of Mount Everest.

Ⓓ Brian reached Camp Four.

5. Why did Brian carry twelve empty oxygen canisters down the mountain?

Ⓐ He believed even small efforts are important in keeping the Earth clean.

Ⓑ He thought they are valuable.

Ⓒ He planned to organize a party.

Ⓓ He needed to fill the canisters.

Vocabulary

> Find each vocabulary word in the selection. The words and sentences around it will help you figure out its meaning.

Fill in the letter with the best definition of the underlined word.

1. Brian saw his hard work as a preparation for becoming strong and <u>fit</u>.

Ⓐ bad-tempered

Ⓑ in good physical condition

Ⓒ happy

Ⓓ in bad physical condition

2. His <u>lifelong</u> dream was to climb Mount Everest.

Ⓐ during one's life   Ⓒ all one's life

Ⓑ never   Ⓓ favorite

3. Brian planned to bring three oxygen canisters with him to the <u>summit</u>.

Ⓐ meeting place

Ⓑ building in the mountains

Ⓒ steep side of a mountain

Ⓓ top of a mountain

4. Empty canisters <u>littered</u> the camp area.

Ⓐ covered with trash   Ⓒ sparkled

Ⓑ made small   Ⓓ sad

5. Reaching the "roof of the world" was a great <u>achievement</u>.

Ⓐ good exercise

Ⓑ something done poorly

Ⓒ large meal

Ⓓ something done well

Name _____ Date _____

Word Work

Antonyms are words that have opposite meanings. For example, *hot* and *cold* are antonyms.

Read each sentence. Write the letter of the antonym of the word in dark type.

1. Climbers **littered** the mountain.
Ⓐ covered   Ⓒ trashed
Ⓑ cleaned up   Ⓓ scattered

2. We saw hundreds of **empty** soda cans along the trail.
Ⓐ dirty   Ⓒ small
Ⓑ old   Ⓓ full

3. He suffered many **hardships** on his way to the top.
Ⓐ difficulties Ⓒ comforts
Ⓑ injuries   Ⓓ burdens

4. Exercise keeps you **healthy**.
Ⓐ strong   Ⓒ fit
Ⓑ sickly   Ⓓ running

5. I was **proud** of my achievement.
Ⓐ pleased Ⓒ unaware
Ⓑ glad   Ⓓ ashamed

A **suffix** is a word part that comes at the end of a base word. The suffixes **-ship**, **-ment**, and **-hood** can be added to base words to form new words. For example:

friend + ship	=	friendship
agree + ment	=	agreement
boy + hood	=	boyhood

Add the suffix -ship, -ment, or -hood to each base word to make a new noun. Write the new word.

6. where neighbors live   neighbor_____

7. state of being hard   hard_____

8. something achieved   achieve_____

9. something that entertains entertain_____

10. time when one is a child   child_____

Write Now

"A Trash Collector's Work Is Never Done" is about Brian Kane, who realized that his daily job as a trash collector was important. It was useful even on Mount Everest. What activities do you do that you feel are important and worthwhile?

- Plan to make a Certificate of Achievement for yourself in recognition of an important activity. First, make a list of all the things you do in a typical day. Which activity do you think makes a difference to you, your family, or your community?

- Make your Certificate of Achievement and write a short paragraph explaining why one of the things you do every day deserves recognition.

THE ANIMALS OF THE ARCTIC TUNDRA

Set Your Purpose

What would you do to stay alive on the Arctic tundra? Read to find out how animals survive on this treeless, frozen plain.

The Arctic tundra is a cold, windy, treeless plain that encircles the globe just below the north pole. Winters on the tundra are bitterly cold. Temperatures can drop to -94 degrees F. Most of the birds and animals have migrated to warmer climates. But the polar bear, Arctic fox, Arctic hare, and lemming have stayed behind. They burrow beneath the snow or make dens to survive. Their thick layers of stored fat keep them warm and provide **nourishment** during the long, cold, dark winter months.

In late February, the sun peeks over the horizon. Spring slowly returns. The weather warms and the top layer of soil thaws. The bottom layers, called permafrost, stay frozen. Melting ice and snow form pools in which hordes of insects breed. Moss, lichen, and low shrubs come to life. Thousands of small plants bloom, covering the tundra with a blanket of color, as if to welcome the millions of returning birds and animals.

Female polar bears and their cubs emerge from their dens. After the long, lean winter months, they hunt for food. Millions of migrating birds return and fight for good nesting sites on the nearby rocky cliffs.

Caribou herds begin the migration north to their summer feeding grounds. Here the females will give birth. There is an abundance of vegetation, and few predators will follow the herds that far north. In summer, the sun never sets, so both young and the old feed around the clock. Food is **plentiful**. The young grow quickly and reach **maturity** before winter returns.

In early September, the hours of sunshine each day are noticeably fewer, signaling the departure of the migrating wildlife. Birds fly to winter nesting sites, caribou begin the long **trek** to the south. Arctic foxes and female polar bears begin searching for sites to make their dens. Male polar bears will continue to hunt throughout the winter. In early December, the sun sinks below the horizon and the long winter night begins. The sun will not appear again until late February. Then the tundra springs to life again.

Think About It

How do the animals of the Arctic tundra manage to survive the long, cold, dark winter months?

DID YOU KNOW?

Caribou herds return to the same place each year to give birth. As many as 100,000 caribou may migrate in a single herd. They may travel up to 1,900 miles.

Name_____ Date _____

Check Your **Understanding**

Fill in the letter with the best answer for each question.

1. What conclusion can you draw about the lack of trees on the Arctic tundra?

   Ⓐ Arctic animals have destroyed the trees.

   Ⓑ Arctic summers are too hot for trees to grow.

   Ⓒ All the trees have been cut down.

   Ⓓ Trees cannot grow in the permafrost.

2. You can conclude that migratory birds return to the Arctic tundra

   Ⓐ when the temperature drops to –94 degrees F.

   Ⓑ in early December.

   Ⓒ only when food is plentiful.

   Ⓓ at any time of year.

3. Which statement best describes polar bears?

   Ⓐ They migrate with the caribou.

   Ⓑ They look for nesting sites on rocky cliffs.

   Ⓒ They are well adapted to live in a cold climate.

   Ⓓ They cannot survive severe weather.

4. Which statement is true of the Arctic tundra?

   Ⓐ It is found only in North America.

   Ⓑ It is in the far north.

   Ⓒ It has short, cold winters.

   Ⓓ It is in the far south.

5. What is another good title for this article?

   Ⓐ Survival on Top of the World

   Ⓑ Summer in the Tundra

   Ⓒ Polar Bears of the Arctic

   Ⓓ Animals: Safe and Sound

Vocabulary

> Find each vocabulary word in the selection. The words and sentences around it will help you figure out its meaning.

Fill in the letter with the best definition of the underlined word.

1. Thick layers of stored fat keep the animals warm and provide <u>nourishment</u>.

   Ⓐ fur   Ⓒ heat

   Ⓑ food   Ⓓ life

2. The weather warms and the top layer of soil <u>thaws</u>.

   Ⓐ freezes   Ⓒ melts

   Ⓑ slides   Ⓓ grows

3. At this time of year, food is <u>plentiful</u>.

   Ⓐ abundant   Ⓒ colorful

   Ⓑ scarce   Ⓓ crunchy

4. The young reach <u>maturity</u> before the frigid winter returns.

   Ⓐ territory

   Ⓑ companions

   Ⓒ full development

   Ⓓ old age

5. Caribou begin the long <u>trek</u> to the south.

   Ⓐ song

   Ⓑ hunt

   Ⓒ place

   Ⓓ journey

Hi-Lo Nonfiction Passages for Struggling Readers: Grades 6–8 • Scholastic Inc.

Name _____ **Date** _____

Word Work

The letters **-le** or **-al** often appear at the end of a word and follow a consonant. When they do, the consonant plus -le or -al usually form the final syllable.

$$\text{eagle} \rightarrow \text{ea/gle}$$
$$\text{signal} \rightarrow \text{sig/nal}$$

Read each sentence. Circle the word that ends in -le or -al and underline the final syllable in that word.

1. The Arctic tundra is a geographical land type.

2. Arctic tundra regions encircle the globe.

3. The snowy owl is a white, meat-eating animal of the tundra.

4. It is almost invisible when it flies against a snowy background.

5. This adaptation is critical to its success as a hunter.

Synonyms are words that have similar meanings. For example, *begins* and *starts* are synonyms.

Read each sentence. Write the word from below that has almost the same meaning as the word in dark type.

freezing   gorge   recognizes   single   large

6. The wolf **acknowledges** her mate's call.

   _____

7. Large animals roam **vast** areas searching for food. _____

8. Some animals **feast** on the first summer plants. _____

9. Winter temperatures can be **frigid**.

   _____

10. A **lone** male polar bear searches for food.

    _____

Write Now

In the article "The Animals of the Arctic Tundra," you read about animals that survive in this harsh environment. Imagine that you are making a TV documentary about the tundra.

- Plan to write the narration (background words) that will accompany a scene focusing on one animal. Copy and complete a web like the one shown to help you organize our ideas.

- Write your narration. Use active voice with lively verbs and descriptive words to help your audience understand the images they are seeing on screen. If you like you may include a storyboard with your narration.

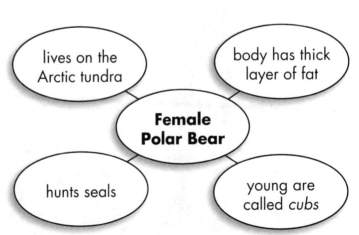

lives on the Arctic tundra

body has thick layer of fat

Female Polar Bear

hunts seals

young are called *cubs*

Wildlife for Sale

Set Your Purpose

Do you have an unusual pet? Read this article to find out if your pet is one of those animals that need protecting.

adapted by Patrick Holford

Have you ever dreamed of owning a pet python or a clever monkey? It's fun to imagine, but in reality wild animals don't make good pets. They belong in their own habitat. Unfortunately, some people will pay thousands of dollars to own an **exotic** pet. They buy snakes and tortoises from Madagascar, monkeys from Brazil, and parrots from Australia and Mexico. Collectors will also pay for dead animals, such as butterflies from Southeast Asia. Still others want animal parts to use in traditional medicines.

Some people pay huge amounts of money to own rare **species** that are protected by law. Smugglers are in the business of stealing these rare animals and plants. Buyers around the world spend billions of dollars to purchase endangered wildlife.

The Tortoise Dilemma

The rare radiated tortoise is one of the world's most-wanted pets. It sells for as much as $10,000 in the United States. It can be found only in the wilds of Madagascar, an island off the coast of Africa. The people who catch the tortoises there earn 30 cents per tortoise.

Think About It

Why do you think people want to buy endangered animals? What do you think should be done to solve the problem?

The tortoise catchers know that it's **illegal** to take the tortoises. One catcher says, "The tortoises are here and my children have to eat. My people have always collected what is nearby for food and money." The tortoise catcher thinks it is crazy that people pass laws to protect certain animals. "To me, they have the problem backwards—let the tortoise live so I can starve," he says.

An Environmental Problem

In many countries, including the United States, people smuggle snakes, lizards, spiders, centipedes, and butterflies out of national parks. Some people have been arrested for **poaching**. But most people who steal and smuggle animals don't get caught. And if they do, their punishment usually isn't very **severe**.

Taking endangered animals out of the wild threatens the environment. It can lead to extinction. When a species becomes extinct, other plants and animals are affected, too. The species that used to eat the extinct species may no longer have food. And the plants and animals that the extinct species used to eat could grow out of control.

Scientists worry about what will happen if people continue to steal animals. Who knows how many ways the loss will upset the balance of life? Despite warnings, animal smugglers aren't likely to stop. When the animals disappear, what will the tortoise catcher do for food?

Name _____   Date _____

Check Your Understanding

Fill in the letter with the best answer for each question.

1. Why do you think people steal endangered animals?

   Ⓐ They want to put the animals in a zoo.

   Ⓑ They want to save the endangered species from becoming extinct.

   Ⓒ They can make a lot of money.

   Ⓓ They plan to breed the animals.

2. Why do you think people in Madagascar take tortoises even though it is against the law?

   Ⓐ They don't know that it is against the law to take the tortoises.

   Ⓑ They think the tortoises are better off as pets.

   Ⓒ They eat the tortoises.

   Ⓓ They sell the tortoises for money to feed their families.

3. What kinds of animals do poachers take?

   Ⓐ common animals, such as rabbits and squirrels

   Ⓑ farm animals, such as cows and sheep

   Ⓒ rare animals, such as monkeys and parrots

   Ⓓ pests, such as rats and mosquitoes

4. What do you think Madagascar is like?

   Ⓐ It is a very poor place where jobs are scarce.

   Ⓑ It is a place where most people are wealthy.

   Ⓒ It is a big place with many job opportunities.

   Ⓓ It is a desert.

5. What might happen if too many endangered snakes are taken out of the wild?

   Ⓐ Nothing will happen.

   Ⓑ The snakes could disappear from the wild.

   Ⓒ People will get tired of snakes.

   Ⓓ The smugglers will get caught.

Vocabulary

Find each vocabulary word in the selection. The words and sentences around it will help you figure out its meaning.

Fill in the letter with the best definition of the underlined word.

1. Some people will pay thousands of dollars to own an <u>exotic</u> pet.

   Ⓐ unusual   Ⓒ common

   Ⓑ extra   Ⓓ friendly

2. It is <u>illegal</u> to buy endangered wildlife in some countries.

   Ⓐ legal   Ⓒ not healthy

   Ⓑ not recommended   Ⓓ against the law

3. There are laws to protect rare <u>species</u>.

   Ⓐ kind of animal or plant

   Ⓑ all animals

   Ⓒ special plants

   Ⓓ people who work in pet stores

4. <u>Poaching</u> rare animals is against the law.

   Ⓐ petting or feeding

   Ⓑ hunting or taking

   Ⓒ photographing

   Ⓓ owning

5. The punishment usually isn't very <u>severe</u>.

   Ⓐ many   Ⓒ apart

   Ⓑ harsh   Ⓓ accurate

Name _____ Date _____

Word Work

A **suffix** is a word part that comes at the end of a base word. Adding the suffix *-ion*, *-tion*, *-ation*, or *-ment* to the end of a base word usually turns a verb into a noun. Sometimes the final *e* is dropped before adding the suffix.

invite → invitation

Add the suffix *-ion* or *-ment* to the base word in dark type to complete the sentence. Write the new word.

1. Sometimes the **punish**_____ for poaching is not strict enough.

2. If people don't protect endangered animals, it can lead to **extinct**_____.

3. Sometimes zoos give endangered animals **protect**_____.

4. The buyer made a large **pay**_____ to the poacher for a rare snake.

5. The man has a **collect**_____ of rare butterflies.

Add the suffix *-ation* or *-ment* to the base word in dark type to complete the sentence.

6. Many animals face the danger of **starve**_____.

7. We need to make an **explore**_____ of that cave.

8. The buyer made an **appoint**_____ to see the rare animals.

9. There was great **excite**_____ when the smugglers were caught.

10. The **govern**_____ has passed laws against poaching animals.

Write Now

As you read "Wildlife for Sale," you may have asked yourself such questions as these:

> **1.** Would I want an endangered animal for a pet?
>
> **2.** Where would I keep such a pet?
>
> **3.** What will happen if I get caught breaking the law?

- Plan to write a paragraph about owning an exotic pet. Begin by making a list of your questions and answers. See the chart above for some ideas.

- Write your paragraph. Use your list to help you write. Organize your thoughts in a way that makes sense to you.

So, How About Those VIKINGS?

adapted by Jay Dinsmore

When you hear the word *Viking*, what comes to mind? A professional football player from Minnesota? Well, there's a lot more to Viking history than how many touchdowns a football team scored last year. The story of the Vikings begins about a thousand years ago, when the world was a much different, much wilder place.

Ancestors of the people who now live in Norway, Sweden, and Denmark, the Vikings were a group both feared and respected. They were fierce warriors who swept across Europe. Around 700 A.D. they began attacking towns up and down the coast of Europe, **plundering** everything in their path. No one felt safe from them.

Norway, Sweden, and Denmark have long coastlines with many harbors. The Vikings became skilled shipmakers and amazing sailors. They built fast, large wooden ships with tall and curved ends. Each ship had a large and square sail, often striped with bright colors. These **striking**, majestic dragon ships carried the Vikings far from their native shores.

The Vikings traveled without the **benefit** of a compass. Instead, they **calculated** their

Set Your Purpose

Who were the Vikings? Read this article to find out why they were feared and respected.

Think About It

Who were the Vikings? Why were people afraid of them?

location using the sun and stars, the color of the water, and the seaweed they saw. Using their knowledge of the sea, they traveled to lands never before seen by Europeans. Leif Ericson led them west to Greenland around 1002 A.D. From there, most scholars believe, they sailed to North America, the first Europeans to do so.

Leif Ericson and other Vikings began to explore other places because they needed new land. Good farmland was becoming hard to find back home. Greenland, where Ericson lived, had few trees. Without wood, there could be no ships. Without their ships, the Vikings could not control the seas or attack other towns.

After sailing for many days from Greenland, Ericson discovered a vast land with many forests. He called it Markland, which means "woodland." Today we call it Labrador. Labrador is on the northeastern tip of North America. Soon other Vikings arrived in Labrador and built settlements there. But they did not stay long. **Historians** believe the people who already lived in the area drove them away. Perhaps the Vikings finally went up against a team they couldn't beat.

Name _____ Date _____

Check Your Understanding

Fill in the letter with the best answer for each question.

1. The Vikings were both feared and respected
because they

Ⓐ built ships.

Ⓑ didn't use compasses.

Ⓒ had deep harbors and tall trees.

Ⓓ were excellent sailors and warriors.

2. Why would the Vikings attack European towns
along the coast?

Ⓐ Coastal towns were easier for Viking sailors
to reach by ship.

Ⓑ Towns on the coast had more treasure.

Ⓒ Towns on the coast were prettier.

Ⓓ Coastal towns did not expect to be attacked.

3. The Vikings were amazing sailors because they
traveled

Ⓐ in beautiful ships.

Ⓑ without the benefit of a compass.

Ⓒ attacking people along the way.

Ⓓ in large groups.

4. Why did the Vikings travel so much?

Ⓐ They had a lot of vacation time.

Ⓑ The weather was bad in Norway,
Sweden, and Denmark.

Ⓒ They like to make friends in new places.

Ⓓ They could not find the resources they
needed at home.

5. What achievement is Leif Ericson
remembered for?

Ⓐ He led the Vikings west to find new land.

Ⓑ He built ships.

Ⓒ He was the first person to sail around
the world.

Ⓓ He settled in Labrador.

Vocabulary

> Find each vocabulary word in the selection.
> The words and sentences around it will help
> you figure out its meaning.

**Fill in the letter with the best definition of the
underlined word.**

1. They come attacking and <u>plundering</u>
everything in their path.

Ⓐ stealing things by force

Ⓑ picking up

Ⓒ making enemies with

Ⓓ stepping on

2. The <u>striking</u>, majestic dragon ships carried
the Vikings far from their native shores.

Ⓐ swift   Ⓒ dangerous

Ⓑ strong   Ⓓ grand

3. The Vikings traveled without the <u>benefit</u> of a
compass.

Ⓐ weakness   Ⓒ cost

Ⓑ advantage   Ⓓ dream

4. Instead, they <u>calculated</u> their location using
the sun and stars.

Ⓐ figured out   Ⓒ sailed

Ⓑ visited   Ⓓ gave up

5. <u>Historians</u> believe the people who lived in
Labrador drove them away.

Ⓐ people from long ago

Ⓑ people who get upset

Ⓒ people who study the past

Ⓓ people from other lands

Name _____   Date _____

Word Work

> **Synonyms** are words that have similar meanings. For example, *people* and *persons* are synonyms.

Read the sentences and the words below. Write the word that means almost the same as the word in dark type.

> bold   plundering   ancestors   benefit   vast

1. The Vikings gained many treasures by attacking and **stealing**. _____

2. The explorers looked out on a **boundless** country that stretched for miles. _____

3. The **daring** Viking sailors took many risks.
_____

4. The **advantage** of having such large ships was that the Vikings could travel miles from the shore. _____

5. Visiting Sweden gave me a chance to learn more about my **forefathers**. _____

> A **suffix** is an ending that changes the meaning of a base word. Knowing the meaning of a suffix helps you figure out the meaning of the whole word. The suffix **-ment** means "the act of." The suffix **-er** means "a person who."
>
> **settle<u>ment</u>**   the act of settling
> **bak<u>er</u>**   someone who bakes

Write a word that fits the definition by adding the suffix *-ment* or *-er*.

6. someone who builds   **build**_____

7. the act of encouraging   **encourage**_____

8. someone who explores   **explor**_____

9. the act of governing   **govern**_____

10. someone who teaches   **teach**_____

Write Now

Creating a word web can be a good way of organizing your thoughts about a topic. Here is a word web around the word "Vikings."

- Plan to write a postcard home as if you were traveling on a Viking ship. Use the word web and details from the story to help you gather ideas to write about.

- Now write your postcard. Imagine that you're aboard a Viking ship journeying to North America. Using ideas you have gathered, describe some of the details of your journey to your family back home.

HIGH-TECH
HIGHWAYS

adapted by J. R. Frank

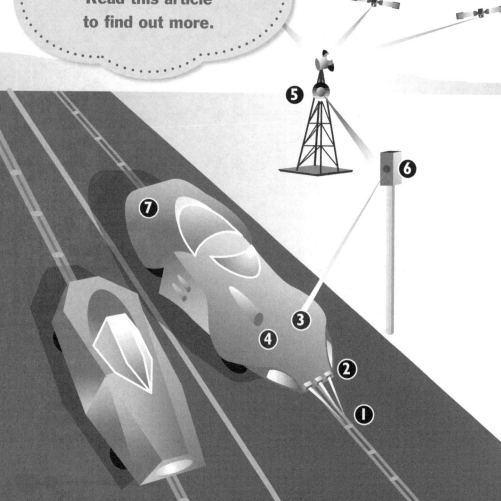

Set Your Purpose

How can computer-controlled cars make our lives better? Read this article to find out more.

How One Automated Highway System Works

1. **Magnetic Markers**
   Magnetized metal disks in the road create a magnetic field.

2. **Magnetometers**
   Sensors under the car bumper tune in to the magnetic field.

3. **Computer Steering**
   This system uses information from magnetometers to steer the car along the magnetic path.

4. **Radar-Connected Brakes**
   When radar identifies an obstacle in the road, the computer hits the brakes.

5. **GPS Satellites**
   A Global Positioning System, or GPS, receiver processes information from satellites orbiting Earth. By calculating your distance from different satellites, a dashboard computer can tell you exactly where you are on the road.

6. **Roadside Guide**
   These guides relay satellite information and local travel warnings.

7. **Central Computer**
   The "brain" of your car's automatic system, the central computer processes all information and tells your car what to do.

Imagine playing a board game with your mom as she drives you to school. Wait! Shouldn't your mom keep her hands on the wheel and her eyes on the road? Not if she's driving a computer-controlled car down a high-tech highway of the future.

Someday, moms may be able to do it. In 1997, scientists and engineers tested new computer-controlled cars that drove themselves along a special high-tech highway called a "smartway." Computers in the cars used information from magnets, light sensors, and radar detectors built into the smartway.

Scientists hope that drivers of the future will simply drive up to a smartway, then switch on the car's automated driver. The human driver will sit back and enjoy the ride. A computer system will do the rest. Satellites and magnets will help **navigate** the car along the highway. Sensors will **alert** the car to other vehicles nearby. The car's central computer will **process** information and instruct the car what to do. For example, if a car is too close to the car in front of it, the computer will tell it to slow down or change lanes. When the car's human driver decides to exit the smartway, he or she will take over the controls and return to the regular highway.

Engineers hope the smartways will save time for commuters and cut down the number of car accidents and traffic jams. Most accidents are caused by human **error**, according to the U.S. Department of Transportation. Computer-controlled cars should **eliminate** those kinds of crashes because a computer, not a human, will determine what the car will do next.

But some car makers aren't sure the smartway will be the safest way to travel. What would happen if a deer jumped into the road? Or if the car's computer broke down? Engineers are trying to answer these questions now.

Until they find the answers, your mom will have to keep her eyes on the road.

Think About It

What did you learn about high-tech highways? What do you think about the idea?

Name _____   Date _____

Check Your Understanding

Fill in the letter with the best answer for each question.

1. According to this selection, how will highways and cars change in the future?

    Ⓐ All roads will become smartways.

    Ⓑ All cars will be computer-driven.

    Ⓒ Some highways will be built for computer-controlled cars only.

    Ⓓ All highways will require computer-driven cars.

2. Why are these highways called smartways?

    Ⓐ Drivers using them must be smart.

    Ⓑ Drivers will enjoy the ride.

    Ⓒ They are the safest way to travel.

    Ⓓ Smartways have built-in magnets and sensors that help the computer drive the car.

3. Which of the following is <u>not</u> true about smartway driving?

    Ⓐ Cars will be computer-controlled.

    Ⓑ Drivers can sit back and relax.

    Ⓒ Satellites will help control the cars.

    Ⓓ Drivers must drive very fast.

4. If a car on a smartway gets too close to another car, what happens?

    Ⓐ The computer tells the car what to do.

    Ⓑ The driver returns to the regular highway.

    Ⓒ The driver exits the smartway.

    Ⓓ The car's automatic driver switches on.

5. What do engineers hope will be the biggest advantage of smartway driving?

    Ⓐ faster driving

    Ⓑ more students working on school nights

    Ⓒ fewer car crashes

    Ⓓ more traffic jams

Vocabulary

> Find each vocabulary word in the selection. The words and sentences around it will help you figure out its meaning.

Fill in the letter with the best definition of the underlined word.

1. Satellites and magnets will help <u>navigate</u> cars along the highway.

    Ⓐ move fast   Ⓒ repair

    Ⓑ guide   Ⓓ sail

2. Sensors will <u>alert</u> the car to other vehicles nearby.

    Ⓐ warn   Ⓒ listen carefully

    Ⓑ stop   Ⓓ slow down

3. The car's central computer will <u>process</u> information and instruct the car what to do.

    Ⓐ sort out   Ⓒ develop

    Ⓑ procedure   Ⓓ see

4. Most accidents are caused by human <u>error</u>.

    Ⓐ feelings   Ⓒ mistakes

    Ⓑ intelligence   Ⓓ greed

5. Computer-controlled cars should <u>eliminate</u> many crashes.

    Ⓐ increase

    Ⓑ ignore

    Ⓒ get in the way of

    Ⓓ get rid of

Name _____ Date _____

Word Work

A **compound word** is made of two shorter words. To understand a compound word, separate it into the two shorter words and think about the meaning of those words.

| rooftop | = | **top** of a **roof** |
| doorbell | = | **bell** of a **door** |

Make compound words by combining each word on the left with a word on the right. Write the compound words.

1. high   work   _____
2. snow   dream   _____
3. home   crow   _____
4. day   flake   _____
5. scare   way   _____

Look at the compound words below. Write the word that best completes each sentence. Then draw a line between the two shorter words that make up each compound word.

sidewalk motorcycle flashlight goldfish sunrise

6. The _____ this morning was very beautiful.

7. It is safer to walk on the _____ than in the middle of the street.

8. The boy used a _____ to light his way down the dark steps.

9. The police officer rode a _____ through the traffic jam.

10. My brother went to the pet store to buy three _____.

Write Now

In "High-Tech Highways" you learned about smartways. How are driving on a smartway and driving on a regular highway alike? How are they different? The Venn diagram below shows some comparisons.

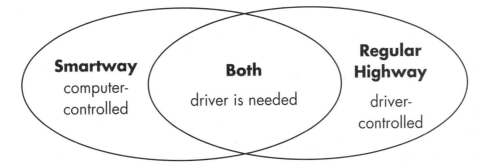

- Plan to write a short paragraph about why you would or would not like to drive on a smartway. Think about which is better: a smartway or a regular highway. Make a diagram like the one above to help you organize your thoughts.

- Write your paragraph. Explain why you think smartways sound great or not so great. Give details to support your opinions. Use your diagram to help you.

Distinguishing Fact & Opinion

❖ When reading a story or an article, it's helpful to evaluate whether what you are reading is a fact or an opinion.

- As you read, ask yourself: "Can this statement be proven?" and "Is this what someone believes or feels?"
- A statement based on evidence that can be checked or proven true is a **fact**.
- A statement of what someone believes or feels is an **opinion**.
- Words such as *think, believe, probably, beautiful,* and *good* are clues that a statement expresses an opinion.

❖ Read this paragraph. Look for **facts** and **opinions**.

Opinion
The first sentence cannot be proven. The words *seems* and *unlikely* are signals that this is an opinion.

Facts
These sentences are based on evidence that can be checked, or proven true.

Desert People: The Papago

➤ The Sonoran Desert of southwestern Arizona seems an unlikely place for anyone to live in. Yet it has long been the home of the Papago, who call themselves the Desert People. Over the centuries, they have adapted to the desert by taking advantage of the seasonal rains to grow crops, by trading with their Pima neighbors, and by collecting the fruit of wild desert plants.

❖ You could chart the **facts** and **opinions** in this paragraph like this:

Statement	Fact	Opinion	Clue
The Sonoran desert seems an unlikely place for people to live.		✓	seems, unlikely
It has long been home to the Papago.	✓		can be checked
The Papago take advantage of seasonal rains, trade with the Pima, and gather fruit of desert plants.	✓		can be checked

Your Turn

❖ Read this passage. Look for **facts** and **opinions**. Make a chart like the one above.

Who Came First?

It is this author's belief that Christopher Columbus was not the first explorer to set foot in North America. There is evidence that others got here first.

Stone anchors found off the California coast resemble those used by the Chinese more than a thousand years ago. I think it's likely that Chinese sailors crossed the Pacific and landed on the West Coast.

Vikings, or Norsemen, were also early explorers. According to Norse sagas, or stories, a seaman named Bjarni Herjolfsson was blown off course by strong winds. He sighted unknown land to the west, but didn't land. If he had, he would probably have been the first European to walk on American soil. Another Viking, Leif Ericson, sailed off to find Bjarni's new land. Ruins found in Canada offer evidence of Viking settlers.

A Panda
for a Pet?

by Constance L. Garvin

Pandas look so cute and cuddly sitting on a toy store shelf. Admit it, you just want to take one home, don't you? You don't just want a stuffed one, though. A real live black-and-white panda is what you want. Well, you might want to be careful about

Set Your Purpose

Pandas look cute and cuddly. But that doesn't mean they make great pets. Read this article to find out why not.

what you wish for. Real giant pandas grow to be about five feet long. An **adult** panda can weigh more than 300 pounds. One of those wouldn't just steal your covers. It would take over your entire bed!

Your pet panda would undoubtedly want a bedtime snack. These gentle giants love to eat. But don't go padlocking your refrigerator just yet. Pandas are very particular about their choice of food. They like to eat bamboo. **Occasionally** they eat meat, but mostly they eat lots and lots of bamboo, a type of plant. Pandas sit up to eat their food. They have thumbs on their front paws so they can hold the bamboo stalks and munch away. In fact, pandas spend about 16 hours a day munching.

All that eating can cause **fatigue**. So, pandas try to get lots of sleep. At home in the wild, they will pretty much lie down and stay **dormant**. They nap wherever and whenever they get the urge. They sometimes nap in trees, and sometimes they find a nice cool cave for a midday nap.

Think About It

Why is a panda not a good choice as a pet?

Pandas are favorite animals not only in toy stores, but also in zoos. However, giant pandas are extremely rare. There are very few pandas either in captivity or in the wild. Scientists **estimate** that there are only about 1,000 giant pandas left in the entire world. So, while giant pandas are furry and fascinating, it is definitely best to stick with the toy-store variety. Real live pandas belong in their own home—the wild bamboo forests found in the highlands of China and Tibet.

Name _____ **Date** _____

Check Your **Understanding**

Fill in the letter with the best answer for each question.

1. Which of the following statements is a fact?

  Ⓐ Pandas look cute and cuddly.

  Ⓑ Pandas are fascinating animals in the zoo.

  Ⓒ Giant pandas often grow to be five feet tall.

  Ⓓ A panda is the best house pet you could possibly buy.

2. Which of the following statements is an opinion?

  Ⓐ Pandas eat up to 16 hours a day.

  Ⓑ The giant panda is black and white.

  Ⓒ It's really annoying when a panda just lies down and falls asleep.

  Ⓓ Pandas sometimes eat meat.

3. Which fact supports the idea that pandas are <u>not</u> ideal pets?

  Ⓐ An adult panda can weigh more than 300 pounds.

  Ⓑ Pandas are favorite animals in zoos and in toy stores.

  Ⓒ Pandas sit up to eat their food.

  Ⓓ Pandas look cute and cuddly.

4. Besides a toy store, a good place to see a panda would be a

  Ⓐ pet store.

  Ⓑ playground.

  Ⓒ school.

  Ⓓ zoo.

5. What is the main idea of this selection?

  Ⓐ Pandas are the most fascinating animals in the world.

  Ⓑ A pet panda would take over your bed.

  Ⓒ Pandas are fascinating animals, but they don't make good pets.

  Ⓓ The giant panda lives in the mountains of China.

Vocabulary

> Find each vocabulary word in the selection. The words and sentences around it will help you figure out its meaning.

Fill in the letter with the best definition of the underlined word.

1. Baby pandas are tiny, but the <u>adult</u> can weigh more than 300 pounds.

  Ⓐ tree   Ⓒ pet

  Ⓑ grown-up Ⓓ animal

2. <u>Occasionally</u> they eat meat, but mostly they eat lots and lots of bamboo.

  Ⓐ very often   Ⓒ a few times

  Ⓑ in a sweet way Ⓓ in a cool manner

3. All that eating causes <u>fatigue</u>, so pandas often take naps.

  Ⓐ hunger   Ⓒ tiredness

  Ⓑ breathing out Ⓓ running around

4. Because they are tired, pandas stay <u>dormant</u>.

  Ⓐ asleep   Ⓒ dumb

  Ⓑ active   Ⓓ wet

5. Scientists <u>estimate</u> that there are only about 1,000 giant pandas in the world.

  Ⓐ hope   Ⓒ imagine

  Ⓑ promise   Ⓓ make an educated guess

Hi-Lo Nonfiction Passages for Struggling Readers: Grades 6–8 • Scholastic Inc.

Name _____ Date _____

Word Work

> **Antonyms** are words that have opposite meanings. For example, *giant* and *tiny* are antonyms.

Read the sentences and the words below. Write the word that means the opposite of the word in dark type.

expensive   chubby   shy   sleep   often

1. Pandas are not **bold** animals. They are very

_____.

2. Even if you shaved a panda, it would not be **thin**. It would still be _____.

3. Pandas do not like to **awaken**. They like to

_____.

4. They **rarely** eat meat. Bamboo is the food they eat most _____.

5. Keeping a panda as a pet would not be **cheap**. It would be very _____.

> A **compound word** is made of two shorter words. Combining the meanings of the two shorter words often explains the compound word.
>
> **fire + fighter = firefighter**

Make compound words by combining each word on the left with a word on the right. Write the compound words.

6. bed   doors   _____

7. out   time   _____

8. rattle   ever   _____

9. sun   shine   _____

10. when   snake   _____

Write Now

In "A Panda for a Pet?" you learned some facts about why the answer to the question is "Definitely not!" These facts could be organized in a word web like the one shown.

- Plan to write a brief how-to instruction card on how to keep an animal of your choice as a pet. Make a word web to help you organize what you know about the animal and its care.

- Write your brief how-to instruction card on how to keep an animal of your choice as a pet. Use your word web to help. Remember that some kinds of animals need a lot of attention and care, while others do not.

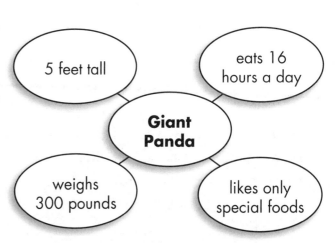

FAITHFULLY OURS

adapted by George Chase

The crowd presses against the railing. Voices are hushed and breaths are held. It'll by any minute now.

Whoosh! A stream of water shoots into the sky. The breeze sprays the closest people with mist. The **spectacle** continues for a few seconds more and then is gone. Applause and cheers burst from the crowd. Old Faithful did it again —right on schedule!

Set Your Purpose

Read this newspaper article to find out about the world's most famous geyser.

As geysers go, Old Faithful in Wyoming's Yellowstone National Park is probably the world's most famous. Geysers are hot springs that shoot water into the air. They're all named after Geysir, Iceland's largest geyser. It can shoot water over 195 feet.

The trouble is, no one knows when a geyser will decide to spout off. They're an **unpredictable** lot. Some erupt often. Others, like New Zealand's Waimangu, spout a few times and then stay quiet for ages. It hasn't been active since 1917. Another geyser, called Giant, spouts water up to 200 feet. Too bad it does it any old time it feels like. The length of time between eruptions varies from a week to three months. Who can make plans around a **schedule** like that?

Old Faithful, however, lives up to its name. Records show that for the past 125 years it hasn't skipped a single performance. About every 76 minutes or so, it shoots its water stream between 125 and 170 feet into the air. Park ranger Sandra Kinzer says it's possible to tell within ten minutes when it will erupt. That kind of **reliability** is what draws millions of people to see it every year.

The rangers' predictions are right 90 percent of the time. How do they do it? In 1938, a ranger noticed a connection between the length of the geyser's eruptions and the **interval** between eruptions. "Long eruptions are followed by long intervals," says Sandra. "Short eruptions are followed by short intervals."

All in all, Old Faithful seems pretty faithful to us!

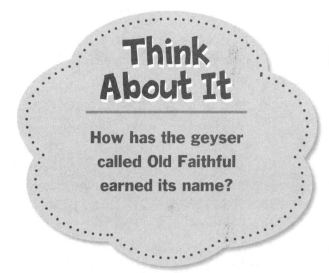

Think About It

How has the geyser called Old Faithful earned its name?

GAGGING THE GEYSERS

Some geysers at Yellowstone may never erupt again. That's because they're clogged with trash! Signs ask visitors not to throw things into the geysers. But some visitors ignore the signs. It's a shame that a few careless individuals can ruin the enjoyment of these natural wonders for the rest of us.

Name _____   Date _____

Check Your **Understanding**

Fill in the letter with the best answer for each question.

1. Which of the following statements is an opinion?

  Ⓐ Old Faithful's eruptions have been recorded for 125 years.

  Ⓑ There are geysers in New Zealand.

  Ⓒ The Giant geyser is prettier than Old Faithful.

  Ⓓ Millions of people come to watch Old Faithful every year.

2. Which of the following statements is an opinion?

  Ⓐ Some geysers do not spout for weeks or months at a time.

  Ⓑ It would be great if Waimangu started spouting again.

  Ⓒ The word *geysers* is taken from the name of a geyser in Iceland.

  Ⓓ Rangers can predict Old Faithful's eruptions within ten minutes.

3. One fact about Old Faithful is that it

  Ⓐ shoots water up to 170 feet into the air.

  Ⓑ is a wonderful geyser.

  Ⓒ is not as impressive as the Grand Canyon.

  Ⓓ is worth a visit.

4. How are all geysers alike?

  Ⓐ Some erupt often; others stay quiet.

  Ⓑ All geysers can shoot water into the air.

  Ⓒ They are all clogged with trash.

  Ⓓ All geysers are faithful.

5. Why is the geyser called "Old Faithful?"

  Ⓐ because it's a nice name

  Ⓑ because it spouts about every 76 minutes

  Ⓒ because it is old

  Ⓓ because it is in Yellowstone

Vocabulary

> Find each vocabulary word in the selection. The words and sentences around it will help you figure out its meaning.

Fill in the letter with the best definition of the underlined word.

1. The <u>spectacle</u> continues for a few seconds more and then is gone.

  Ⓐ guess   Ⓒ unusual sight

  Ⓑ spray of water   Ⓓ park tour

2. The time that a geyser shoots water is <u>unpredictable</u>.

  Ⓐ changeable   Ⓒ regular

  Ⓑ colorful   Ⓓ wet

3. Who can make plans around the Giant geyser's <u>schedule</u>?

  Ⓐ spray of water

  Ⓑ list of times for an event

  Ⓒ old, inactive geyser

  Ⓓ unexpected problem

4. Old Faithful's <u>reliability</u> has made it very popular.

  Ⓐ strength   Ⓒ location

  Ⓑ colorfulness   Ⓓ dependability

5. A long eruption is followed by a long <u>interval</u>.

  Ⓐ park ranger training programs

  Ⓑ space between two geysers

  Ⓒ small rooms used for storage

  Ⓓ period of time between events

Name _____ Date _____

Word Work

A **suffix** is an ending that changes the meaning of a base word. The suffix **-able** means "capable of." The suffix **-ous** means "having." The suffix **-ful** means "full of."

read<u>able</u>	able to be read
danger<u>ous</u>	having danger
faith<u>ful</u>	full of faith

If a base word ends with a consonant and *y*, we usually change *y* to *i* before adding the suffix *-ous* or *-able*.

glory → **glorious**

Write a word that fits the definition by adding the suffix *-able*, *-ous*, or *-ful* to the base word.

1. capable of being predicted _____

2. having victory _____

3. full of play _____

4. capable of being laughed at _____

5. full of care _____

Add the suffix *-able*, *-ous*, or *-ful* to the word in dark type. Write the new word.

6. rely Old Faithful is quite _____ about erupting on time.

7. thought Vandals are not very _____ of others.

8. work We need a _____ plan for keeping the geysers clean.

9. fury When people throw junk in the geysers, it makes me _____!

10. mystery There is nothing _____ about Old Faithful's eruptions.

Write Now

In "Faithfully Ours," you read about Old Faithful and other geysers. Have you ever seen a geyser? What do you imagine it's like?

	Waiting for Old Faithful to erupt	Watching Old Faithful erupt
I see		
I hear		
I feel		
I think		

- Plan to write a poem about Old Faithful. Imagine you are in Yellowstone Park, waiting to watch Old Faithful erupt. What are some things you might see, hear, feel, and think? Copy the chart shown and complete it with your ideas.

- Write your poem about Old Faithful, using the ideas from your chart. Your poem doesn't have to rhyme.

CLEOPATRA'S CITY—LOST & FOUND

by Patrick Lynch

Set Your Purpose

What treasures lie hidden under the sea? Read this article to find out about one underwater discovery.

ALEXANDRIA, Egypt. An ancient sphinx came up from the Mediterranean Sea. Inch by inch it rose. Divers slowly brought it onto the deck of a research ship. The stone sphinx had spent 1,600 years beneath the waves. Here, 20 feet (6.1 m) below the surface, lie the ruins of a city. Long, long ago, Queen Cleopatra had a palace here.

Over 200 years before Cleopatra was born, Alexander the Great founded the city. Then, some 1,600 years ago, a series of earthquakes and tidal waves struck. The city sank beneath the sea.

French **marine** expert Franck Goddio found the city's ruins. His team had the aid of the best high-tech equipment. Still, the search took three years. Goddio's team mapped the **submerged** royal quarters. The maps show columns, statues, and other features. The sphinx was just one sample of what the team found.

Experts believe that the sphinx's head shows Cleopatra's father. The great queen was born in 69 B.C. She was 17 when her father died. Cleopatra was the last of Egypt's pharaohs. Following her death in 30 B.C., Egypt came under Roman rule.

The divers also brought up a statue of the Great Priest of Isis. "This is one of the most beautifully preserved statues of its kind and very rare," Goddio said. The statue weighs 550 pounds (249 kg). It dates from the first century A.D.

Despite all of the interest in bringing the ruins up from the water, some people in Egypt want them left untouched. They would like the site to be an underwater museum. They want to build a **network** of glass-walled tunnels. Tourists would go down into the tunnels. Strolling along underwater, they could view the **sunken** wonders.

At this writing, the Egyptian government has not approved the plans. The cost would be great. The museum may never be built. And Cleopatra's palace may stay unseen beneath the waves.

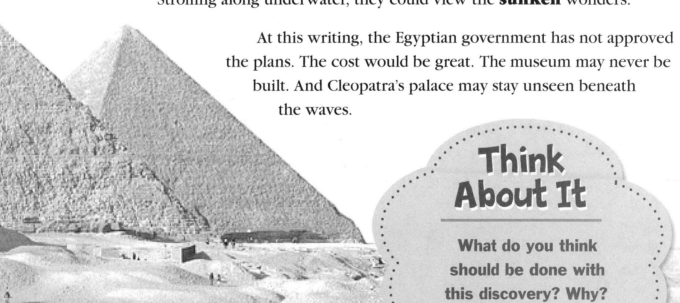

Think About It

What do you think should be done with this discovery? Why?

Name _____ **Date** _____

Check Your Understanding

Fill in the letter with the best answer for each question.

1. Which of the following states an opinion about Cleopatra?

Ⓐ Cleopatra was the last of Egypt's rulers.

Ⓑ Cleopatra was born in 69 B.C.

Ⓒ Cleopatra had a palace in the sunken city.

Ⓓ Cleopatra was the greatest of Egypt's rulers.

2. Which of the following statements is <u>not</u> a fact?

Ⓐ The sphinx was underwater for 1,600 years.

Ⓑ The sphinx's head is probably that of Cleopatra's father.

Ⓒ The sphinx is made of stone.

Ⓓ Franck Goddio found the sphinx.

3. Which of the following statements is a fact?

Ⓐ Viewing the ruins underwater would be the best way to see them.

Ⓑ The museum should be built right away.

Ⓒ The city is under 20 feet of water.

Ⓓ An underwater museum is too expensive.

4. Which statement best summarizes the selection?

Ⓐ Earthquakes sank a Roman city.

Ⓑ Divers brought up a sphinx from the sunken ruins of an Egyptian city.

Ⓒ Cleopatra had a palace in the sunken city.

Ⓓ Experts found the ancient ruins of an Egyptian city sunk by earthquakes.

5. The author of this article wants to

Ⓐ present facts about a recent discovery.

Ⓑ persuade people to build an underwater museum.

Ⓒ persuade tourists to visit the ruins of the sunken city.

Ⓓ describe an ancient statue.

Vocabulary

Find each vocabulary word in the selection. The words and sentences around it will help you figure out its meaning.

Fill in the letter with the best definition of the underlined word.

1. Franck Goddio, a <u>marine</u> expert, found the ruins beneath the waves.

Ⓐ having to do with ships or the sea

Ⓑ having to do with mountains

Ⓒ having to do with Egyptian ruins

Ⓓ having to do with the desert

2. Tourists could view the <u>sunken</u> wonders.

Ⓐ in a dark place

Ⓑ located beneath the water

Ⓒ forgotten

Ⓓ beautiful

3. The <u>submerged</u> palace was found 20 feet below the surface.

Ⓐ made with sand

Ⓑ totally destroyed

Ⓒ able to float

Ⓓ covered with water

4. A <u>network</u> of tunnels would allow tourists to view the ruins.

Ⓐ cloth woven together

Ⓑ system of connecting parts

Ⓒ long line

Ⓓ television station

5. Some want the ruins to stay underwater <u>despite</u> the interest in raising them.

Ⓐ in addition to

Ⓑ against

Ⓒ because of

Ⓓ regardless of

Name_____   Date_____

Word Work

> Some words have more than one meaning. You can often figure out the meaning of a word by looking at how the word is used in a sentence. For example, the word *rose* has different meanings.
>
> **1. rose** (*noun*) – a garden flower
> Look at the *rose* by the tree.
>
> **2. rose** (*verb*) – past tense of rise
> The bubbles *rose* to the surface.

Read the sentences below. Decide if each underlined word has meaning A or B. Fill in the letter with the correct answer.

1. Divers brought the sphinx onto the <u>deck</u>.
Ⓐ the floor of a boat or ship
Ⓑ a full set of playing cards

2. Earthquakes and tidal waves <u>struck</u> the city.
Ⓐ hit
Ⓑ suddenly discovered

3. The city's ruins lie below the water's <u>surface</u>.
Ⓐ the outside or outermost layer of something
Ⓑ to come to the top

4. The statue was extremely <u>rare</u>.
Ⓐ not often seen or found
Ⓑ very lightly cooked

5. Cleopatra is considered a <u>great</u> queen.
Ⓐ very big or large
Ⓑ very important and famous

6. The maps show <u>columns</u>, statues, and more.
Ⓐ articles by a writer
Ⓑ long, usually round, upright supports

7. The sphinx had <u>spent</u> 1,600 years under water.
Ⓐ tired out
Ⓑ used up, as in time

8. The divers were <u>spent</u> after the long work day.
Ⓐ tired out
Ⓑ used up, as in time

9. The statue was one of the rarest of its <u>kind</u>.
Ⓐ sort or variety
Ⓑ always ready to help others

10. I wonder if Cleopatra was a <u>kind</u> woman.
Ⓐ sort or variety
Ⓑ always ready to help others

Write Now

The web at the right shows information from "Cleopatra's City—Lost and Found."

- Plan to write a one-page travel brochure advertising the proposed underwater museum. Brainstorm a list of features that would attract tourists.

- Write your brochure. Use the most persuasive ideas from your list. Draw pictures to illustrate the brochure.

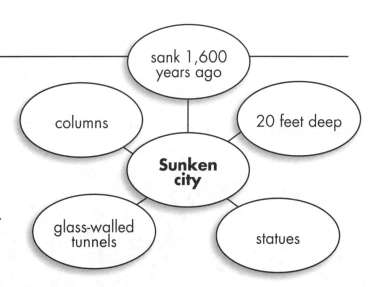

Searching for the "Real" King Arthur

by Gienna Matson

A boy sprints into the clearing, searching for a sword to help his stepbrother. There! Jutting out from a boulder, the sword gleams like a beacon. Without pausing, the boy pulls the sword from the stone.

On the stone is the **inscription**: *Only the rightful king shall be able to pull this sword from this stone.* The sword was called Excalibur (eks KAL uh ber). The boy was Arthur, who became England's heroic king. The story of Arthur goes back to the sixth century.

Set Your Purpose

Have you ever heard the story of King Arthur? Read this article to find out more about a boy who became a king.

Many authors have written about King Arthur, Merlin, and the Knights of the Round Table. Some stories explained that Merlin was a magician and that he helped raise and educate young Arthur. Some legends tell that only the bravest of knights were honored with a seat at the Round Table. This famous table was said to have been chosen intentionally by Arthur. A round table ensured that each knight was considered an equal to all the others seated around him. There was no "head" of the table.

Not everyone thinks that Arthur stories are **credible**. Some say he never lived. Tales about Arthur's **exploits** didn't begin until 300 years after he would have ruled. As time passed, the tales were **embellished** with details about magic and wizards.

Still, the stories may be based on real people and places. In 1191, monks at Glastonbury Abbey were said to have dug up two bodies and an ancient cross. The cross bore the names Arthur and Guinevere, Arthur's wife. Although there is an early burial site at the abbey, the cross and the bodies have been lost.

Arthur is said to have had many different residences. Camelot, considered his favorite place to live, was a castle in Southern England. In more recent times, findings have led some to believe that Camelot was actually Cadbury Castle. There, a slab of rock was found that dates back to the sixth century. A name similar to Arthur was carved into it.

We may never know the truth about the **legendary** Arthur. True or made up, the stories will continue to be enjoyed by people for years to come.

Think About It

Do you know any other tales of people who may or may not be real? Who are they?

Name _____ Date _____

Check Your Understanding

Fill in the letter with the best answer for each question.

1. Which statement is a fact?

Ⓐ Monks found an ancient cross bearing Arthur and Guinevere's names.

Ⓑ Arthur was a very strong boy.

Ⓒ You can't believe stories about events that took place so long ago.

Ⓓ Most kings are heroes to their people.

2. Which statement is an opinion?

Ⓐ Many authors have written about the legend of King Arthur.

Ⓑ Some people believe that part of the King Arthur story is true.

Ⓒ The whole King Arthur story is silly.

Ⓓ The slab at Cadbury Castle dates back to the sixth century.

3. Some people doubt that Arthur lived because

Ⓐ his story is still so popular today.

Ⓑ the story could not possibly be true.

Ⓒ there is very little real proof that Arthur ever existed.

Ⓓ no one has found Arthur's sword.

4. Which event happened first in the story of King Arthur?

Ⓐ Arthur pulls a sword from a stone.

Ⓑ Arthur becomes King of England.

Ⓒ Arthur marries Guinevere.

Ⓓ Arthur learns about magic and wizards.

5. Arthur might have been real because

Ⓐ the stories about him sound real.

Ⓑ a slab of rock dating to the sixth century with a name similar to Arthur carved into it has been found.

Ⓒ the first tales about Arthur were written 300 years after he would have ruled.

Ⓓ the stories were embellished over time.

Vocabulary

> Find each vocabulary word in the selection. The words and sentences around it will help you figure out its meaning.

Fill in the letter with the best definition of the underlined word.

1. The <u>inscription</u> on the stone told who would become king.

Ⓐ moss   Ⓒ writing

Ⓑ painting   Ⓓ material

2. Not everyone thinks the Arthur stories are <u>credible</u>.

Ⓐ believable   Ⓒ numerous

Ⓑ ordinary   Ⓓ amazing

3. The tales of Arthur's <u>exploits</u> were written 300 years after he would have ruled.

Ⓐ writings   Ⓒ speeches

Ⓑ actions or deeds   Ⓓ feelings

4. As time passed, the tales were <u>embellished</u> with details about magic and wizards.

Ⓐ painted   Ⓒ taken away

Ⓑ given   Ⓓ made more interesting

5. We may never know the truth about the <u>legendary</u> Arthur.

Ⓐ scientific   Ⓒ scary

Ⓑ recent   Ⓓ fabled

Name_____ Date_____

Word Work

> **Synonyms** are words that have similar meanings. For example, *large* and *big* are synonyms.

> **Antonyms** are words that have the opposite meanings. For example, *old* and *new* are antonyms.

Fill in the letter of the synonym of the word in dark type.

1. The sword **gleams** like a beacon.
   Ⓐ shines   Ⓑ hides

2. Arthur **resided** in a number of places.
   Ⓐ reigned   Ⓑ lived

3. The Round Table **ensured** that all knights were seen as equal.
   Ⓐ betrayed   Ⓑ guaranteed

4. The sword Excalibur was **lodged** firmly in the stone.
   Ⓐ stuck   Ⓑ sharpened

5. Was Arthur one of England's **heroic** kings?
   Ⓐ weakest   Ⓑ courageous

Read the sentences and the words below. Write the word that means the opposite of the word in dark type.

shame unknown dull unimportant began

6. The story of King Arthur is **famous** in several countries. _____

7. The Knights of the Round Table were men of **honor**. _____

8. Lancelot was one of Arthur's **chief** knights.
_____

9. Excalibur was a **sharp** sword. _____

10. Arthur's own nephew **ended** the story of Camelot. _____

Write Now

In the article "Searching for the 'Real' King Arthur," you read about the legendary ruler of England. Pretend you have visited Camelot castle.

- Plan to write a postcard to a friend describing what you learned and what you believe about King Arthur. Make a chart like the one shown to help organize your thoughts.

- Write your postcard. Don't forget to include your own opinion and the facts to back it up.

I learned...	I think...
Some people say King Arthur was real because... • a slab with a name like Arthur's was found at a castle. • monks said they found his burial site and a cross with his name. Some people say King Arthur was not real because... • the stories were written too long after his time. • there is not enough real evidence he existed.	King Arthur was real because... King Arthur wasn't real because...

ROCK AROUND THE CLOCK

by Perry Lee

Most high school kids go from one class to the next, never getting a break from the books. What if kids had a chance to run a school radio station? Nathan Hill High School has an **advanced** radio class that gives its students that very opportunity.

Set Your Purpose

Can you imagine running a radio station? Some high school students do it every day. Read this article to find out how.

The students play the hottest music, take requests, **produce** ads, air music countdowns, and run **testimonials**. KNHC is known for playing up-and-coming dance hits before any other stations in the nation. KNHC-FM has 60,000 listeners a week. Tim Green, the 18-year-old music director for KNHC, says, "For me, radio is a break from the normal school day. It is something I enjoy."

Running a radio station is not all play. There is real work to do. The radio station stays on a **precise** schedule called an hour clock. The hour clock shows the time at which music and different

announcements will be **aired**. The 17-year-old program director, Shirstie Schmidgall, says, "All of that material airs within one minute, give or take, of the time that it's written."

Like any other job, radio broadcasting has special lingo, or language, for the students to learn. Below is a list of radio lingo used at KNHC.

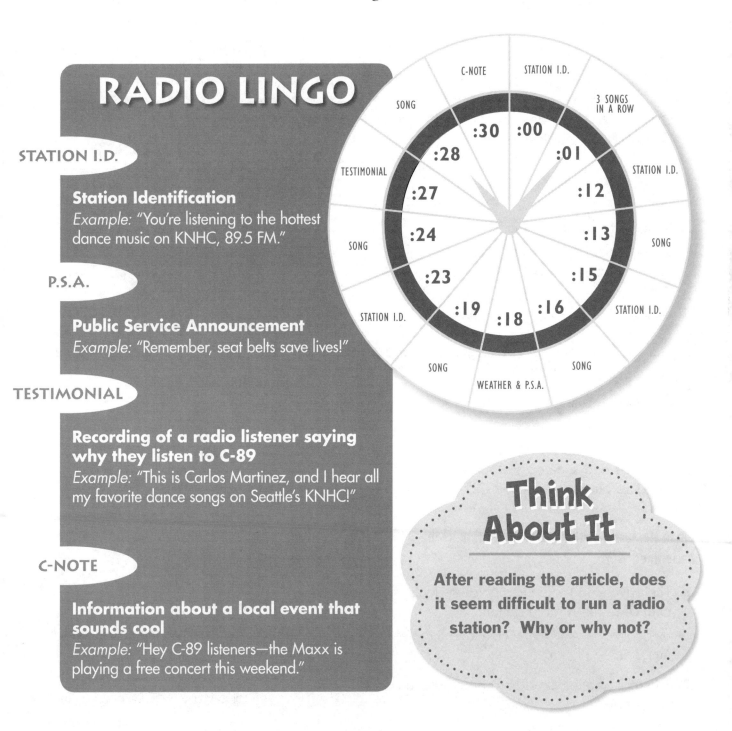

RADIO LINGO

STATION I.D.

Station Identification
Example: "You're listening to the hottest dance music on KNHC, 89.5 FM."

P.S.A.

Public Service Announcement
Example: "Remember, seat belts save lives!"

TESTIMONIAL

Recording of a radio listener saying why they listen to C-89
Example: "This is Carlos Martinez, and I hear all my favorite dance songs on Seattle's KNHC!"

C-NOTE

Information about a local event that sounds cool
Example: "Hey C-89 listeners—the Maxx is playing a free concert this weekend."

Think About It

After reading the article, does it seem difficult to run a radio station? Why or why not?

Name _____ Date _____

Check Your Understanding

Fill in the letter with the best answer for each question.

1. Which statement is an opinion?

   Ⓐ KNHC has 60,000 listeners per week.

   Ⓑ KNHC is run by high school students.

   Ⓒ KNHC is the best radio station in the nation.

   Ⓓ KNHC disc jockeys play dance music.

2. Which statement is a fact?

   Ⓐ Disc jockeys use a schedule called an hour clock.

   Ⓑ Only the hottest music is played on KNHC.

   Ⓒ Teenagers make better disc jockeys than adults.

   Ⓓ Other radio stations should be more like KNHC.

3. Which statement is a fact?

   Ⓐ The radio lingo is difficult to learn.

   Ⓑ Nathan High School offers a radio class.

   Ⓒ Working at the station is always fun.

   Ⓓ The program director's job is the easiest one to do.

4. Which of the following statements is a testimonial?

   Ⓐ "You're listening to KNHC, 89.5 FM, Seattle!"

   Ⓑ "It's going to be cold and damp this morning, so bundle up."

   Ⓒ "My name is Carrie and I always listen to KNHC. It's the greatest!"

   Ⓓ "Remember to wear your helmet every time you bike."

5. How many songs does KNHC play in a half-hour? Look at the hour clock.

   Ⓐ 30 songs

   Ⓑ 6 songs

   Ⓒ 8 songs

   Ⓓ 13 songs

Vocabulary

Find each vocabulary word in the selection. The words and sentences around it will help you figure out its meaning.

Fill in the letter with the best definition of the underlined word.

1. The <u>advanced</u> radio class gives students a chance to run a radio station.

   Ⓐ beginner   Ⓒ at a high level

   Ⓑ late-night   Ⓓ outside

2. The radio station stays on a <u>precise</u> schedule.

   Ⓐ flexible   Ⓒ unsure

   Ⓑ incorrect   Ⓓ strict

3. The students <u>produce</u> ads.

   Ⓐ create

   Ⓑ make music

   Ⓒ bring something closer

   Ⓓ cause people to buy something

4. Famous athletes made <u>testimonials</u> for the radio station.

   Ⓐ secrets

   Ⓑ complaints

   Ⓒ arguments for or against

   Ⓓ statements praising something

5. The hour clock shows the time at which music will be <u>aired</u>.

   Ⓐ played on the radio   Ⓒ thrown out

   Ⓑ taken for a walk   Ⓓ made a mistake

Name _____ **Date** _____

Word Work

A **prefix** comes at the beginning of a word and changes the meaning of the word. Knowing the meaning of a prefix helps you figure out the meaning of the whole word. The prefix **re-** means "again." The prefix **inter-** means "between or among." The prefix **mono-** means "having just one."

reopen	to open again
international	between or among several nations
monotone	having just one tone

Read the definition below. Add the prefix *re-*, *inter-*, or *mono-* to the base word to make a new word that fits the definition.

1. to lock between _____ _____lock

2. having just one rail _____rail

3. to turn and come back again _____turn

4. able to speak just one language _____lingual

5. to play again _____play

6. between continents _____continental

Fill in the letter with the correct definition of the word in dark type.

7. retest
- Ⓐ to test well
- Ⓑ to test first
- Ⓒ to test again
- Ⓓ to test wrongly

8. monosyllable
- Ⓐ having one syllable
- Ⓑ having the best syllable
- Ⓒ having two syllables
- Ⓓ having silent syllables

9. intercommunication
- Ⓐ by communication
- Ⓑ not communicating
- Ⓒ communication between
- Ⓓ electrical communication

10. rename
- Ⓐ to name after
- Ⓑ to name again
- Ⓒ to name in advance
- Ⓓ to forget a name

Write Now

In "Rock Around the Clock," you learned about some of the things involved in producing a radio show.

- Plan to create your own hour clock, or schedule, for a radio show. What sorts of things do you want to include in your program—music, news, weather? Use a form like the one at the right to plan your program.

- Create an hour clock for your station. List all the material you will air during the first 30 minutes. List the names of the songs you will play. Give your station a name. Write a script for your station I.D.

Hour	Clock
4:00	News Break
4:03	
4:05	Song:_____
4:06	
4:10	Station I.D.

349

Answer Key

Rocket Man! (pp. 14–15)
Check Your Understanding
1. C 2. B 3. D 4. C 5. D
Vocabulary
1. C 2. B 3. C 4. D 5. A
Word Work
1. noise 2. peaceful 3. glide 4. amazing
5. compliment 6. shuttle 7. shake 8. choose
9. reach 10. thrill
Write Now Answers will vary.

Quiet Creatures: Two Poems (pp. 18–19)
Check Your Understanding
1. C 2. D 3. C 4. A 5. B
Vocabulary
1. D 2. A 3. B 4. C 5. D
Word Work
1. creeps 2. dumb 3. markings 4. powerful
5. skip 6. A 7. B 8. A 9. A 10. B
Write Now Answers will vary.

Kids Help Pass Safety Laws (pp. 22–23)
Check Your Understanding
1. D 2. C 3. D 4. B 5. A
Vocabulary
1. A 2. C 3. D 4. C 5. B
Word Work
1. C 2. A 3. A 4. B 5. A 6. beach
7. shake 8. hopscotch 9. thunder 10. squash
Write Now Answers will vary.

The Talking Otter (pp. 26–27)
Check Your Understanding
1. D 2. B 3. C 4. A 5. D
Vocabulary
1. C 2. B 3. C 4. B 5. A
Word Work
1. sometimes 2. oxcart 3. teamwork
4. faraway 5. storytellers 6. faraway
7. oxcart 8. sometimes 9. teamwork
10. storytellers
Write Now Answers will vary.

She Climbed to the Top (pp. 30–31)
Check Your Understanding
1. C 2. B 3. A 4. D 5. B
Vocabulary
1. A 2. D 3. C 4. A 5. D
Word Work
1. top 2. leader 3. hazardous 4. dropped
5. adventure 6. C 7. B 8. A 9. C 10. B
Write Now Answers will vary.

Who Says Ball Games Are for the Birds? (pp. 34–35)
Check Your Understanding
1. B 2. B 3. C 4. C 5. B
Vocabulary
1. C 2. A 3. A 4. B 5. D
Word Work
1. B 2. A 3. A 4. B 5. B 6. A 7. C
8. A 9. B 10. D
Write Now Answers will vary.

Written by Anonymous (pp. 38–39)
Check Your Understanding
1. C 2. C 3. D 4. B 5. C
Vocabulary
1. A 2. C 3. D 4. A 5. B
Word Work
1. boring 2. puzzled 3. wondering 4. nest
5. crack 6. hot 7. fresh 8. sad 9. strange
10. freed
Write Now Answers will vary.

Lights! Camera! Invention! (pp. 42–43)
Check Your Understanding
1. B 2. D 3. C 4. D 5. B
Vocabulary
1. C 2. D 3. C 4. B 5. A
Word Work
1. harsh 2. delay 3. indoors 4. succeed
5. advantages 6. invent 7. dream 8. direct
9. invent 10. act
Write Now Answers will vary.

Giants of the Earth (pp. 48–49)
Check Your Understanding
1. B 2. D 3. B 4. D 5. A
Vocabulary
1. C 2. D 3. A 4. B 5. B
Word Work
1. kinder 2. tallest 3. prettiest 4. greener
5. richer 6. old 7. lazy 8. wise 9. sleepy
10. hard
Write Now Answers will vary.

Long Ago in Timbuktu (pp. 52–53)
Check Your Understanding
1. A 2. C 3. A 4. D 5. A
Vocabulary
1. B 2. C 3. A 4. C 5. B
Word Work
1. faraway 2. strong 3. journeyed 4. traders
5. enormous 6. ruined 7. old 8. C
9. C 10. D
Write Now Answers will vary.

Astronauts Walk on the Moon
(pp. 56–57)
Check Your Understanding
1. C 2. D 3. A 4. B 5. D
Vocabulary
1. B 2. C 3. D 4. A 5. A
Word Work
1. B 2. C 3. D 4. A 5. B 6. landed
7. watched 8. walked 9. carried 10. waved
Write Now Answers will vary.

Rain-Forest Medicines (pp. 60–61)
Check Your Understanding
1. D 2. A 3. C 4. B 5. A
Vocabulary
1. B 2. B 3. C 4. D 5. A
Word Work
1. headache 2. cookbook 3. snakeskin
4. sunlight 5. doorbell 6. ear/ache 7. tree/
tops 8. rattle/snake 9. note/book
10. back/pack
Write Now Answers will vary.

Baseball Is a Hit in Japan (pp. 64–65)
Check Your Understanding
1. B 2. A 3. A 4. C 5. C
Vocabulary
1. A 2. D 3. D 4. C 5. A
Word Work
1. baseball 2. noontime 3. windshield
4. toothbrush 5. sunglasses 6. team/mates
7. flag/pole 8. ball/park 9. ball/games
10. under/foot
Write Now Answers will vary.

May You Have a Long Life (pp. 68–69)
Check Your Understanding
1. C 2. D 3. A 4. B 5. C
Vocabulary
1. A 2. B 3. C 4. B 5. C
Word Work
1. official 2. general 3. quiet 4. mental
5. final 6. unusually 7. hardly 8. physically

9. Actually 10. really
Write Now Answers will vary.

The Truth About AIDS (pp. 72–73)
Check Your Understanding
1. C 2. D 3. B 4. A 5. C
Vocabulary
1. B 2. B 3. A 4. D 5. C
Word Work
1. sick 2. fame 3. danger 4. love 5. weak
6. curable 7. dangerous 8. sadness
9. famous 10. washable
Write Now Answers will vary.

Hail to the Chief! (pp. 76–77)
Check Your Understanding
1. D 2. A 3. B 4. B 5. A
Vocabulary
1. B 2. A 3. D 4. C 5. B
Word Work
1. A 2. B 3. A 4. B 5. B 6. Kennedy
7. cleaver 8. equal 9. freedom 10. shield
Write Now Answers will vary.

Not Just Black or White (pp. 80–81)
Check Your Understanding
1. B 2. C 3. C 4. A 5. A
Vocabulary
1. A 2. C 3. A 4. B 5. B
Word Work
1. multiculturalism 2. multiple 3. bilingual
4. biannual 5. multilingual 6. high 7. Mariah
8. white 9. identify 10. Tiger
Write Now Answers will vary.

The Real Dracula (pp. 84–85)
Check Your Understanding
1. D 2. B 3. D 4. C 5. A
Vocabulary
1. A 2. B 3. A 4. B 5. D
Word Work
1. B 2. A 3. A 4. A 5. B 6. C 7. B
8. D 9. A 10. B
Write Now Answers will vary.

Old Bones Dug Up (pp. 88–89)
Check Your Understanding
1. C 2. D 3. B 4. C 5. C
Vocabulary
1. B 2. D 3. A 4. D 5. B
Word Work
1. realized 2. whole 3. covered
4. discovered 5. location 6. astounding
7. pointed 8. around 9. cow 10. boy
Write Now Answers will vary.

Creatures of the Deep (pp. 92–93)
Check Your Understanding
1. A 2. C 3. A 4. A 5. B
Vocabulary
1. C 2. B 3. C 4. D 5. A
Word Work
1. fascinating 2. unexpected 3. harsh
4. unusual 5. wonder 6. seafood 7. waterfall
8. wetland 9. jellyfish 10. boathouse
Write Now Answers will vary.

One Cool-Looking Cowhand (pp. 98–99)
Check Your Understanding
1. A 2. C 3. D 4. C 5. B
Vocabulary
1. A 2. B 3. A 4. C 5. D
Word Work
1. B 2. A 3. B 4. B 5. G 6. D 7. A
8. F 9. C 10. E
Write Now Answers will vary.

Americans Discover TV (pp. 102–103)
Check Your Understanding
1. A 2. B 3. B 4. C 5. A
Vocabulary
1. A 2. A 3. C 4. B 5. A
Word Work
1. monkeys 2. flies 3. days 4. parties
5. supplies 6. preview 7. prepay
8. substandard 9. preteen 10. submarine
Write Now Answers will vary.

Collectors Strike It Rich! (pp. 106–107)
Check Your Understanding
1. A 2. C 3. C 4. A 5. D
Vocabulary
1. B 2. A 3. D 4. A 5. A
Word Work
1. B 2. B 3. C 4. C 5. D 6. collectible
7. hopeful 8. foolish 9. careful 10. softness
Write Now Answers will vary.

Victory at Sea (pp. 110–111)
Check Your Understanding
1. A 2. C 3. C 4. B 5. B
Vocabulary
1. B 2. A 3. D 4. B 5. C
Word Work
1. D 2. A 3. D 4. C 5. C 6. undefeated
7. resend 8. unready 9. unfriendly
10. reinvade
Write Now Answers will vary.

The Earth Heats Up (pp. 114–115)
Check Your Understanding
1. C 2. C 3. A 4. A 5. D
Vocabulary
1. D 2. A 3. B 4. D 5. D
Word Work
1. A 2. B 3. B 4. B 5. campground
6. windshield 7. checklist 8. handball
9. mailbox 10. sunlight
Write Now Answers will vary.

Fire in Their Eyes (pp. 118–119)
Check Your Understanding
1. C 2. A 3. C 4. A 5. D
Vocabulary
1. D 2. A 3. A 4. B 5. B
Word Work
1. D 2. B 3. C 4. A 5. B 6. day
7. takes 8. aid 9. airplane 10. flames
Write Now Answers will vary.

Children at Work (pp. 122–123)
Check Your Understanding
1. C 2. A 3. B 4. D 5. B
Vocabulary
1. C 2. D 3. D 4. B 5. A
Word Work
1. isn't 2. don't 3. aren't 4. It's 5. That's
6. cannot 7. She is 8. there will
9. would have 10. we will
Write Now Answers will vary.

The California Gold Rush (pp. 126–127)
Check Your Understanding
1. B 2. B 3. C 4. B 5. A
Vocabulary
1. C 2. C 3. D 4. C 5. B
Word Work
1. B 2. A 3. B 4. A 5. A 6. Sutter's mill
7. the mill's water channel 8. San Francisco's
growth 9. these events' importance
10. the forty-niners' wagons
Write Now Answers will vary.

Deborah Samson, Secret Soldier
(pp. 130–131)
Check Your Understanding
1. C 2. A 3. C 4. B 5. B
Vocabulary
1. B 2. C 3. B 4. A 5. A
Word Work
1. secretly 2. foolish 3. personally 4. hopeful
5. sadness 6. real 7. truth 8. mean 9. free
10. red
Write Now Answers will vary.

Stories That Reach Toward the Sky
(pp. 136–137)
Check Your Understanding
1. C 2. B 3. A 4. C 5. C
Vocabulary
1. B 2. C 3. A 4. A 5. D
Word Work
1. barnyard 2. bathtub 3. bookworms
4. classroom 5. driveway 6. eyeglasses
7. playpen 8. sandbox 9. earring
10. bedroom
Write Now Answers will vary.

A Bridge to a New World (pp. 140–141)
Check Your Understanding
1. C 2. B 3. D 4. C 5. B
Vocabulary
1. C 2. D 3. B 4. B 5. C
Word Work
1. sturdy 2. clumsy 3. descendants
4. celebrated 5. die 6. A 7. C 8. B
9. C 10. D
Write Now Answers will vary.

Saving the Sphinx (pp. 144–145)
Check Your Understanding
1. B 2. C 3. B 4. C 5. D
Vocabulary
1. A 2. B 3. D 4. A 5. C
Word Work
1. A 2. C 3. B 4. D 5. C 6. believe, see
7. feel, near 8. seems, easy 9. treat, see
10. pleaded, teacher, meet, feet
Write Now Answers will vary.

Scum Energy (pp. 148–149)
Check Your Understanding
1. C 2. A 3. D 4. B 5. D
Vocabulary
1. C 2. B 3. B 4. A 5. D
Word Work
1. B 2. A 3. B 4. B 5. B 6. smokestack
7. airtight 8. daylight 9. downtown
10. treetop
Write Now Answers will vary.

Condor Comeback (pp. 152–153)
Check Your Understanding
1. C 2. A 3. B 4. B 5. D
Vocabulary
1. C 2. D 3. B 4. A 5. D
Word Work
1. hadn't 2. don't 3. it's 4. There's 5. you're
6. C 7. D 8. A 9. A 10. B
Write Now Answers will vary.

Exploring Jupiter (pp. 156–157)
Check Your Understanding
1. C 2. B 3. B 4. D 5. B
Vocabulary
1. C 2. C 3. D 4. A 5. D
Word Work
1. poisonous 2. airless 3. dangerous
4. wishful 5. hopeful 6. careless 7. wonderful

8. waterless 9. weightless 10. courageous
Write Now Answers will vary.

The King's Things (pp. 162–163)
Check Your Understanding
1. C 2. B 3. A 4. D 5. B
Vocabulary
1. D 2. A 3. C 4. B 5. B
Word Work
1. B 2. A 3. D 4. C 5. A 6. C 7. I've
8. could've 9. Wouldn't 10. haven't
Write Now Answers will vary.

What's It Like to Live in China?
(pp. 166–167)
Check Your Understanding
1. C 2. A 3. C 4. B 5. C
Vocabulary
1. A 2. D 3. A 4. B 5. D
Word Work
1. B 2. A 3. A 4. B 5. arrangement
6. friendship 7. soften 8. enjoyment
9. weaken 10. apartment
Write Now Answers will vary.

Unsolved Mysteries (pp. 170–171)
Check Your Understanding
1. A 2. B 3. A 4. C 5. A
Vocabulary
1. B 2. A 3. C 4. C 5. D
Word Work
1. footprint 2. hillside 3. thunderstorm
4. moonlight 5. newspaper 6. air/port
7. sky/writing 8. take/off 9. down/pour
10. under/water
Write Now Answers will vary.

The Galápagos—Can They Survive?
(pp. 174–175)
Check Your Understanding
1. C 2. D 3. D 4. B 5. D
Vocabulary
1. D 2. C 3. A 4. B 5. C
Word Work
1. rupt (to break) 2. tract (to draw, to pull)
3. spect (to look) 4. rupt (to break) 5. port
(to carry) 6. transportation 7. subtract
8. abrupt 9. inspection 10. interrupt
Write Now Answers will vary.

What's the Word? (pp. 178–179)
Check Your Understanding
1. B 2. A 3. D 4. A 5. C
Vocabulary
1. A 2. C 3. A 4. B 5. B
Word Work
1. carpool 2. knockdown 3. spaceship
4. snowstorm 5. classroom 6. mountainside
7. B 8. A 9. A 10. B
Write Now Answers will vary.

Who Dropped the Ball? (pp. 182–183)
Check Your Understanding
1. B 2. C 3. A 4. A 5. D
Vocabulary
1. B 2. C 3. A 4. C 5. B
Word Work
1. B 2. A 3. B 4. D 5. A 6. players
7. boxes 8. matches 9. wishes 10. glasses
Write Now Answers will vary.

Triathlon: The Sport That Does It All
(pp. 188–189)
Check Your Understanding
1. C 2. B 3. A 4. B 5. C

Vocabulary
1. B 2. C 3. A 4. D 5. C
Word Work
1. thorn 2. arm 3. north 4. shark 5. thirty
6. sport 7. short 8. hard 9. first 10. Start
Write Now Answers will vary.

Life in the Comics (pp. 192–193)
Check Your Understanding
1. D 2. D 3. A 4. A 5. C
Vocabulary
1. A 2. D 3. B 4. C 5. A
Word Work
1. wonderful 2. snowy 3. respectful
4. colorful 5. lacy 6. dirty 7. careful 8. easy
9. joyful 10. thoughtful
Write Now Answers will vary.

Driving Through Time (pp. 196–197)
Check Your Understanding
1. B 2. C 3. A 4. D 5. C
Vocabulary
1. C 2. D 3. B 4. B 5. A
Word Work
1. parked 2. happened 3. raked 4. turned
5. cared 6. assembled 7. started 8. saved
9. required 10. called
Write Now Answers will vary.

**Marie Curie: A Woman Ahead of
Her Time** (pp. 200–201)
Check Your Understanding
1. A 2. D 3. C 4. B 5. A
Vocabulary
1. A 2. B 3. B 4. C 5. D
Word Work
1. science 2. treated 3. honored 4. piano
5. hypnotizes 6. interests 7. emits 8. Often
9. basic 10. notice
Write Now Answers will vary.

Lost & Found: The First Fort
(pp. 204–205)
Check Your Understanding
1. C 2. D 3. B 4. D 5. A
Vocabulary
1. D 2. C 3. B 4. A 5. A
Word Work
1. throw 2. phone 3. slope 4. groan
5. elbow 6. closed, roads 7. holes, stones
8. broken, bowls, bones 9. notes 10. hoped,
shown
Write Now Answers will vary.

The Case of the Missing Globe
(pp. 208–209)
Check Your Understanding
1. B 2. B 3. D 4. A 5. C
Vocabulary
1. A 2. D 3. C 4. A 5. B
Word Work
1. 3 2. 3 3. 4 4. 4 5. 2 6. peo/ple
7. sim/ple 8. prac/ti/cal 9. puz/zle
10. o/ri/gi/nal
Write Now Answers will vary.

Jim Carrey: Class Clown Makes Good
(pp. 212–213)
Check Your Understanding
1. A 2. B 3. D 4. D 5. D
Vocabulary
1. C 2. A 3. C 4. B 5. A
Word Work
1. classroom 2. homeowners 3. nightclubs
4. moviegoers 5. worldwide 6. grew
7. found 8. overcame 9. brought 10. said

Write Now Answers will vary.

Making Stories Come Alive (pp. 216–217)
Check Your Understanding
1. B 2. C 3. A 4. B 5. A
Vocabulary
1. B 2. A 3. C 4. D 5. B
Word Work
1. interlock 2. enclose 3. transplant
4. submarine 5. transform 6. interaction
7. transport 8. encase 9. substandard
10. encircle
Write Now Answers will vary.

Yo-yos Are Forever (pp. 222–223)
Check Your Understanding
1. C 2. B 3. C 4. D 5. B
Vocabulary
1. D 2. D 3. C 4. A 5. B
Word Work
1. B 2. C 3. C 4. B 5. A 6. similar
7. unusual 8. appealing 9. quickly
10. durable
Write Now Answers will vary.

Giving TV the Boot! (pp. 226–227)
Check Your Understanding
1. B 2. B 3. A 4. C 5. D
Vocabulary
1. A 2. B 3. A 4. C 5. B
Word Work
1. B 2. C 3. A 4. D 5. A 6. decided
7. laughed 8. played 9. planted 10. jumped
Write Now Answers will vary.

Sports: For Fun or Money? (pp. 230–231)
Check Your Understanding
1. B 2. A 3. C 4. C 5. D
Vocabulary
1. C 2. D 3. A 4. B 5. B
Word Work
1. B 2. D 3. E 4. A 5. C 6. inspect
7. tractor 8. spectacle 9. distract 10. suspect
Write Now Answers will vary.

The Water Festival (pp. 234–235)
Check Your Understanding
1. B 2. B 3. C 4. D 5. C
Vocabulary
1. C 2. A 3. B 4. B 5. A
Word Work
1. B 2. C 3. D 4. C 5. C 6. music
7. bright 8. less 9. region 10. fright
Write Now Answers will vary.

Cartoons Come to Life (pp. 238–239)
Check Your Understanding
1. B 2. C 3. B 4. C 5. D
Vocabulary
1. A 2. D 3. C 4. B 5. A
Word Work
1. checkers 2. width 3. shape 4. path
5. depth 6. invention 7. possession
8. expression 9. animation 10. connection
Write Now Answers will vary.

Foods With a Difference (pp. 242–243)
Check Your Understanding
1. D 2. A 3. C 4. B 5. D
Vocabulary
1. A 2. D 3. A 4. C 5. A
Word Work
1. louder 2. oldest 3. greatest 4. faster
5. sharpest 6. higher 7. reddest 8. longest
9. smaller 10. brightest
Write Now Answers will vary.

Presidential Pets and Kids (pp. 248–249)
Check Your Understanding
1. B 2. A 3. D 4. B 5. A
Vocabulary
1. A 2. C 3. B 4. B 5. C
Word Work
1. C 2. B 3. D 4. A 5. A 6. countries
7. foxes 8. tigers 9. guides 10. businesses
Write Now Answers will vary.

History of Marbles (pp. 252–253)
Check Your Understanding
1. A 2. B 3. B 4. A 5. C
Vocabulary
1. A 2. B 3. A 4. D 5. C
Word Work
1. amusement 2. impressive 3. government
4. secretive 5. improvement 6. grasses
7. wishes 8. foxes 9. latches 10. bunches
Write Now Answers will vary.

Flying Friends of the Air Force
(pp. 256–257)
Check Your Understanding
1. A 2. B 3. D 4. C 5. B
Vocabulary
1. B 2. A 3. D 4. B 5. C
Word Work
1. find 2. flight 3. sky 4. time 5. right
6. fly, high, sky 7. fine, mind 8. dives, frighten
9. Bright, sunlight, blind, while 10. tire, flight
Write Now Answers will vary.

Flying Machine (pp. 260–261)
Check Your Understanding
1. C 2. D 3. B 4. C 5. A
Vocabulary
1. C 2. C 3. A 4. B 5. D
Word Work
1. invent 2. tiny 3. dull 4. smell 5. photos
6. rapidly 7. finalist 8. guitarist 9. differently
10. cartoonist
Write Now Answers will vary.

Fighting for Their Lives (pp. 264–265)
Check Your Understanding
1. C 2. B 3. A 4. B 5. D
Vocabulary
1. D 2. A 3. C 4. D 5. B
Word Work
1. wet 2. create 3. ancient 4. future
5. endangered 6. arriving 7. recognize
8. vital 9. young 10. scarce
Write Now Answers will vary.

Crunchy Critters (pp. 268–269)
Check Your Understanding
1. B 2. D 3. B 4. B 5. A
Vocabulary
1. D 2. A 3. A 4. C 5. C
Word Work
1. disgusting 2. fancy 3. before 4. cooked
5. ask 6. D 7. A 8. C 9. B 10. C
Write Now Answers will vary.

Children Who Ruled (pp. 272–273)
Check Your Understanding
1. C 2. B 3. C 4. C 5. D
Vocabulary
1. D 2. B 3. C 4. B 5. D
Word Work
1. throughout 2. plow 3. crowns 4. spouse
5. count 6. grave 7. gems 8. king 9. jailed
10. nation
Write Now Answers will vary.

Friendly Rooms (pp. 276–277)
Check Your Understanding
1. B 2. C 3. D 4. B 5. A
Vocabulary
1. B 2. A 3. C 4. C 5. D
Word Work
1. C 2. A 3. D 4. B 5. computer's
6. human's 7. friends' 8. family's 9. sisters'
10. neighbors'
Write Now Answers will vary.

Pedal Power (pp. 280–281)
Check Your Understanding
1. A 2. D 3. B 4. A 5. B
Vocabulary
1. C 2. B 3. B 4. A 5. C
Word Work
1. A 2. B 3. A 4. A 5. B 6. B 7. B
8. A 9. B 10. A
Write Now Answers will vary.

The Story That Stretched (pp. 284–285)
Check Your Understanding
1. A 2. D 3. C 4. B 5. C
Vocabulary
1. A 2. D 3. B 4. C 5. D
Word Work
1. B 2. A 3. B 4. A 5. B 6. A 7. A
8. B 9. A 10. B
Write Now Answers will vary.

Mary McLeod Bethune (pp. 290–291)
Check Your Understanding
1. D 2. B 3. D 4. C 5. B
Vocabulary
1. A 2. D 3. C 4. B 5. B
Word Work
1. invention 2. action 3. completion
4. instruction 5. concentration 6. creation
7. connection 8. construction 9. collection
10. election
Write Now Answers will vary.

Does Music Make You Smarter?
(pp. 294–295)
Check Your Understanding
1. B 2. D 3. B 4. A 5. D
Vocabulary
1. D 2. A 3. B 4. C 5. D
Word Work
1. A 2. B 3. A 4. A 5. A 6. B 7. B
8. A 9. A 10. B
Write Now Answers will vary.

Grant Hill: Straight Shooter
(pp. 298–299)
Check Your Understanding
1. C 2. B 3. A 4. D 5. D
Vocabulary
1. D 2. A 3. C 4. B 5. A
Word Work
1. dragonfly 2. everyone 3. birdhouse
4. basketball 5. airport 6. playground
7. thunderstorm 8. snowball 9. nighttime
10. doorbell
Write Now Answers will vary.

Surf's Up—Way Up! (pp. 302–303)
Check Your Understanding
1. C 2. B 3. A 4. C 5. D
Vocabulary
1. A 2. D 3. B 4. D 5. A
Word Work
1. B 2. A 3. B 4. A 5. A 6. A 7. B
8. A 9. B 10. A
Write Now Answers will vary.

Coral Crisis (pp. 306–307)
Check Your Understanding
1. C 2. D 3. D 4. A 5. D
Vocabulary
1. D 2. A 3. B 4. A 5. C
Word Work
1. bodies 2. nutrients 3. creatures
4. diseases 5. activities 6. reefs 7. Rays
8. fins 9. tentacles 10. enemies
Write Now Answers will vary.

A Trash Collector's Work Is
Never Done (pp. 310–311)
Check Your Understanding
1. C 2. C 3. B 4. C 5. A
Vocabulary
1. B 2. C 3. D 4. A 5. D
Word Work
1. B 2. D 3. C 4. B 5. D 6. neighborhood
7. hardship 8. achievement 9. entertainment
10. childhood
Write Now Answers will vary.

The Animals of the Arctic Tundra
(pp. 314–315)
Check Your Understanding
1. D 2. C 3. C 4. B 5. A
Vocabulary
1. B 2. C 3. A 4. C 5. D
Word Work
1. geographical 2. encircle 3. animal
4. invisible 5. critical 6. recognizes 7. large
8. gorge 9. freezing 10. single
Write Now Answers will vary.

Wildlife for Sale (pp. 318–319)
Check Your Understanding
1. C 2. C 3. C 4. A 5. B
Vocabulary
1. A 2. D 3. A 4. B 5. B
Word Work
1. punishment 2. extinction 3. protection
4. payment 5. collection 6. starvation
7. exploration 8. appointment 9. excitement
10. government
Write Now Answers will vary.

So, How About Those Vikings?
(pp. 322–323)
Check Your Understanding
1. D 2. A 3. B 4. D 5. A
Vocabulary
1. A 2. D 3. B 4. A 5. C
Word Work
1. plundering 2. vast 3. bold 4. benefit
5. ancestors 6. builder 7. encouragement
8. explorer 9. government 10. teacher
Write Now Answers will vary.

High-Tech Highways (pp. 326–327)
Check Your Understanding
1. C 2. D 3. D 4. A 5. C
Vocabulary
1. B 2. A 3. A 4. C 5. D
Word Work
1. highway 2. snowflake 3. homework
4. daydream 5. scarecrow 6. sun/rise
7. side/walk 8. flash/light 9. motor/cycle
10. gold/fish
Write Now Answers will vary.

A Panda for a Pet? (pp. 332–333)
Check Your Understanding
1. C 2. C 3. A 4. D 5. C
Vocabulary
1. B 2. C 3. C 4. A 5. D

Word Work
1. shy 2. chubby 3. sleep 4. often
5. expensive 6. bedtime 7. outdoors
8. rattlesnake 9. sunshine 10. whenever
Write Now Answers will vary.

Faithfully Ours (pp. 336–337)
Check Your Understanding
1. C 2. B 3. A 4. B 5. B
Vocabulary
1. C 2. A 3. B 4. D 5. D
Word Work
1. predictable 2. victorious 3. playful
4. laughable 5. careful 6. reliable
7. thoughtful 8. workable 9. furious
10. mysterious
Write Now Answers will vary.

Cleopatra's City—Lost and Found
(pp. 340–341)
Check Your Understanding
1. D 2. B 3. C 4. D 5. A
Vocabulary
1. A 2. B 3. D 4. B 5. D
Word Work
1. A 2. A 3. A 4. A 5. B 6. B 7. B 8. A
9. A 10. B
Write Now Answers will vary.

Searching for the "Real" King Arthur
(pp. 344–345)
Check Your Understanding
1. A 2. C 3. C 4. A 5. B
Vocabulary
1. C 2. A 3. B 4. D 5. D
Word Work
1. A 2. B 3. B 4. A 5. B 6. unknown
7. shame 8. unimportant 9. dull 10. began
Write Now Answers will vary.

Rock Around the Clock (pp. 348–349)
Check Your Understanding
1. C 2. A 3. B 4. C 5. C
Vocabulary
1. C 2. D 3. A 4. D 5. A
Word Work
1. interlock 2. monorail 3. return
4. monolingual 5. replay 6. intercontinental
7. C 8. A 9. C 10. B
Write Now Answers will vary.